D0291866

A Celebration of Excellence

SEVEN

OTHER BOOKS BY ALAN ROSS

The Yankees Century
Voices and Memories of the Pinstripe Past

The Red Sox Century
Voices and Memories from Fenway Park

Packer Pride
For the Love of Lambeau, Lombardi, and Cheeseheads

Cubs Pride
For the Love of Ernie, Fergie, and Wrigley

Cardinals Glory
For the Love of Dizzy, Ozzie, and The Man

Browns Glory
For the Love of Ozzie, The Toe, and Otto

I Remember Reggie White

Twins Pride
For the Love of Kirby, Kent, and Killebrew

White Sox Glory
For the Love of Nellie, Shoeless Joe, and Konerko

The New Yankees Century
For the Love of Jeter, Joltin' Joe, and Mariano

Steelers Glory
For the Love of Bradshaw, Big Ben, and The Bus

Lakers Glory
For the Love of Kobe, Magic, and Mikan

Mets Pride
For the Love of Mookie, Mike, and David Wright

A Celebration of Excellence

SEVEN

The National Championship Teams of the
TENNESSEE LADY VOLS

ALAN ROSS

CUMBERLAND HOUSE
NASHVILLE, TENNESSEE

SEVEN
PUBLISHED BY CUMBERLAND HOUSE PUBLISHING, INC.
431 Harding Industrial Drive
Nashville, TN 37211–3160
Copyright © 2007 by Alan Ross

Cover design: Gore Studio, Inc.
Text design: John Mitchell

Library of Congress Cataloging-in-Publication Data

Ross, Alan, 1944–
  Seven : the national championship teams of the Tennessee Lady Vols / Alan Ross.
    p. cm.
  Includes bibliographical references and index.
  ISBN-13: 978-1-58182-625-8 (hardcover : alk. paper)
  ISBN-10: 1-58182-625-7 (hardcover : alk. paper)
  1. University of Tennessee, Knoxville—Basketball. 2. Lady Volunteers (Basketball team) I. Title.

  GV885.43.U58R67 2007
  796.323'630976885—dc22

                                                        2007034778

Printed in the United States of America

1 2 3 4 5 6 7—13 12 11 10 09 08 07

Contents

Preface 11

1
1986–87
Raising the Corn-fed Chicks 17

2
1988–89
"God Bless Her, Graduate
and Get Out of Tennessee" 49

3
1990–91
Head of the Class 83

4
1995–96
Chamique, as in Unique-wah 115

5
1996–97
R-E-S-P-E-C-T 141

6
1997–98
Perfect 167

7
2006–07
Lucky Seven 197

8
The Lady Vols All-Time
Championship Team 227

References 231
Index 245

Preface

For way too long, both genders have dealt with the suppositions, realities, and unfairness of life in "a man's world."

If you are a woman, your perspective on these matters has no doubt been influenced by instances seared into your consciousness as a result of countless inequities and incongruities with the system in place as you know it. For men, a patriarchy has been the conveyor to power, might, money, and position—elements many would be reluctant to give up unless forced to.

That tumultuous climate received a jolt in 1972, when Congress passed the now legendary Title IX amendment—a law banning sexual discrimination by any school receiving federal money. Schools, colleges, and universities would ante up in many ways, but mostly by guaranteeing that the number of athletes would hereafter equal the gender ratio of a school's student population and by increasing opportunities for athletes of both sexes.

Into this extraordinary environment walked young Pat Head in 1974, hired as the new head coach for the University of Tennessee women's basketball team. Surely the author of Title IX,

Hawaii Congresswoman Patsy T. Mink, before her death in 2002, witnessed the marvels of her law come to magnificent fruition. As a consequence of Mink's foresight, women were introduced to parity with the gods of collegiate athletic income—the men. After the dust eventually settled, women's sports began a slow climb to respectability. And if you had to pick one person in the whole of America most responsible with putting women's athletics not only on the map but also on the A Train to success, it certainly would be none other than Pat Head Summitt, the winningest basketball coach in NCAA history, male or female.

In her 33 years at the helm of the UT program, Summitt has made her Lady Vols synonymous with the best in sport. They are the New York Yankees of women's collegiate basketball, the champion nonpareil.

While so many of Summitt's great athletes have benefited from her unequalled coaching skills—Holly Warlick, Patricia Roberts, Bridgette Gordon, Daedra Charles, Dena Head, Michelle Marciniak, Chamique Holdsclaw, Tamika Catchings, Kara Lawson, Michelle Snow, Shanna Zolman, Candace Parker—all have Title IX to thank for the eventual opportunity to showcase their substantial talents, Summitt included.

One only has to think back to a Nera White or a Babe Didrikson Zaharias to fully appreciate the situation. While today's collegiate star performers head off to the WNBA after glistening NCAA careers, pioneering women athletes such as White and Zaharias had to find solace in amateur competition (White was a 15-time consecutive AAU All-American, from 1955 through 1969) or change sports entirely. Zaharias, voted the top female athlete of the first half of the 20th century, was an All-America basketball player and jaw-dropping Olympic track and field gold medalist who ultimately had to take up the game of golf to make a living in pro sports. About White, no less an accomplished figure than LSU's former women's basketball coach, the late Sue Gunter, once said, "I've coached two Olympic teams and I've seen the best players in the world. Nera White is the best of them all."

If people like White and Zaharias paved the way, superstars like Holdsclaw and Parker redefined it, their otherworldly athleticism electrifying the women's game and elevating it to heights initially unthinkable. Holdsclaw holds the distinction of powering three straight national championship teams; Parker has one ring . . . and counting.

Both standouts have played important roles in weaving the on-going tapestry of Lady Vols basketball. There are many other contributors, whether they represent a single strand or an entire section of that tapestry. *Seven* looks at the herculean courage, indomitable will, and persevering dedication of the seven Tennessee Lady Vols national championship teams, each title squad possessing its own unique identity and character. Throughout it all, the guiding hand of Pat Summitt has kept the UT rudder steady and on course. Each season of conquest has held its own wildly varying range of possibilities, from dismal disaster to dramatic victory. Even the perfect season of 1997–98 wasn't without its struggles. The collective components of each banner year seem sealed together for all time. Summitt's women are the ultimate combatants; relentless warriors weathering challenging foes, vengeful rivals, and their own hard-driving coach to ultimately hoist the trophy. They are the Lady Volunteers, and they are champions.

—*A. R.*

1

1986–87

Raising the
Corn-fed Chicks

FOLLOWERS OF UNIVERSITY OF TENNESSEE Lady Vols basketball have become comfortable with—in fact, many expect—national rankings that place the team atop the college hoops heap, as well as the traditional cutting-down of the nets that follows another national title.

But that familiar spot in the rarefied air at the pinnacle of women's college basketball wasn't fashioned overnight. Tennessee had knocked on the championship door many times, perched on the doorstep without seeing the door swing wide open.

"Looking back on it," says Lady Vols head coach Pat Head Summitt in *Reach for the Summitt*, her personal view of the landmark program she has developed at Tennessee, "when I arrived in 1974, Tennessee basketball could have been compared to a 'start-up' organization. We had no budget to speak of. But we developed a good program despite our limitations, thanks to people like Nancy Darsch, who was integral to laying the foundation. But in 1985, after nearly ten years, we wanted to get to the next level. In those years, Tennessee had a stigma. We were the perennial bridesmaid, never the bride. At that point, in 1985, we'd been to the Final Four six times. And we'd never won. Boy, I wanted it. I couldn't stand it."

Summitt and her Lady Vols would endure one final rejection, in the 1986 women's NCAA Final Four, before knocking the championship door off its hinges with the school's first national crown in 1987.

But when Summitt's group rose to No. 1 in mid-December 1986 to start that breakthrough season, it had been 10 long years since the Lady Vols had occupied the hallowed top spot in the ratings. In fact, right there on the UT bench, alongside Summitt, sat an icon from that era. Lady Vols assistant coach Holly Warlick was a vital cog on a team that clawed its way to a No. 1 ranking in the final Associated Press poll of 1977-78, Summitt's fourth year at the Tennessee helm. Warlick, a decorated Lady Vol point guard, had been honored as a Kodak All-American, a 1980 Olympian, had led her Lady Vols to three Final Four appearances, and was the first Volunteer, male or female, to have her jersey (No. 22) retired, in 1980.

Now, on the afternoon of Sunday, December 14, 1986, after Tennessee had vanquished its first four opponents to open the 1986–87 season, Warlick, in her second year as an assistant to Pat Summitt, watched from the bench as Tennessee found itself in the atypical position of underdog.

Out on the floor of the Frank Erwin Center in Austin, Texas, the No. 1 women's college basketball team in the country took the court. They were wearing orange, all right. Burnt Orange. The University of Texas Lady Longhorns, the 1986 national champions, were riding a 40-game winning streak, a 50-game regular-season winning streak, and had won their last 43 games at home. Expectations were high that No. 3-ranked Tennessee would be the next Lady Longhorns victim. At forward for Texas was one preseason publication's pick for player of the year, a daunting 6-foot-2 physical specimen, All-American Andrea Lloyd.

"When Lloyd gets the ball up there," noted Lady Vols sophomore forward Bridgette Gordon, assigned to guard the Texas star, "she's like a quarterback on the team. All I've been hearing is Andrea Lloyd, this All-American."

After the game, though, all Lloyd would be hearing about was Bridgette Gordon. The 6-footer from DeLand, Florida, came into her own at Austin with a dominating performance against the Lady Longhorns, scoring 26 points, pulling down nine rebounds, grabbing six steals, logging four assists, and committing no turnovers in 36 minutes of play in Tennessee's stunning 85–78 upset of Texas.

Dazzling as those statistics were, they were dwarfed by one surprising yet significant element of Gordon's play. Incredibly, Gordon, not at all known for her defense, limited Lloyd to just a pair of free throws. The Texan went 0-for-3 from the floor, failing to attempt more shots because of Gordon's tenacity in denying her the ball. The resulting frustration forced Lloyd to turn the ball over nine times.

"Gordon's defensive pressure was indicative of the whole team's defensive pressure," said Lloyd after the game. "We were thinking about that so much, I think that hurt us. I wasn't getting the opportunities to go to the basket a lot. I was getting myself in situations I didn't need to be in."

Gordon added: "I knew I had to come in the game and deny Andrea Lloyd the ball. My defense came along with my maturity in basketball. In high school, defense was nonexistent to me."

Summitt, generally wary in praising her younger players, didn't skimp in commending Gordon's performance. "She did a tremendous job on Andrea Lloyd," said the Lady Vols' mentor. "She's just really becoming an all-around player. I personally think she's one of the best forwards in the country."

Overshadowed in the glare of Gordon's brilliance was Sheila Frost's 8-of-11 shooting from the field and four steals. As a team, Tennessee forced a dramatic 27 turnovers, with Summitt's suffocating defense befuddling the Lady Longhorns all afternoon. In addition, the well-conditioned Lady Vols stole a page from the Texas playbook, running the Lady Longhorns ragged.

The game started ominously for UT, with Texas running up a quick 4–0 lead, before Summitt substituted freshman Tonya Edwards at point guard for Dawn Marsh, the junior from Alcoa, Tennessee, who labored against the Lady Longhorns' full-court pressure defense. Texas held a slim 78–76 lead with 3:01 remaining but never scored again. The exhausted

Lady Longhorns failed time after time at the free-throw line, while Tennessee converted nine charity tosses to seal the game.

In a historical but ultimately meaningless footnote to the game, it was the first time that the Tennessee women played with a three-point rule. Incredibly, not one player from either team even attempted a shot from beyond the arc.

Though Summitt called the triumph one of her top 10 victories of all time, she stated that she would vote No. 2 Louisiana Tech to the top spot over her third-rated Vols in the following week's polls. But over the next 24 hours, assistants Mickie DeMoss and Warlick successfully talked their boss into voting for Tennessee, bringing to an end Texas's superlative run of 26 straight weeks at No. 1.

"The last couple of years is finally paying off," exclaimed Shelley Sexton, a starting senior guard from Lake City, Tennessee, who contributed eight points and four rebounds against Texas. "This is one of the most exciting wins I've played in. Being ranked No. 1, to hear it from your own coach, that means more than anything."

Finally, Warlick was left to muse over the feeling of being No. 1 again, experiencing the honor for the first time as a coach. "They have worked so hard, they deserve to be No. 1," she said. "They're the type of team that can defend a No. 1 ranking."

Orange Bowling

A week after the huge road victory over Texas, the Lady Vols hosted and defeated UCLA before packing their swimsuits and heading south for the post-Christmas holidays to Coral Gables, Florida, site of the Orange Bowl Invitational, a tournament that drew women's college basketball's biggest teams to an impossibly tiny little gym called the Knight Complex, seating capacity: 800.

So small was the facility that teams were literally shoulder to shoulder trying to ferret out pregame and halftime areas to conduct their talks; so small that teams were required to dress in their hotel rooms before the games and had to postpone post-game showers until their return to their hotel rooms; so small that there were no concession stands, and attendees had to visit restrooms outside the gym.

UT dispatched St. Joseph's 76–66 in the tournament opener on December 27 before facing rugged Southern California, the team that had ousted the Lady Vols from the previous year's Final Four, the last time Tennessee had lost a game.

The seventh-ranked Women of Troy ran up a 17-point lead in the first half, but the Trojans, barren on the bench, with illness knocking out two of their players, were a flat tire waiting to happen. Pat Summitt, ever the strategist, eyed the depleted Southern Cal corps and ordered her Lady Vols to run, run, run—substituting frequently and ultimately leaving the exhausted Trojans in their wake. Also, for the first time in four years, USC was without the services of its spectacular All-American, Cheryl Miller, to bolster its attack.

With Bridgette Gordon again leading the way, matching her career-high 26 points posted two weeks earlier in the upset of Texas, the Lady Vols roared off to an 8–0 start in the second half. Point guard Dawn Marsh contributed a game-high 10 assists, and Sheila Frost, the 6–4 sophomore center from Pulaski, Tennessee, converted eight of 14 shots from the field, tallying 20 points and blocking three shots. Her baseline jump shot just before the half gave UT a one-point lead it never relinquished.

"I looked up at the clock, and it was 30–15," said Frost of USC's early lead. "I thought, *No! We're not really down this much! You've got to do it now!* I looked up again after we got out front and said, 'This looks a lot better.'"

Over the last 5:33 of the first half, Tennessee buried the Trojan women 25–7. The 89–75 win set up a rematch with the Texas Lady Longhorns in the finals. Tournament director Lin Dunn couldn't have scripted a better finale: The Orange Bowl Invitational had two Orange-clad finalists, and they just happened to be the No. 1- and No. 2-ranked teams in the country.

Messin' with Texas

Monday evening, December 29, the air was electric inside the bursting Knight Complex, where 400 additional spectators beyond the little gym's capacity of 800 squeezed in to witness the titanic clash of the two UTs: No. 1 Tennessee vs. No. 2 Texas. With neither team's band present inside the primitive facility, fans of both clubs had to content themselves with a cappella versions of "The Eyes of Texas" and barely audible, boom-box renderings of "Rocky Top."

But if Tennessee was expecting a repeat of the exhilarating earlier triumph in Austin, it didn't consult the Lady Longhorns, who protected the ball, placed five players in double figures, avoided serious foul trouble, and received strong bench support throughout its 88–74 win. Texas sophomore forward Clarissa Davis, who had posted a game-high 32 points in the Lady Longhorns' loss to Tennessee a fortnight ago, again claimed scoring honors, knocking down 29 points and grabbing 12 rebounds, on her way to being named Orange Bowl Invitational Tournament MVP.

"Obviously, they were really motivated to play us," explained Pat Summitt. "I thought Texas played harder for 40 minutes than Tennessee did."

Texas All-America forward Andrea Lloyd, completely shut down by Bridgette Gordon in the earlier meeting, hung 11 points and collared 10 rebounds. "They used their post players to get open," noted Gordon of her inside rematch with Lloyd. "They did the little things tonight to get open."

Certainly, there was no lack of motivation on the part of the Lady Longhorns. "There's no question that when Tennessee beat us earlier, they really humiliated us," said Texas coach Jody Conradt. In retaliation, her team connected on 54.2 percent of its shots and hit 24 of 35 from the free-throw line, in denying Summitt her 300th career victory and in reestablishing the Lady Longhorns as the top team in the country. In addition, the Lady Vols turned the ball over 25 times, the exact total of turnovers in their first two tournament games. But most Tennessee players credited the Texas defense as the key element that decided the outcome.

"I just think their defense affected us," noted Karla Horton, the 6–2 junior forward/center from Kershaw, South Carolina. "When we tried to get in an offense, they were in our uniforms."

Lisa Webb, a 5–9 junior from Milledgeville, Georgia, moved to the inside by Summitt for this contest, nailed all five of her shots, while Gordon, who led Tennessee with 14 points, and Frost were named to the all-tournament team. If there was a bright spot in the Orange Bowl tournament, it

AP IMAGES

Shelley Sexton

was the discovery of 6-foot-3 freshman forward Carla McGhee, whose raw potential in preseason transformed into much-needed inside speed and jumping ability in two of the team's tournament games—Southern Cal and Texas.

"That was my first major playing time in college," said McGhee, who logged a total of 36 minutes in the two contests. "It felt good, because I was really into the game. I was mentally into the game on the bench."

Though her point totals were relatively insignificant, McGhee pulled down five rebounds in her brief on-court stint. "You're going to see us play her early a lot," said Summitt. "Carla is the athlete that can give us that quickness."

But the Lady Vols' coach left Florida scratching her head with some standing concerns: "I'm just really searching for what we need to do with our post game," she said. "I've been searching since October 15."

If turnabout is fair play, then the two UTs were dead even. But for Tennessee, the top rating was not just gone for a while; it disappeared for the remainder of the year. But such was the developing state of the "T for Texas-T for Tennessee" rivalry that when the two teams met the next time, on December 9, 1987, at the brand-new Thompson-Boling Arena in Knoxville, a world record for attendance at a women's basketball game was set, with 24,563 fans packed into the venue.

In the eye of the tiger

The Lady Vols christened the New Year with a dominant 19-point win over North Carolina at home, on January 4, before heading out of town to face old adversary Old Dominion. In Norfolk, Virginia, before a paltry crowd of 970 at the ODU Fieldhouse, Tennessee, outgunned by 12 points from the field, converted 33 of 41 charity tosses, including eight of nine foul shots in the last minute, to ward off the Lady Monarchs 99–90.

Just as she had done against the Tar Heel women in the Vols' preceding game, frosh guard Tonya Edwards came off the bench to set her career high, this time canning 20 points, with 5-of-6 shooting from the field and netting all 10 free throws against ODU. Edwards's late hot hand was crucial. In the final 3:30 of the game, she tallied eight points.

"We had a lot of poise when we could have folded," commented Pat Summitt. "The freshman, Tonya Edwards, showed a lot of poise."

Old Dominion kept it interesting. With 2:32 left, the Lady Monarchs were down by just two points. Defensively, ODU resorted to a successful scheme they had employed in their national championship year just two seasons earlier, in which three players down low played zone, while Lady Vols Bridgette Gordon and Shelley Sexton played man-to-man coverage. The packed inside opened up the outside for UT, and point guard Dawn Marsh made the most of it, sinking seven long jumpers.

"I think Old Dominion confused us a bit with their defense," said Summitt. "But Dawn really came through for us. We needed her to make some big shots and she did."

Marsh was delighted and even somewhat surprised by her sterling performance. "I don't think I've ever shot that much," said the 5-foot-6 point guard, who had been averaging just 4.7 points. "They left me open, so I shot the ball. I'm just glad I was hitting." Marsh added six assists and a pair of steals to go with her 14 points.

"We were a little flat," noted Summitt after the foul shot-producing victory. "But ODU may have made us look flat."

The win over Old Dominion primed UT for the start of its demanding conference schedule, tackled head-on four nights later in Stokely Athletic Center with a crisp and efficient win over Kentucky's Lady Wildcats, 76–64.

But the good start ran afoul just four nights later in a game of historic conference proportions. It was the No. 2 Lady Vols versus No. 3-ranked Auburn. A crowd of 5,089—10 times the size of a normal turnout for the Lady Tigers—packed Memorial Coliseum at Auburn to witness the showdown of the SEC's two finest women's hoops programs.

For Auburn, it was a coming-of-age affair. The Lady Tigers entered the game with an unblemished 12–0 mark, the best start in team history. But naysayers pointed to the weakness of the school's competition in suggesting that AU wasn't worthy of being on the same floor with Tennessee, making its first appearance in the "Loveliest Village on the Plains."

"It's the biggest game in the state of Alabama," Auburn head coach Joe Ciampi stumped before the contest. "We've played some big teams in here, but we haven't won. It's a big game to help us leapfrog and become a better team."

The Lady Tigers didn't just leapfrog, they rocketed to a whole new level of respect in the women's game, taking down the Lady Vols 75–69 in a match that showed just a slim one-point AU edge with six seconds remaining. That's when it suddenly turned all Orange and Blue.

With Auburn attempting to inbound the ball from the side court, the Tigers' Mae Ola Bolton charged into UT's Shelley Sexton. Tennessee's senior guard made the front end of a one-and-one to whittle the AU lead to one, at 70–69. Wrestling for the rebound after Sexton's missed second shot, Lady Vol Lisa Webb was fingered for a foul when it appeared a jump ball would be the correct call. Pat Summitt vociferously protested the decision, and official Doug Cloud quickly issued the Tennessee coach a technical. It seems Summitt had ample reason for an objection.

"She [official June Corteau] made a jump-ball call before he [Cloud] ever blew the whistle!" said Summitt afterward.

The argument was to no avail, as Auburn went to the line, hitting three shots on the foul plus the technical. A final Tigers basket at the buzzer accounted for the closing six-point margin.

"We had ample opportunities," Summitt stated. "I thought we kept our poise in the second half."

On-court presence as well as bench composure required near-superhuman concentration by the Tennessee contingent. Auburn's well-wishers shattered the decibel meter throughout the game, forcing Summitt and her team to gather at the foul line during timeouts in the second half.

"Tonight, the volume alone made it difficult to communicate," she told reporters after the game. "That's their sixth player. I wish we had one every night."

The Lady Vols hung on through a subpar first half, surviving 33.3 percent shooting and digging out from a 13-point deficit to enter the second stanza just six points down. A slew of Auburn offensive fouls aided the Vols, not to mention UT's precision from the line, where they canned 13 of 14 shots.

Sexton dramatically punctuated the first 20 minutes with a 50-foot buzzer-beater.

"It would be nice if we could have that lead at halftime," said Bridgette Gordon, who logged 14 points, 12 in the second half. "Getting that jump early in the game tells us how much we mature down the road."

The Tennessee star briefly brought the Lady Vols the lead on an 18-foot baseline jumper with 4:46 to go, and twice in the final four minutes UT closed the lead to one, but they couldn't offset Auburn point guard Helene Baroody's hot hand at the end. The Lady Tigers playmaker hit four of five total shots, dished out five assists, and didn't commit a single turnover in the epic victory.

"Baroody was the difference," said Summitt, in admiration of the Auburn star's Houdini-like escapes from UT's defensive traps and her resultant clutch baskets. "She bailed them out twice when they were in dead-ball situations."

Gordon appeared to have a clairvoyant picture of the Vols' next two and a half months: "We play the toughest schedule in the nation," she said. "I just hope when we get to the postseason that we'll be able to pull out close games like this one."

Vols in Vandyland

Three more SEC tilts plus non-conference bouts with Northwestern and Georgia Tech filled the Lady Vols field of view through January and on into February. Their worksheet would have been a perfect 6–0 during this run had it not been for a tumble at home against No. 8 Ole Miss. Tennessee dispatched Florida, Northwestern, Georgia, and Memphis State, before falling by four points to the Rebels at Stokely. UT rebounded with a triple-digit win over the Yellow Jackets, a 100–74 mauling, before heading west on I-40 to Nashville for a meeting with No. 14 Vanderbilt, on February 4, before 4,297 fans—the largest home crowd in Lady Commodores history.

Tennessee, having fallen to No. 5 in the national rankings with the loss to Mississippi, glided to a secure 43–34 first-half lead. But just as it had wilted in the second half the previous Saturday against Ole Miss, the Lady Vols, committing 25 turnovers, crumbled at Memorial Gym in the final 20 minutes.

"Sports is a funny thing," sympathized Vandy coach Phil Lee. "You can come off a loss so low that you've got to reach up to grab the gutter."

But if Tennessee ever had a hold on the gutter in the second half it wasn't able to hang on, as they went down to their second consecutive SEC loss in a heartbreaker, 77–76. Even UT's mainstay, Bridgette Gordon, was ineffective, totaling only five points. The lackluster performance broke Gordon's personal string of 13 straight games scoring in double figures.

"It hurts," said UT guard Shelley Sexton, who had her best scoring night of the season, with 17. "It's a game we should have won, and it cost us." Unfortunately for the Lady Vols, Sexton's two turnovers in the final minute and a half figured critically in the one-point loss.

Filling Gordon's gap production-wise was center Sheila Frost, who came through with 24 points, including 15 in the first half—her best offensive first half of the season. With family and friends in the stands from her hometown of Pulaski, Tennessee, rooting her on, Frost missed her first four shots before catching fire and netting her next seven in a row.

Forward Karla Horton stepped up, bringing UT back from a 72–62 deficit with six straight points that tied it at 72. But her 14-point contribution also fell short.

"We beat ourselves," Horton remarked. "When nine seconds were left, I thought there was a minute. It seemed like we still had time."

With the loss, Summitt appeared surprisingly upbeat. "I was really pleased with our effort," she said. "I really feel like our team over the past week has been tested. If I could capitalize one thing, I would say unforced errors beat Tennessee." The near future, however, was no breeding ground for optimism, with No. 9 Louisiana State and No. 5 Louisiana Tech waiting in the wings.

Though UT still overwhelmingly led the overall series between the two schools 10–2, Summitt's reaction to the loss was in sharp contrast to her now-legendary response after Vandy's victory two years earlier. Following that 1985 loss at Memorial Gym, Summitt had run her girls through a 3 a.m. practice session when the team returned to Knoxville after the three-hour bus ride home.

Techs-ture

Now having lost two of their last four games, the Lady Vols hit the road for Cajun country and back-to-back games with LSU and Louisiana Tech, both Top 10 teams. UT rebounded from its loss at Vanderbilt, handily beating the Lady Tigers in Baton Rouge, 84–73, before facing daunting Louisiana Tech, owners of a formidable 10–1 series record over Tennessee. If the Lady Techsters had UT's number before, then they were still dialing it without a problem. For the 11th time in 12 meetings, the Lady Vols went down at the hands of the Ruston, Louisiana, residents, 72–60.

"As poorly as we played, we're probably fortunate to be leaving town only 12 points down," Summitt said attempting to find some levity in the defeat. "The bottom line is they're very well coached. They play a smart game, and they're mentally tough."

The game scenario followed the pattern of earlier Vols losses to Tech: poor shooting and poor rebounding. Tennessee shot its series average against the Lady Techsters, hitting 37.7 from the field. Inside, they were outrebounded 50–33.

"Louisiana Tech killed us on the boards," Summitt stated. "They're the best rebounding team we've faced, comparable to Texas. A fundamental thing like not boxing out probably cost us 16 points."

Contributing to UT's demise were 30 fouls, including three personals in the first five minutes that took star forward Bridgette Gordon out of the game completely. For the second time in three games, she was held to single-digit scoring, collecting only eight points in just 15 minutes of playing time. It was the first time in her career she had been held scoreless in the first half.

"Certainly, foul trouble was a factor for Tennessee," Louisiana Tech coach Leon Barmore noted in an understatement. Joining Gordon on the pine were Karla Horton, who sat early because of four fouls. In addition to the two forwards, center Sheila Frost picked up four fouls, while guard Shelley Sexton fouled out. Carla McGhee came off the bench to post 10 points for the Lady Vols, who incredibly sliced the margin to four points twice during the second half even without Gordon and Horton, who both registered their fourth fouls within the first three minutes of the second half.

But the real damage was sustained in the final seven minutes of the first period. Gordon and Horton watched from the bench as UT failed to record a field goal during that eternal stretch. Louisiana Tech took full advantage, going on a 13–3 tear to take a 10-point halftime lead. For the Lady Vols, the indignity could have been worse: Tech's subpar free-throw shooting netted only 18 of 34 from the line.

As usual, Tennessee beat a hasty retreat from Ruston. In looking for a positive, UT fans could point to Frost's four steals and two blocked shots, both game highs for either club. Though it's unlikely it salved any immediate wounds from the Tech game, the Lady Vols, now sitting at No. 7 nationally with a 17–5 record, could look forward to three straight contests back at Stokely. And they would win them all, including a conference game against Mississippi State, before heading to Tuscaloosa to bury the Crimson Tide women with their highest offensive output of the season—a 108–77 blowout.

Tennessee concluded the regular season at home, on March 1, with an even bigger margin of victory against UNC-Charlotte, a monstrous 47-point whitewashing that prepped the team for the start of the annual SEC Tournament, to be held in Albany, Georgia. In the five games after the loss at Louisiana Tech, the Lady Vols had run the table, outscoring their competition by a combined 453 to 285, an average of 33.6 points per game over their foes.

The Orange was ripening in Big Orange Country. It was tournament time!

Auburn in the headlights

With an opening-round match scheduled against Louisiana State to kick off the tourney, it appeared the Lady Vols might have a breather of sorts, even though the women of LSU were ranked 14th in the country. Only a month before, Tennessee had claimed an 11-point victory in Baton Rouge. Such was definitely *not* to be the case this go-round. UT escaped with the narrowest of wins, 64–63, to set up a tournament semifinal showdown against SEC nemesis Auburn.

But the highly anticipated rematch against the regular-season SEC champion Lady Tigers turned out to be a near rerun of the two teams' earlier meeting—a six-point win that opened with AU burning the floor and running the Lady Vols out of Memorial Coliseum. Auburn apparently liked the script for that one, so it used it again, reeling off a 12–2 run that set UT back on its heels. Just as in the late-season loss at Louisiana Tech, Tennessee got zero performance from its starting five. Bridgette Gordon picked up two quick fouls and sat down, while Shelley Sexton could not solve the riddle of the Lady Tigers' defense. Center Sheila Frost went cold, not hitting her first basket until the 3:15 mark.

Enter Summitt's Subs. The trio of Tonya Edwards, Lisa Webb, and Kathy Spinks triggered a Tennessee comeback. Edwards bucketed 12 first-half points, with Spinks and Webb contributing nine each. Edwards, the SEC's leading free-throw shooter, connected on four foul shots in the waning seconds of the first stanza to cut Auburn's lead to 49–45 at halftime. Encouraging, it would seem. Especially in light of Auburn's 14 first-half turnovers, its average for an entire game.

But it was déjà vu all over again. With Tennessee's starters reinserted to begin the second half, the Lady Tigers roared out of the blocks to score 11 unanswered points.

"It's always frustrating when you have to play catch-up," professed Webb, who came up big with 15 points off the bench. "It's like Pat said: The first three minutes of the second half are the most important. We needed to jump on them, and we didn't do that. It was very frustrating."

Spinks, who was selected to the SEC All-Tournament Team, threw in 15 second-half points for UT, en route to her team-high 24. But there was no holding back Auburn, which again won by six, this time 102–96. After the defeat, Summitt simmered.

"I'm definitely going to change the starting lineup," announced the UT mentor. "We had the people starting who we felt like were going to get this team off to a good start. Basically, you look at the stat sheet, and it tells the story."

Statistically, four of the Lady Vols' top five scorers in the contest came off the bench. Defensively, Gordon and Frost recorded game-high totals, with four steals and four blocks respectively. If there was a consolation prize, at season's end Tennessee could take heart in the fact that its 96 points against the Lady Tigers, ranked sixth nationally in defense, would be the highest point total recorded against Auburn all season.

No. 8 Tennessee (23–6), then, was at the mercy of the NCAA Tournament Selection Committee as to where it would wind up, having no idea into which region it would fall. But the team's appearance seemed assured, thanks to having played the nation's most difficult schedule. There was little doubt that No. 2 Auburn (28–1) would be a contender for the national crown all the way.

"Auburn's going to be a top-four seed," Summitt believed. "I would expect them to be in Knoxville [site of the Mideast Regional]. To me, they're definitely a Final Four team. Our goal right now is to be in the Mideast. We've got to win a first- or second-round game. Otherwise, we'll just be hostess."

Auburn in the rearview mirrors

The gods of bracket placement shined kindly on Tennessee, inserting the Lady Vols into, indeed, the Mideast Regional bracket, which of course meant they would have an unofficial home-court advantage at Stokely Athletic Center.

UT drew a first-round bye and opened in the second round against instate non-rival Tennessee Tech, whom they creamed 95–59. In the regional semifinals they were strong in a 66–58 victory over Virginia. And then . . . well, well, what have we here?

Looks like Auburn on the radar, back for its third taste of Orange. What kind of strange karma or odd bit of NCAA scheduling had the Lady Tigers again blocking the door to the Final Four?

When you get the chance for perspective, it usually comes at the expense of time. Looking back now at the '87 season, it's easy to see which game was the turning point in the season, which was the high-water mark, the low. Twice the Lady Tigers had done away with Tennessee like so much clutter in its path. In both games, though, UT, stymied offensively, hung in and lost by only six. The issue of solving Auburn's well-publicized full-court press occupied a lot of pregame attention, with even a solution offered to Pat Summitt in the local *Knoxville News-Sentinel* by the top high school woman's basketball coach in the area. Good night.

But AU's 2-2-1 zone press was no joke, figuring strongly in both earlier Auburn wins. In those matches, the Lady Vols trailed early then fell short despite gutsy comebacks.

"The times before, they executed very well and outre-bounded us," guard Dawn Marsh noted. "We need to execute better and for sure beat their zone press." That dreaded press featured the athletic Lady Tigers clogging up the passing lanes and quickly covering a lot of the court. "It's just so active," added Marsh. "It's very rare that you see a press that's so active."

Auburn's Baroody wasn't shy in telling how to beat the press. "Don't get flustered with our press," she began. "Take your time, pass it around. Use a lot of pass fakes." Would Summitt and her Lady Vols take the suggestion?

Auburn's No. 2-ranked Lady Tigers (31–1, losing only to Georgia by a single point) were taking aim at their first Final Four appearance. The tradition-rich Lady Vols (25–6), at No. 7, were attempting to make their second straight visit to the Final Four, which would also be their third time in four seasons and eighth time in 11 seasons.

"We played catch-up with them both games," said Summitt prior to the two teams' third meeting of the year. "We can't afford to play catch-up tomorrow night. Obviously, we're going to have to make a few changes. The bottom line is it comes down to execution. Turnovers always play a significant role in the outcome of a basketball game."

Barely gaining notice was a small announcement made just before the big Mideast Regional final that ran in the papers as an end-of-story add-on: Drug testing would be introduced for the first time in women' basketball history after all four regional championship games, according to the NCAA, which was conducting the tests. Five starters and three random players from the winner's roster would be tested after each final.

Holy Stokely!

The old cliché "If at first you don't succeed, try, try again" was never more in evidence than in the 1987 NCAA Mideast Regional championship game. While mystics may feel that the third attempt at an endeavor is charmed, in the Lady Vols case that number was eight. If nothing else, Tennessee's big 77–61 win in the regional final over archrival Auburn at Stokely Athletic Center was a paramount example of perseverance at work.

At the outset, it appeared that No. 7 UT (26–6) had learned nothing from its previous two losses to the Lady Tigers. Auburn opened with its efficient web-like zone press in full working order, forcing Tennessee into five turnovers in the first three and a half minutes, four of them committed by freshman guard Tonya Edwards that enabled the Lady Tigers to run off to a 15–8 lead. Same old, same old. But early foul trouble for three of its starting five eventually undid Auburn. With AU's star forward Mae Ola Bolton, guard Diann McNeil, and center Vickie Orr all sitting at times throughout the first half, the Lady Vols began to chew away at Auburn's advantage just past the half's midpoint.

Coming through with her second straight breakout game, Lady Vol forward Bridgette Gordon couldn't have regained her old form at a better time. The DeLand, Florida, sophomore took over the game, ripping the cords for 33 points, hitting nine of 10 from the charity line, and pulling down 10 rebounds. At her sides were solid contributions from center Sheila Frost and forward Karla Horton, who poured in five and four points respectively during Tennessee's hot 11–0 first-half run that produced some of the team's best basketball since UT's big win at Austin in December over then-top-ranked Texas. At game's end, Frost had totaled 15 points and grabbed a game-high 13 boards. Horton added 13 points.

"The last two times, to borrow one of Pat's phrases, it seemed like I was hiding," remarked Frost, on the two earlier losses to the Lady Tigers. "Tonight, I wanted people to know I was playing." Her performance in the regional placed her on the all-tournament team.

Gordon was equally effusive about her own play. "They were giving me the ball when I was hot," she said. "You're seeing a different Bridgette Gordon."

Coupled with its foul troubles, a lack of conversion at the free-throw line doomed Auburn. Though they started hot, going seven for eight from the stripe before the half, the Lady Tigers cooled after intermission, making only six of their final 18 foul shots. Overall, Tennessee shut down AU from the field as well, holding Auburn to just a 39.3 shooting percentage. Conversely, UT shot 50.0 percent, getting strong help from a bench that supplied 28 points. In the end, the happy home crowd of 7,533 clamored as the Lady Vols pulled away.

Lady Tigers coach Joe Ciampi was glib about factors influencing the game's outcome. "Nobody went out there and helped Tennessee play defense," he said. "The way they played tonight, they could have probably gone on top of the Holiday Inn and done a job." Finally, the sizable task of what his team had attempted became unavoidable. "It's difficult to beat any good team three times," Ciampi admitted.

A mix of determination and relief poured from Gordon, after being held to eight points and fouling out in the SEC Tournament semifinals loss to the Lady Tigers. "Tonight, I had just one thing in mind: Auburn wasn't going to beat me on my home court," she said. "In the beginning of the game, I couldn't have fun. I was talking to myself, saying, 'Relax.'"

For the Lady Vols, good fortune seems to follow whenever they host the Mideast Regional. The '87 triumph became the school's third crown in as many times of hosting the event. UT also took the region from its home court in 1982 and '84.

So, it was on to the Final Four, in of all places, Austin, Texas, where as fate would have it, the Lady Longhorns had progressed through their bracket to land a spot on their home court for the NCAA semifinals and possibly even the title game.

But UT had already made its presence felt in Austin with the big upset win in December. If they were thinking of Texas, they still had to get by an extraordinarily talented Long Beach State team that had ousted Ohio State in the West Regional championship game to enter the Final Four with an impressive 33–2 record.

But on this night, confidence oozed from Tennessee. "If we play the way we played tonight," said Gordon, "we'll bring home a national championship."

Final Four

In Austin, excitement before the Final Four was building to a fever pitch, with tickets to the women's event on the tough-to-get list. Texas officials announced that a sold-out, NCAA Final Four-record crowd of 15,615 would be on hand for the two bonanza games.

Long Beach State, a cadre of talkative and gifted athletes, featured the superb play of All-America forward Cindy Brown, a 6-2 senior who had established the women's single-game NCAA scoring record with 60 points against San Jose State earlier in the season. She would earn a unique infamy from the contest aside from her outstanding play. It was Brown who coined the now-legendary phrase "corn-fed chicks" used to describe the 1986–87 Lady Vols. The phrase stuck as a nickname for the team that would hand Pat Summitt her first NCAA crown. Brown's comment was a result of comparing the two semifinalists' physical attributes: Tennessee wide bodies versus the 49ers' sleek, lean, lithe athletes.

"You may be big and thick, but I'm skinny and quick," she rhymed. "With corn-fed chicks like that . . . they use it to a great advantage. If they're bigger, I'll stay away from them defensively. I just don't like that physical contact. If they stay too close, I'll just go around them." Brown then added a thought-provoking comment about her fellow 49ers: "Our team plays so fast, it's like international ball."

And so it was that Tennessee's "corn-fed chicks" took the floor against a runnin', gunnin' bunch of Californians that had spectacularly beat up on several opponents during the regular season. So preposterous were some final scores that they looked like misprints: Long Beach State over San Jose State, 149–69; a 105–25 rout of Cal-Santa Barbara; a repeat mugging of San Jose State, 120–53.

The Lady Vols would assign a quick and large post player, 6-2 Kathy Spinks, to guard the highly productive Brown. And Summitt, to her great credit, scrupulously prepared her team by running the 49ers' feared run-and-press attack all week in practice.

"We knew their plays better than they did," Bridgette Gordon would say after the game.

Summitt, looking for her 318th career victory but first

national championship, said: "I look at Long Beach as having a lot of similarities to Auburn. We've played a lot of people who enjoy running the basketball this year."

Joan Bonvicini, head coach of the 49ers women, indicated that her plan was to stick with their strengths against UT. "Our game is to press and run," she said. "We're going to press from the beginning of our game until the end."

The Lady Vols were unanimous in their feelings surrounding Summitt's presence in the Final Four for the eighth time. Bridgette Gordon's words seemed to hang in the air until tipoff: "This year we're on a mission," said the sensational sophomore forward. "It would mean a lot [to win the national title]. She has done a tremendous job with me. I would like to give that back to her."

Friday night at the Frank Erwin Center, No. 7 Tennessee, with six losses—more than the other three teams' losses combined—broke from the gate and eased to a 25–15 lead, before Long Beach State switched defenses and began to shut down the Lady Vols offensively. In fact, the 49ers took a 30–28 half-time lead. But Tennessee pounded the boards, working tough inside, and outmuscled Long Beach State on rebounds 47–37. Tonya Edwards, the freshman guard, came through with a career-high 21 points. But the big ace up the Lady Vols' sleeve turned out to be 5-foot-10 Melissa McCray, a minister's daughter from Johnson City, Tennessee, known more for her defense.

McCray produced a season-high 14 points, connecting on five of seven long-range shots from beyond the three-point arc. Of course, they didn't count as threes. That wouldn't happen until the following year, as the NCAA announced during the Final Four weekend that the three-point rule would be in effect for all of women's college basketball in 1987–88. (Some conferences, among them the Southwest Conference, employed it in 1986–87 as part of a trial run. The women's arc would be the same as the men's, 19 feet, 9 inches.) Still, McCray's performance surprised the 49ers, who admitted that UT's sophomore guard/forward was a bit off their radar.

"McCray hurt us, and we didn't expect that," conceded Bonvicini. "She had not been a factor in the games we scouted. She hit very key baskets."

McCray's dependableness down the stretch ignited Tennessee. With just over four minutes remaining, she hit from the top of the key to put UT up 57–55. Another McCray 18-footer stretched the lead to four. Then, with just 1:17 left, she canned both ends of a one-and-one to ensure the 74–64 victory.

"I like the confidence she has," said Summitt. "Melissa has never hesitated to shoot the ball in a pressure situation." McCray's marksmanship ultimately affected other areas of the game.

"It really opened up the inside," said Gordon of her roommate McCray. "We were telling her at halftime she needed to shoot the ball, because they weren't respecting her at all." Gordon benefited highly from McCray's effectiveness, finishing with 21 points and 11 rebounds.

The 49ers were held to their lowest scoring output of not only the 1986–87 season but over their past 73 games, shooting just 38.8 percent, and failed to lead at any time by more than four points. Tennessee was golden at the free-throw line, hitting 24 of 29 overall and 10 of 11 in the final 2:49, with the reliable Edwards going six for six.

"They showed a lot of poise when they needed to show poise," Bonvicini said of UT's performance. Her own all-star, the talented Brown, had been commanding, registering game highs in scoring (27 points), rebounding (an NCAA semifinals record 18), blocks (4), and steals (tied, with 2).

For Summitt, it would be her fourth NCAA final, having come up short in 1980, '81, and '84. One of those previous title game losses was to the Lady Vols' foe in the upcoming 1987 championship game: Louisiana Tech, which in 1981 had soundly thrashed the Lady Vols by 20 points, 79–59, for the national crown. The same night that Tennessee ousted Long Beach State, the Lady Techsters stunned No. 1 Texas to set up the Sunday afternoon showdown in Longhorn Country.

Here's looking at you, Tech

How many Goliaths does David have to slay!

It wasn't enough to finally overcome an Auburn squad that had taken two earlier games from Tennessee with its nearly impenetrable zone press. Then the highest scoring team in the nation strolls into the gym, and UT has to outdraw this quickest of gunslingers, in Long Beach State. Now the top of the mountain is barred by a team that literally owns the Lady Vols.

Everyone in the world of women's college basketball was aware of the 11–1 stranglehold that Louisiana Tech had on Tennessee, including the 1981 national championship game defeat. In fact, the only time the Lady Vols had ever beaten Louisiana Tech was at home in 1979–80, when they barely edged the Lady Techsters by two points. In sharp contrast, the average margin of victory by Louisiana Tech in the 11 victories over the Lady Vols was an intimidating 14.9 points per game.

During the past 1986–87 season, Louisiana Tech was 29–1 in games in which it had outrebounded the other team. In Ruston, in February, Tech had outmuscled UT on the boards, 50–33. Even beyond the national crown itself, the Lady Techsters had additional incentive. One more win would give them their 400th lifetime victory, their 399–63 worksheet to that point representing the highest winning percentage in women's college basketball history. Between them, Tennessee and Louisiana Tech had amassed 15 Final Four appearances, two national titles (both Louisiana Tech's), and five second-place finishes in the championship game.

"They're not going to beat themselves," intoned Summitt before the title contest. "They play with a lot of poise. We've had the least amount of success against Louisiana Tech as we've had with any of the top teams in the country. We're overdue."

Louisiana Tech coach Leon Barmore noted that the clash portended a physical game by both teams: "I think you'll see a backstreet brawl," he said. "We gave up 20 offensive rebounds to Texas. If Tennessee gets 20 offensive rebounds, they'll take the trophy home to Knoxville. For us to be 11–1 against them is really incredible. There's no explanation for that."

Part of Summitt's game plan would be to rotate her post people. "They'll have their work cut out for them," she said. "And I'm real concerned about the point position. When we were down there, I thought she [Lady Techster guard Teresa Weatherspoon] did a job on all three of our point guards."

Though Coach Barmore's crew had the longest current winning streak in the women's game, at 19, still, there was a clairvoyant feeling in the air among some of the Lady Vols. "I think this is our year," offered Gordon before the big game. "Lately, I've just been feeling that way. I daydream about going back to school, walking around campus as national champs."

Summitt optimistically summed it up: "Talent-wise, these two teams match up very well."

National champions

It may not have matched Joe Namath's famous "guarantee" to beat the Baltimore Colts in Super Bowl III for sheer drama, but freshman Tonya Edwards's pre-NCAA-championship-game remark came pretty close.

"Like I told Pat before I signed with her," said Edwards on the eve of the national title game against Louisiana Tech, "'You've won everything but a national championship. I want to help you win a national championship.'" All Edwards did was back up her promise to Summitt with an NCAA Final Four MVP performance.

The evening of March 29, 1987, was the tale of the little engine that could; the little guy that beat the big guy, with an attacking defense the preferred weapon of choice rather than the biblical slingshot. Before a championship game-record crowd of 9,823 in Austin's Erwin Center, the Tennessee Lady Vols handed head coach Pat Summitt the pinnacle moment of her 13-year coaching career. Mighty Louisiana Tech had fallen. The conquering seventh-ranked Lady Vols were national champions, having upset No. 2 Auburn, No. 4 Long Beach State, and No. 3 Louisiana Tech.

"I think Tennessee played as good a defensive game as I've ever seen or ever played against," praised Louisiana Tech coach Leon Barmore, after the Lady Vols buried his Lady Techsters 67–44.

UT (28–6) posted balanced scoring and rebounding muscle to augment a tight defense, with Edwards, forward Bridgette Gordon, and center Sheila Frost each contributing 13 points. The Lady Vols' big three also set the pace under the boards, where Tennessee claimed dominance with a 47–36 advantage over Louisiana Tech, the trio logging seven, 12, and eight rebounds respectively. Ironically, Barmore's earlier mention that UT might take home the title if they collected 20 offensive rebounds proved to be on the money.

If the Lady Techsters (30–3 overall) were rattled, it showed. They hit just 12 of 22 from the free-throw line and committed 20 turnovers. Barmore found more.

"One element of the game—and I knew it was a problem for us going in—was the ability to pass the basketball," he said. "When we got someone open, we didn't get the ball to them on time." Normally high-scoring Louisiana Tech forward Nora Lewis was kept in check by a tenacious Gordon. Lewis ended with 12 points on just 4-of-11 shooting, team-high for Tech. Two egregious pockets of time elapsed when the Lady Techsters were silent, going without scoring for three minutes and 31 seconds in the first half followed by a near-eternal five-minute lapse without points in the second half. The poor production was Louisiana Tech's lowest scoring output since an 81–44 loss to Southeastern Louisiana way back in 1974. The Vols' 23-point victory was also Tech's second-worst margin of defeat in school history.

"The monkey's off my back!" yelled Summitt. Then she talked about her team. "Everybody said they'd win it next year. This young team may never have another opportunity like this. . . . I told them today, 'Don't approach this game like, Hey, this is the national championship and we've got to win it. Approach it like any other game.' It was a matter of fact they were going to win it. They didn't want to go to the movies this week, go to the mall. They wanted to win it."

Summitt was classic Summitt down the stretch of the title game, getting after her charges right up until the final buzzer. "I did not want to let up," she said amidst the jubilation of the post-game celebration. "You can celebrate too early." The woman who had an Olympic gold medal for her role as head coach of the 1984 U.S. women's basketball team (America's first gold in that event), who had played as an Olympian in 1976, now had a national championship to go along with her 319th coaching win at Tennessee.

"Winning the gold medal was a great moment. That was for the country," said Summitt. "This one is just as special. The University of Tennessee has been so good to me and women in sports. There are a lot of people who have believed in Tennessee. This win is for them."

The UT icon's belief in her team as possible championship contenders escalated as tournament time approached. "I'm a dreamer, and I'm also a believer," said the Lady Vols mentor. "In the last two weeks, I believed our team could do it."

The euphoria of the milestone victory—Tennessee became the first SEC school to win an NCAA title in women's basketball—was pictured sweetly as Summitt and Shelley Sexton, whom Summitt had recruited four years earlier from Lake City, Tennessee, embraced when the senior guard was removed 42 seconds from the end of the game.

"I told Shelley I wanted to be the first to ride in the Mercedes her father promised to buy her if we ever won a national championship," quipped Summitt. As events turned out there was little need for that. Though Sexton's father came through on his promise to his daughter, Summitt was given her own Mercedes Benz convertible by a local dealership upon the Lady Vols' triumphant return to Knoxville. Summitt had additional words for the woman she said reminded her a lot of her younger self.

"We're both overachievers," said Summitt of Sexton. "We're both competitors. We're both fighters. It's a victory she has wanted as badly as me. She's a Tennessean. It's special to her. I tell you, Shelley looked good in orange today."

Sexton noted those likenesses in her own comments: "I'm sure there are similarities between Coach Summitt and me," acknowledged the Lady Vols' co-captain. "We're both intense. We're both from small towns. We're both winners. We've shared this dream for four years. I'm serious when I say I love her."

The Lady Vols all credited Summitt's game plan and its implementation by the assistant coaches as critical to the outcome. "Pat, Mickie [DeMoss], and Holly [Warlick] busted their butts day in and day out going over game films," acknowledged Gordon, selected to the NCAA All-Tournament Team along with Edwards. Summitt, in turn, recognized her players for their execution, saying that the 1986–87 Lady Vols gave the best back-to-back defensive performances of any of her UT teams on record: "I haven't had a team carry out a game plan any better," she stated proudly.

It was also noted that the women's title triumph was Tennessee's third national crown claimed in Austin, hailed alongside the 1974 men's track national champions and the women's track titlists of 1981.

Summitt had the wisdom to know the future impact of this special game on her young players. "I told them in the locker room, 'This championship will mean as much or more in the days and years to come than it will today. I don't think you can really grasp what this means to the state of Tennessee and the university.'"

That seemed evident with some of the new national champions, who initially couldn't comprehend the magnitude of the event. A fatigued Sheila Frost felt like taking a nap. "I'm mentally drained," the 6–4 center said after the championship game. "It just seems like we won another game." Freshman Carla McGhee's reality check didn't occur until the team arrived back in Knoxville. "Until we rode limos on campus, that's when it really sunk in," she said. "We got on the Strip, and you could see people waving to you on the streets. No one can take that ring and championship from us."

Twenty years later, guard Shelley Sexton, now assistant athletic director and head women's basketball coach at Knoxville's Webb High School, recalled her thoughts about the long road she and her teammates had traveled to finally bring UT women's basketball its first national championship.

"We were just feeling humiliated, getting beat by Southern Cal [the year before, in the 1986 Final Four semifinals at Lexington]," said Sexton at the 20-year reunion of the 1987 national champion team in Knoxville. "I can remember just wanting it *so* bad that I couldn't move. Living with that feeling the whole rest of the next year through practice and the season, knowing that you were a senior and that you're supposed to be a leader and set the tone. Feeling the pressure of making sure you were doing all you could do just to get back to that point and have a chance.

"It was just an unbelievable team. The chemistry; coming back my last year, my senior year; how everybody just played their role. It didn't matter who did what. We just wanted to win."

Summitt, in 2007, was equally reflective on her first national championship team. "Obviously, I remember the players," she said. "As you reflect, you think more about the relationships that you had with the student-athletes. I think, with this group in particular, it was the journey more than anything. The ultimate goal was to win a championship, but when we lost at Louisiana Tech [72–60, February 9, 1987], I just told 'em that they were too nice to win a national championship and that nice girls finish last. I wasn't sure we had it. But then, we began to prepare for Long Beach State in the Final Four. They had the No. 1 offensive team in the country, and they were *fast*! They scored all the time off transition. I just remember our whole preparation. I remember getting upset with Bridgette because she wasn't real inspired to practice one day—one of many days! You've got to love her, though. Come game time, she played!"

Upset at her team's lack of energy in practice, Summitt remembers huddling with her players before that '87 title game. "'What do you think Auburn would be doing now?' [Tennessee had beaten the Lady Tigers in the regional finals.] They'd *love* to be out here working!'" Summitt told her attentive team. "'*We're* sure not working!' So when we got [to the Final Four in Austin, Texas], Mimi Griffith, who was in charge of our press conference, said after it, 'I've never seen you this calm in a Final Four.' And I said, 'Well, Mimi, I've decided Tennessee's going to win a championship. I don't know when it's going to be. I just hope I'm the coach. I just hope I get to see it.' I had a good feeling. When we got to the hotel, I ran into Karla [Horton] coming off the elevator. I said, 'Hey, how y'all doin', you ready to go?' And I'll never forget the look on Karla's face. She said, 'Coach, we're on a mission.' And I believed her. I got out of her way! It was just a neat group. I think they just have something inside that was really special."

It was left to Summitt's father, Richard, to place the final stamp on the 1987 national champions. "Trish," he said to his daughter, "tell them girls we're planting two acres of corn, and we're going to plant three more."

Yes, Tennessee's corn-fed chicks had come home to roost.

1986–87
(28–6, 6–3 SEC, 4th)
Final AP Ranking: 7th
NCAA Mideast Regional Champions
NCAA NATIONAL CHAMPIONS

ROSTER

No.	Player	Yr.	Pos.	Ht.	Hometown
4	**Dawn Marsh**	**Jr**	**G**	**5–6**	**Alcoa, TN**
11	Kathy Spinks	Jr	F/C	6–2	Forest Hills, KY
12	**Sheila Frost**	**So**	**C**	**6–4**	**Pulaski, TN**
14	Gay Townson	Jr	F	5–9	Loudon, TN
23	**Shelley Sexton**	**Sr**	**G**	**5–7**	**Lake City, TN**
24	Carla McGhee	Fr	F	6–3	Peoria, IL
30	**Bridgette Gordon**	**So**	**F**	**6–0**	**DeLand, FL**
32	Jennifer Tuggle	So	F	6–2	Etowah, TN
33	Tonya Edwards	Fr	G	5–10	Flint, MI
34	Lisa Webb	Jr	F	5–9	Milledgeville, GA
35	Melissa McCray	So	G/F	5–10	Johnson City, TN
40	Sabrina Mott	Fr	G	5–9	Brentwood, TN
44	Cheryl Littlejohn	Sr	C	6–3	Gastonia, NC
55	**Karla Horton**	**Jr**	**F/C**	**6–2**	**Kershaw, SC**

(starters in bold)

SEASON STATS

Player	PPG	RPG	FG-Pct.	FT-Pct.
Bridgette Gordon	16.4	6.8	.484	.719
Sheila Frost	11.3	6.4	.590	.598
Karla Horton	9.8	6.8	.459	.717
Tonya Edwards	8.9	2.7	.432	.788
Shelley Sexton	8.2	2.8	.459	.689
Melissa McCray	5.5	2.2	.438	.743
Dawn Marsh	5.2	1.6	.484	.723
Lisa Webb	4.5	2.2	.467	.769
Carla McGhee	4.3	3.3	.474	.688
Kathy Spinks	4.1	2.7	.455	.532
Jennifer Tuggle	2.5	1.1	.468	.571
Cheryl Littlejohn	1.9	1.3	.467	.692
Gay Townson	0.8	0.2	.500	1.000
Sabrina Mott	0.7	0.4	.000	.700

1986–87 UT POLL HISTORY

Starting position:	3rd (11/18/86)
Highest 1986–87 ranking:	1st (three times)
Lowest 1986–87 ranking:	9th (2/16/87)
Final 1986–87 position:	7th (3/10/87)
NCAA Tournament finish:	NCAA CHAMPIONS

1986–87 SCHEDULE

Date	Rank	Site	W/L	Score	Opponent
11/29/86	3/nr	N	W	86–70	Providence
11/30/86	3/8	A	W	74–56	Iowa
12/4/86	3/nr	H	W	66–40	Dayton
12/6/86	3/20	H	W	86–65	N.C. State
12/14/86	3/1	A	W	85–78	Texas
12/20/86	1/nr	H	W	81–58	UCLA
12/27/86	1/nr	N	W	76–66	St. Joseph's
12/28/86	1/7	N	W	89–75	Southern Cal
12/29/86	1/2	N	L	74–88	Texas
1/4/87	1/nr	H	W	87–68	North Carolina
1/7/87	2/nr	A	W	99–90	Old Dominion
1/11/87	2/nr	H	W	76–64	Kentucky
1/14/87	2/3	A	L	69–75	Auburn
1/17/87	2/nr	A	W	90–72	Florida
1/20/87	3/nr	A	W	74–71	Northwestern
1/24/87	3/12	H	W	78–72	Georgia
1/28/87	3/nr	H	W	91–81	Memphis State
1/31/87	3/8	H	L	65–69	Mississippi
2/2/87	5/nr	H	W	100–74	Georgia Tech
2/4/87	5/14	A	L	76–77	Vanderbilt
2/7/87	5/9	A	W	84–73	Louisiana State
2/9/87	7/5	A	L	60–72	Louisiana Tech
2/14/87	7/nr	H	W	90–55	Notre Dame
2/19/87	9/nr	H	W	80–56	South Carolina
2/21/87	9/nr	H	W	84–53	Mississippi State
2/25/87	8/nr	A	W	108–77	Alabama
3/1/87	8/nr	H	W	91–44	UNC-Charlotte
SEC TOURNAMENT (3rd), Albany, Ga.					
3/5/87	8/14	N	W	64–63	Louisiana State
3/6/87	8/2	N	L	96–102	Auburn

(rankings are for UT/opponent)

NCAA FIRST ROUND, Knoxville, Tenn.

3/15/87	7/nr	H	W	95–59	Tennessee Tech

NCAA MIDEAST REGIONAL CHAMPIONSHIPS, Knoxville, Tenn.

3/19/87	7/11	H	W	66–58	Virginia
3/21/87	7/2	H	W	77–61	Auburn

NCAA FINAL FOUR, Austin, Texas

3/27/87	7/4	N	W	74–64	Long Beach State
3/29/87	7/3	N	W	67–44	Louisiana Tech

(BRAZILIAN TOUR)

6/14/87		A	L-ex	71–104	UNIMEP Sao Paulo (Brazil)
6/17/87		N	L-ex	62–85	Prague Univ. (Czechoslovakia)
6/18/87		N	W-ex	88–44	Argentinian Natl. Team
6/19/87		N	L-ex	74–86	South Korean Natl. Team
6/20/87		A	L-ex	68–105	Brazilian Natl. Team

2

1988–89

"God Bless Her, Graduate and Get Out of Tennessee"

THE 1987 NATIONAL CHAMPIONSHIP HAD become just a warm memory by the end of the following season. But once again, Tennessee was in the hunt for the national title. For the third straight year, and ninth time in head coach Pat Summitt's sterling 14-year coaching career on The Hill, the Lady Vols were in the Final Four. Some things never change. But appearances in the Final Four aren't the only events occasionally set in stone. Old rivalries, too, have a way of sticking around in the same inexorable way.

Yes, the Lady Vols were Final Four bound in March of 1988. No, they would not leave with another NCAA crown. Yes, they fell once again to their bitterest rival and ultimate national champion. An old familiar refrain reverberated in the rafters of the Tacoma Dome in Washington, as UT felt the sting of elimination at the hands of archnemesis Louisiana Tech in the semifinals. The loss, denying Tennessee a second straight title shot, left the Lady Vols wrestling with their eternal demon from

Ruston, Louisiana, through the off-season and into late November of the 1988–89 campaign, when, as fate would have it, the two adversaries were paired in the finals of the Rainbow Wahine Classic in Honolulu.

"Revenge was going through my mind the whole time," admitted senior Sheila Frost, the 6–3 center from Pulaski, Tennessee. Frost had a particularly painful seven months to endure since the galling defeat the previous April: She had been shut out, failing to score a single point in the nightmarish 68–59 loss to the Lady Techsters. "That's the only thing that was going through my mind."

Frost's chance at redemption now came in the 1988 rematch in Hawaii. With a single point separating the two teams at halftime, the contest went neck and neck, the lead changing hands throughout the first 10 minutes of the second half. Both defenses were superb, so tenacious that for a period of three and a half minutes late in the game neither side scored. Eventually, junior guard Tonya Edwards hit a short seven-footer to knot the contest at 52, forcing the game into overtime.

Throughout the extra period, the teams battled back and forth, and with 15 seconds left in overtime, Frost went to the line for two free throws. She sank them both to carry the Lady Vols to a one-point victory, 62–61, over the defending national champions. Only a paltry 450 spectators at Klum Gym actually witnessed the big moment, but it mattered little to UT's rangy center, lost in concentration.

"When I got to the free-throw line, all I did was relax," said Frost. "I knew they were in the moment I touched the ball."

Louisiana Tech head coach Leon Barmore was impressed. "I thought it was pretty clutch shooting on Frost's part," he said. Frost, who closed with 12 points, was selected to the all-tournament team, along with Edwards and Bridgette Gordon, who admitted to no small case of payback herself.

"The loss [in the '88 Final Four to Louisiana Tech] was in the back of my mind. I had to live with that," said Gordon. "I had to sleep and eat and think about it all the time, how they beat us in Tacoma."

That motivation fired up the 6–0 senior forward, who responded with a 16-point performance, in the process becoming

Tennessee's all-time leading scorer, with 1,778 points to that point in her luminous career. Gordon's play earned her the tournament's most valuable player award.

"I couldn't let Tennessee lose," she said. "I don't think they should have beaten us then, either. It's great that we got them back once, but I want to play them again and beat them again. They lead the series [12–4], and it's time for us to turn it around."

Gordon made serious development in all facets of her game during the off-season between her junior and senior years, as one might expect of a member of the U.S. Olympic team. With Gordon and her cronies pocketing the 1988 Olympic gold medal at Seoul, South Korea, the high-level experience of international play brought a new maturity to the veteran forward.

"Bridgette has added another dimension to her game," noticed Heidi VanDerveer, a former graduate assistant with Tennessee through Gordon's junior season. And teammate Tonya Edwards saw the difference, too. "She is more of a threat this season, because she's not just a shooter," said Edwards. "She is now a passer, and she's moving well off the ball. She's a lot smarter player, too.

Gordon's coach also couldn't help but pick up on the growth. "After the Olympic experience, I knew Bridgette would come back as a different player," said Pat Summitt, herself an Olympic player in 1976. "I really feel like she has got to be one of the top two players in the country if not the best."

Twenty years later, former *Knoxville News-Sentinel* sportswriter Kim Boatman would look back at Gordon and remember her work as pioneering. "Bridgette Gordon had electrifying athleticism and great basketball skills," said Boatman. "She was a harbinger of women's basketball to come."

Meanwhile, back at the Rainbow Wahine Classic, Tech's Barmore acknowledged his team's conqueror. "Tennessee is the No. 1 team in the nation, and they played extremely good defense," he said. The same was certainly true of his Lady Techsters, whom Summitt felt, outplayed her Vols.

"The game was a big win for us, but I don't think we played especially well at all," she said of her team that was outrebounded 36–34, committed 24 turnovers, and shot just 43 percent from the field. "We were able to get some key baskets and pull it out when it counted. It was good for us to play competition like this early in the season."

The No. 1 Lady Vols, with the big win, went to 3–0 on the young season, having earlier disposed of Illinois and Washington by 31- and 22-point margins. Maturity marked the club unlike the unseasoned champions of 1987. Senior leadership was at every point on the court, with starters Gordon, Frost, and Melissa McCray robustly weighing in. In the off-season Summitt outdid herself, bringing in an unusually large class of five new freshmen, three from Tennessee.

"They are five different personalities with five different styles," noted Summitt of home-state forwards Debbie Scott, Kelli Casteel, and Debbie Hawhee, along with Michigan guards Dena Head and Regina Clark." As if seeing into her near future, Summitt commented on the particular fan friendliness of future star Head and her sidekick Clark. "I think they're all exciting players, particularly Regina and Dena. They have a flashier style that's very spectator pleasing."

Little could Summitt have known at the time how critical a role Head, a future NCAA All-Final Four Team selection and All-American, would wind up playing in that 1988–89 season.

Running with Long Beach

Heading into December, the No. 1-ranked Lady Vols (3–0) hosted a rematch against the team they had beaten in the NCAA Final Four two seasons earlier. Long Beach State was long on running, and questions before the game, as usual, centered around whether UT could keep up with the fast-paced Californians or would be run out of the relatively new Thompson-Boling Arena, which had replaced aging Stokely Athletic Center as the home for Tennessee's men's and women's basketball programs in 1987–88.

As it turned out, the match was a mismatch, as UT opened up an early 40–19 lead. Though the 49ers cut the bulge to five points in the second half, courtesy of an effective full-court press, Tennessee's powerful front line halted the comeback to close with a resounding 88–74 win.

Incredibly, the Lady Vols outscored their No. 2-ranked

opponent from the coast 63–10 inside, with Sheila Frost and Bridgette Gordon each contributing 20 points, while sophomore Daedra Charles muscled down 11 rebounds and added 13 points. Making even more of a difference, UT sent its players to the foul line 53 times, converting 36 tries, while the 49ers visited the stripe just 13 times, scoring only seven points. That's a 29-point swing on foul shots alone. Amazingly, only one foul was called against the Lady Volunteers in the last 13 minutes of the game.

Frost found herself free at the high post on several occasions and took some unguarded jumpers to augment her inside scoring. "I want to stay low," Frost said, "but if something comes up high I'm not going to stand there like a dummy."

Frost had a surprising fan in the hall, none other than Long Beach State coach Joan Bonvicini. "I don't think she gets enough credit," noted the 49ers' mentor. "She's the heart and soul of the team."

Frost and her frontline mates, Gordon and Charles, proved the decisive force underneath that ultimately brought Long Beach State to its knees, with the threesome totaling 32 points in the first half alone. "With people of Sheila and Daedra's size and capabilities," said Summitt, "you have to take advantage of them."

Not that the dynamic trio did it all by themselves. Guard Tonya Edwards took the fouls that the 49ers gave her, and the free-throw ace connected on 11 of 13 from the line, part of her game total of 19, all scored after the intermission. The brilliant junior showcased her other skills too, leading both clubs in steals, with five, and hauling down 10 rebounds.

And did I mention that the Lady Vols ran? Ran with, according to Pat Summitt, the fastest team in the country? "Tennessee ran more against us than I've ever seen them do," acknowledged Bonvicini after her team's loss, "but they'll have to get used to that with the West Coast teams."

That was a fact, all right. UT's next three opponents, in a scheduling oddity, were all from California, and all were uptempo teams. Southern California, Stanford, and UCLA would each visit Thompson-Boling Arena in December.

In the end, the exasperated 49ers were asking a question

that, ironically, one of their own celebrated teammates just two years earlier could have answered authoritatively.

"What do they feed them?" inquired Long Beach State guard Traci Waites, the game's high scorer with 25. Incredibly, nobody seemed to remember that former 49er All-American Cindy Brown had the answer, which she shared with the world before Tennessee's upset of then-No. 2-ranked Long Beach State in the 1987 Final Four:

Corn. Pure and simple.

Tennessee vs. all of California

Three days later, with the Vols still catching their breath from the full-court dashes against Long Beach State, the second wave from the West Coast hit Knoxville. Southern California, still best known in Big Orange Country as the team that left the Lady Vols in the dust in the semifinals of the 1986 Final Four in Rupp Arena, washed into town sporting a high-scoring center, a running game a notch down from Long Beach State, and a desire to score inside.

"They're probably not going to push the ball as much as Long Beach, but they'll look to push it as much as possible," Pat Summitt surmised before the game. Overall, the Women of Troy had bigger post players than the 49ers but not quite as much speed from the guards. "Bigger, slower," it translated into. And though USC didn't match the speed of Long Beach, UT could still count on some running.

"More running?" laughed Tonya Edwards. "We're already set for that."

There was, however, an X factor in the game. Kris Durham, the 5–8 sophomore guard from Dunellen, New Jersey, had quit the team the day before the game. "Any time you miss someone it has an effect on the team," said Edwards. "Hopefully, we can regroup."

The loss of her best three-point shooter had Summitt, well aware of Durham's perimeter skills, concerned.

She needn't have been.

Summitt's Lady Vols ran up their highest point total of the 1988–89 season—102—in taking a 33-point, 102–69 breather over the No. 17 team in the country.

"Our post game was wide open," observed Bridgette Gordon in the immediate wake of the romp, before 2,115 at Thompson-Boling.

Firing out of the box was center Sheila Frost, who netted 26 points, 21 in the first half, including Tennessee's first seven points. With only 11 minutes gone in the first half, Frost had logged 19 points. She was unstoppable.

"She was responding," commented Gordon of Frost, "so we just gave her the ball." Gordon started slowly, finishing with 16 points and producing game-highs in assists (4, tied with freshman Regina Clark) and steals (6).

The night also called for the smashing debut of Knoxville's five freshmen, who, though perhaps not in the same class with Michigan's famous male quintet of 1992, nonetheless impacted the game with a stirring performance that brought praise from the UT veterans.

"I could see her face from the bench," remarked Frost of frosh replacement, Kelli Casteel. "She wanted the ball so bad. It made us feel good to see them come in tonight and look real confident."

Casteel got the sphere often enough that the first-year forward from Maryville, Tennessee, threw in 19 points, 15 in the final six minutes of play, going 6-for-6 from the field and 7-for-8 from the foul line. After competing against the Women of Troy for 10 minutes, she couldn't resist an opportunity to toot her teammates' horn. "To practice against the best . . . the varsity," Casteel said of her fellow Lady Vols. "If you play well against them, you'll play well against anyone."

Another freshman donating significantly to the cause was Clark, who sank 10 points and came up with a game-high-tying four assists. Collectively the five freshmen posted 38 points in their unofficial welcome to college basketball.

"Pat has gathered together what she has and takes from each player what they're capable of giving her," said Cherie Nelson, Southern Cal's star center, who took game-high scoring honors with 36. "And they give her that."

Freshman Dena Head spoke of the relationship with the upperclassmen and the growing acceptance that the five were experiencing. "The freshmen are accepting their responsibility.

It all starts with the upperclassmen. They get the tempo up, and it's our obligation to take over," stated Head. "For a while, everybody is going to keep separating us from the rest of the team. We are going to make mistakes, but we don't want to be distinguished just as freshmen. Today was the start of what people will be seeing in the future."

The future, indeed. Head couldn't possibly have known at the time that within a month she would be called upon to step up in a major way to replace an injured veteran and ultimately help direct the Vols to two national titles in the next three seasons.

Stanford invaded the Vols' home court a week before Christmas and came away with a rather large dose of Bridgette Gordon. The senior forward led all scorers with 24 points and showed off her other myriad court attributes, setting game-highs in steals (4) and assists (8), as Tennessee whipped up on the Cardinal 83–60. At the conclusion, Stanford's head coach, Tara VanDerveer, was not at a loss to send Gordon gleaming accolades.

"After playing in the Olympics, how is she going to worry about the girl she's going against here?" wondered VanDerveer aloud. "She's played the best. She knows she's a great player. She doesn't have any question marks."

Gordon, as usual, wasn't alone in UT's assault on Stanford. Sheila Frost poured in 22 points and grabbed 10 balls off the boards, Daedra Charles pulled down a game-high 12 rebounds, and Tonya Edwards chipped in with 12 points. Gordon seemed to get a particular kick out of watching the Baby Vols go to work.

"I get excited to see them go in there and have a good game," said Gordon of the freshmen. "I try to get them motivated. They look up to me. When I was a freshman I needed that push. Maybe that's one of my jobs now—to motivate. If they see me get fired up, they get fired up. I have taken that on as one of my responsibilities. When they go out there and work hard, I love it."

A more mature, relaxed Gordon also feels she doesn't have to do it all by herself. "I'm in a unique situation," she said. "I'm on a team with two other preseason All-Americans. So teams can't just key on me. They're going to have to play straight up against all of us. I'm having fun now, because there is always a Tonya Edwards or Sheila Frost behind me."

Two nights later, the Rout of California was complete, when Tennessee handily beat UCLA 82–50: In the span of 18 days, Tennessee had taken down No. 2 Long Beach State, No. 17 Southern California, No. 5 Stanford, and UCLA. UT was now a perfect 7–0 on the season.

Ripping Rutgers

It wasn't really an 18-year prelude to the 2007 NCAA championship game in women's basketball. But you wouldn't have known that by some people's anticipation of the finals of the Bell Atlantic Holiday Tournament at the Louis Brown Athletic Center in Piscataway, New Jersey, home of the 10th-ranked Rutgers Lady Knights. On December 30, the host wound up in the championship round of its own tournament, and many among the 5,084 onlookers predicted an upset of the No. 1-ranked Lady Vols, as Rutgers was riding the nation's longest home unbeaten streak, at 53.

Instead, Tennessee, after a 21-point victory over Wake Forest in the tournament's opening round, inflicted the worst drubbing of Rutgers in three seasons—a 40-point, 93–53, blowout that upped UT's season mark to 9–0 and left head coach Pat Summitt, in a rare display of optimism, handing out A's on her Lady Vols' report card.

"It was an exceptional night for Tennessee," she told reporters afterward. "The first half was one of the most exciting I've ever seen or coached. In that half, there were very few things I would have changed as a coach."

One of the exciting things Summitt witnessed was a 43–18 Tennessee lead at halftime. The score indicated another item of pleasure to the coach: the Volunteers' stonewall defense had resulted in the Lady Knights posting a pathetic 18.9 shooting percentage from the floor.

More thrills came in the form of Bridgette Gordon's 24 points and three steals, game highs in both categories. The DeLand, Florida, senior's productive output created an uncharacteristic projection of confidence as she looked down the road to April.

"If we stay healthy, there's a very high possibility of winning a national championship," said Gordon, the tournament's most valuable player, "if we keep playing the way we did tonight.

Gordon's frontline mates, Sheila Frost and Daedra Charles, were also named to the all-tournament team, with Charles bagging a game-high 10 boards and putting in 19 points. Frost led all players with five blocks.

"We got off to a good, quick start and we kept attacking," said Tonya Edwards. "With our depth on the bench, that's going to be the key to the rest of our season."

The junior point guard had no idea how prophetic just one month later that last statement would turn out to be, not just for the team but for her personally.

The Auburn blues

Just when you thought it was safe to toot your horn and roll down the windows . . .

Coming off 45- and 35-point blowouts of Western Michigan and Old Dominion, the high-flying Lady Vols took their premier act to Auburn, and as the phrase politely goes, had their hats handed to them, in a 67–59 reality check that knocked Tennessee from its season-long spot atop the national rankings.

Everything UT had done right at Rutgers just a week earlier in the holiday tournament seemed to be the reverse at Auburn. The smothering defense so effective against the Lady Knights was absent against the Lady Tigers, whose guards scored on a flurry of easy layups, consistently beating the Volunteers' one-on-one coverage. At the free-throw line, Tennessee went a lame three for 12. Rebounding, a usually reliable strength, came up short on a 41–37 comparison with the Lady Tigers.

"I don't think we had our minds set on stopping Auburn," Summitt said after the loss. "When somebody got beat, nobody helped," she pointed out about UT's inability to rotate on defense. "We were too offensive-minded."

Another generally dependable Lady Vols strongpoint, veteran guard Tonya Edwards, had a miserable game, plagued throughout the match with foul troubles. She finally succumbed

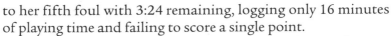

to her fifth foul with 3:24 remaining, logging only 16 minutes of playing time and failing to score a single point.

"This will help us realize that we're not as good as we thought we were," said center Sheila Frost, to which teammate Bridgette Gordon added: "It's important to learn from the loss. We're not going to get down. We've got quite a few veterans on this team."

As fate would have it, they would get their chance at redemption.

Mississippi's Burning

Lady Vols fans could easily be lulled into thinking that Auburn represented the only truly serious SEC competition for UT. But lurking just behind the Lady Tigers was Ole Miss. SEC teams cornered the collegiate market on the top three spots in women's basketball, with Auburn at No. 1, Tennessee second, and Ole Miss third. In the decade from the early 1980s through the early '90s, the Lady Rebels were a perennial Top 10 team when facing the Lady Vols. During Tennessee's 1987 national championship season, Ole Miss hung one of the six defeats over the season on Tennessee, beating UT in Knoxville.

Now, on January 14, 1989, before 10,105 at Thompson-Boling Arena, the second-largest home crowd to ever witness a Lady Vols game, Tennessee took on the No. 3 Lady Rebels, winners of four of their last five meetings with UT. All around campus were indications that this was going to be a big game. Traffic jams lined Neyland Drive extending nearly to the Karnes Bridge, and fans accustomed to showing up at the ticket booths right before tipoff found lengthy lines preventing them from getting to their seats until midway through the first half. The Lady Vols, pioneers in their field who once played to all-but-empty gyms, were becoming a big-ticket item.

After a slow start in which they scored only two baskets in the first seven and a half minutes of the game and shot an inferior 39 percent from the field, the Volunteers (13–1, 1–1 in the SEC) managed to pull within four at the half. They must have put away a case of Jolt cola at intermission, because UT roared out to dominate the second half, grabbing 29 boards to Mississippi's six and out-muscling Ole Miss inside by a 42–26 margin.

The Lady Vols' show of strength inside forced the Rebels back to the perimeter, where they faired poorly.

"We took a step back and invited them to take the outside shot," said Summitt. "We forced them to have to set up and think about things."

Maybe Ole Miss thought *too* much. At any rate, the Lady Vols came alive, forcing four quick turnovers and heading off on a 10–2 run halfway through the second half. Compounding the tight defense, UT's Big Three, all but silent in the first half, stepped up. Daedra Charles, held to just one first-half rebound, pulled down eight in the second period, while frontline mate Bridgette Gordon, the SEC's third-leading scorer, upped her rebound total of one in the first half to finish with seven. Center Sheila Frost led them all with 10 rebounds and hit three straight decisive buckets near the end to salt the game away for Tennessee, 68–61.

"I felt like I owed it to my teammates to make a difference," said Frost, in reference to her subpar performance in the Auburn loss. She finished with 10 points to augment the 15 points apiece posted by Charles and Gordon.

Speaking of Gordon, *Knoxville Journal* columnist Ben Byrd had some glittering things to say about the sensational senior the following day. "I never cease to marvel at Bridgette Gordon," Byrd wrote in his Byrd's Eye View. "The truly great athletes all have one thing in common: they can raise their performance levels when the occasion demands. Gordon was pretty well subdued by the Ole Miss defense in the first half, but after intermission she shifted into high gear. Those big baskets she made at clutch intervals were not easy ones; she draws a crowd wherever she goes."

Two nights later, UT made its destruction of the state of Mississippi complete, rolling out a 25-point margin of victory over Mississippi State, 79–54. But the game was not without its hilarity beforehand, when Lady Bulldogs head coach Brenda Paul quipped: "I'm bringing some Mississippi possum with a bow on it, and I'm giving it to Pat as a peace offering." Fearing the worst for her undersized squad, she added: "We're going to start the game in Stokely Athletic Center without them, and we'll take the lead we have when the Lady Vols get there."

Stokely, of course, had given way to the new Thompson-Boling Arena the season before. Humor is often an antidote for pain, something UT duly inflicted on the Bulldogs that night.

More Lady Bulldogs

Tennessee continued its winning ways, with a 44-point victory over the Kentucky women in UT's second-highest scoring output of the season, 101–57, before trouncing Southern Illinois and Vanderbilt by 34 and 20 points respectively. That set up a conference struggle at home with, for the second time in two weeks, the Lady Bulldogs. But this time Tennessee was facing No. 5 Georgia, not Mississippi State.

The game had special meaning for Bridgette Gordon, who was recruited by both Georgia and Tennessee. The athletic forward stepped up with a game-high 19 points and added six rebounds. "Georgia just brings out the best in me," she said after the 78–64 victory. "I just wanted to show them I made the right choice [in coming to Tennessee]. That gives me extra incentive. I should play like that all the time."

The Lady Vols (18–1, 5–1) established the strong play of its post players underneath, with Daedra Charles's 10 rebounds and Sheila Frost's seven boards. Guard Melissa McCray contributed 15 points, while Frost added 12. And though the lead changed hands six times in the second half, UT made a five-minute 16–2 run midway through the period that sealed the win. In the process, three Georgia starters, including two of its big inside players, fouled out. That seemed to surprise Georgia head coach Andy Landers, who hadn't anticipated Tennessee's stout showing on the boards.

"I thought rebounding was the one thing we'd go to war over, and they just whipped us," said Landers, whose team was overwhelmed by UT's 48–26 rebounding advantage. It was the Lady Vols' fifth consecutive win over the Bulldogs.

"For a game like this one, against a team like Georgia, we knew we had to be ready," Charles commented. "We were very confident at the post. Four minutes before warmup, the post players have a talk. We talk about hitting the boards and boxing out, and that talk motivates us individually. We knew that Georgia loves to rebound, so we put it into our minds, 'Hey, we're going to crash the boards because they like to. We're going to take that from them.'"

Her teammate, Gordon, added: "Georgia was packing in the posts, so we took our shots from the perimeter. It was a combination of good play for all of us. The perimeter allowed the post players an extra second to get in front to rebound, and we all picked up our intensity."

Gordon also mentioned an aspect that was becoming an ever more vital element in the mix of Lady Vols games: "I think conditioning had a lot to do with it," Gordon said of UT's blistering 16–2 run halfway through the second period. "They got tired of pushing the ball, and we didn't. I could see them running by huffing and puffing. They had built a lead and we were able to overcome it because of our conditioning."

In 48 hours, Tennessee's intensity and conditioning would get a severe test. No. 11 Texas lay in wait in their home lair in Austin. The Lady Longhorns leading scorer and rebounder, Clarissa Davis, was rumored to be out of the game with a severe ankle sprain. Davis had achieved her career high of 45 points the previous year, when Texas came into Thompson-Boling Arena and smoked the Lady Vols 97–78. UT had won seven straight since losing at Auburn earlier in the month. But if Pat Summitt's crew thought they might catch the Lady Longhorns in disarray without their star, they didn't know the resuscitative powers of Davis. Nor did they anticipate the exit of one of their key players for the remainder of the season

Going down in Austin

"I felt like my leg was up in the air, then I felt a pop when I was coming down," lamented junior Tonya Edwards.

In one split second, the star point guard's season was over. Before a national television audience and a crowd of 9,614 at the Frank Erwin Center in Austin, Texas, the Lady Vols, up 33–25 over No. 10 Texas at the half but stunned by the loss of their comrade, dropped the intersectional contest by a basket, 69–67. Edwards, who fell clutching her left knee with 17:01 left in the game, was carried from the court.

"When I was on the floor, I was trying to straighten it out, but I couldn't," she said. "Pat came out and was telling me not to fear the worst. But I was like, 'God, what's wrong with me?' It wasn't hurting. Nothing like this has ever happened to me before." To her enduring credit, Edwards, cordoned off in the training room and hearing the roar of the partisan crowd, asked a Lady Vols trainer for a sleeve for her knee so she could go back out and help her teammates. But the serious injury, a tear of the anterior cruciate ligament, instead dictated a knee brace and crutches for the nervy backcourt star. Texas (13–4) took quick advantage of Tennessee's shock, scoring at a 12–4 clip to tie the game at 39.

"Once Tonya went down it hit a lot of us hard," said center Sheila Frost. "We thought about it a lot but pulled together hard. It was in the back of our minds, though. We told her we wanted to win it for her, but Texas played a great game."

But the Lady Vols also played well, well enough to merit praise from Pat Summitt despite finishing on the losing end. "We played our hearts out here," said the Tennessee coach. "We played hard enough to win here. We outrebounded them [54–36] and lost. How do you explain that?"

Two reasons: 1) The Lady Vols (18–2) shot a miserable 3-for-13 from the foul line, and 2) Clarissa Davis. Yes, she of the severely sprained right ankle that was supposed to sideline her for the Tennessee game. Instead the Lady Longhorns' game center came with game, taking over the contest in the second half with an otherworldly performance that at one point included scoring 18 straight points!

"She's a great player," acknowledged the Lady Vols' own player-of-the-year candidate, Bridgette Gordon. "You have to deny her the ball because once she gets it, it's automatic." Davis, who seems to save her best games for Tennessee, scored a season-high 38 points.

Midway through the second half, Texas took a four-point lead and looked to be on the verge of running away with it. But Gordon answered, canning six of the next eight points to put the Lady Vols back in front by four. She totaled 18 for the game, with nine rebounds.

Replacing Edwards was freshman point guard Dena Head, who never looked entirely comfortable with the sudden change of events for her team or herself. "Dena is just going to have to do it," said Summitt of the games ahead, with the young point guard now elevated to starter. "She has to. And she has time to prepare herself mentally. My worry isn't this loss, but how we handle it."

Go-to girl

To begin to describe what Bridgette Gordon meant to the Lady Vols during her gleaming career on The Hill could spill way beyond the constraints of this book. Gold medal Olympian, two-time national champion, two-time All-American. Those are just the headline accolades. But one thing no one could ever doubt about the six-foot forward was her consistent ability to produce in the clutch. As such, call her the go-to girl.

Following three straight victories after the Texas loss, including two wins over Top 20 teams South Carolina (60–54) and Louisiana State (89–65), Gordon and her No. 3-ranked Lady Vol teammates (22–2) were once again embarking on a road trip that generated less than paramount enthusiasm. They were headed for Ruston, Louisiana, and could expect the usual: a tough, physical battle under the boards and power production from the Lady Techsters' formidable group of inside players.

That's what they got, all right. But surprisingly, UT gave back more than it received, heeding Pat Summitt's challenge to "outrebound Louisiana Tech by 10 rebounds." They got close. "That was a little unreasonable," Summitt noted in hindsight, as her Lady Vols posted a 37–34 edge underneath, "but we did outrebound them."

And outscored them. Tennessee, in an upset of the team that owned a 12–5 series edge, handed the No. 2-ranked Lady Techsters a 72–65 defeat on the latter's home court, snapping the defending national champion's 42-game home winning streak.

Center Sheila Frost, a veteran of four years of grueling matchups with Louisiana Tech, felt it was typical Tech. "The inside play was all-out for blood," she said. "It's push, shove, and knock and hit. It was a battle."

Louisiana Tech led by as many as seven points in the first half, before Tennessee answered with a 10–2 run.

Ultimately, though, it was another showcase game by Gordon that spelled the difference. The native Floridian rang up 29 points and pulled down nine rebounds before a national television audience and 7,160 in attendance at the Thomas Assembly Center.

"Lately, I haven't been playing as well as Bridgette Gordon plays," she said. "I needed to respond for my team, and I was more aggressive tonight. I see myself continuing to improve. My teammates need me . . . they need me to do my share. Tonight I did that. Not only was it a good offensive game, but the defense was there, too. My overall game was going."

Going, going, good! Meanwhile, Summitt's evaluation of her star forward referenced the loss in Austin a fortnight ago. "At Texas, Bridgette did not work as hard for the ball," said the UT coach. "After that game, I told her that if we got into that type of situation again, she would have to take over and initiate the attack. I told her to take 50 shots if she needed to. She just needs to take over."

Louisiana Tech coach Leon Barmore, no stranger to Gordon's exceptional level of play the past four seasons, knew there was no halting the Lady Vol forward that night. "If you've got to single out one player on their team, I've got to go with Gordon," Barmore conceded. "She's their go-to player, and they did that over and over. Bridgette came through and we couldn't stop her."

Earning a gold star square in the middle of her young forehead was freshman Dena Head, the heir apparent to the starting point guard position after incumbent Tonya Edwards had been knocked out for the season with a serious knee injury sustained in the loss at Texas. Head ran the Lady Vols offense flawlessly in the second half, after turning the ball over five times in the opening period. She finished with 12 points and eight assists, and more importantly, began to look like the floor leader Summitt envisioned out of necessity after the Texas game.

"Tonya's injury made us realize we have to do more," explained Summitt, who grabbed her first win on Louisiana Tech's home court. "This game should give Dena a lot of confidence. She settled down in the second half and really gave us a boost."

If there was a significant turning point to the game, it happened on the court but not when the ball was in play. Infuriated at watching his standout six-foot post player, Nora Lewis, being held, pushed, and flagrantly fouled, Barmore stormed the court just past the midway point of the second half—with his Lady Techsters holding off UT by a single point—and cried foul to the refs for their lack of calling fouls on Tennessee. A technical was assessed, and Head pushed through two fouls shots to give the Lady Vols a lead they would never relinquish.

Louisiana Tech fans hurled crushed ice onto the playing floor and were warned that continuation could result in a technical against their team. Minutes later, an alert Summitt called for that technical when some ice was indeed thrown on the floor. Though the call inflamed the crowd, it was Tennessee that went on a 7–0 run after the T, lengthening its lead to 59–51 on Melissa McCray's two-pointer.

"I thought the first technical definitely swung the momentum," said Summitt afterward. "It inspired us, but I was worried it would inspire Louisiana Tech more."

Barmore was hardly contrite, refusing to apologize for his technical and even failing to admonish the ice-throwing fans. Instead, the Tech coach elected to sing the praises of his worthy and admirable foe. "Tennessee at this moment is a better team than we are," he stated. "I said going into the season that they were the best team, and Tennessee, to me, still has too many weapons."

Later that night Summitt commented on her team's noteworthy victory in the unfriendly confines of northern Louisiana. "It's about as tough as I thought it would be," she said. "To win down here, to me, is like winning at Texas. Both programs have the crowd and the tradition. This is such a big win for us."

Though the Lady Vols left Ruston for the first time with smiles on their faces, those were short-lived. Because of Summitt's desire to showcase her team on national TV, the Louisiana Tech game had been moved from February 13 to February 14 to accommodate the broadcast. In so doing, she pushed her Lady Vols up against a 5 p.m. start time the following day at home for

Bridgette Gordon

a game against Georgia Tech, a move that made her players none too happy.

"I'll do anything to get on television," quipped Summitt lightheartedly.

Her players failed to see the humor. "I don't even want to think about it," said a disgruntled Sheila Frost on the chartered flight home.

Heading to Albany

Frost needn't have been concerned. Neither Georgia Tech, nor Florida, Notre Dame, Western Kentucky, nor Alabama provided the slightest impediment to Tennessee, as the Lady Vols closed the season with five straight lopsided victories, winning by an average of 26 points. Heading to Albany, Georgia, for the annual SEC Tournament, UT was ranked No. 2 in the nation and boasted a 27–2 overall mark, 8–1 in the SEC regular season.

On consecutive days, March 4 and 5, Tennessee eliminated Alabama by 28 points then Ole Miss by 22. The Lady Vols were in the finals, and of course were matched against their principal conference rival, top-ranked Auburn, the only SEC team and one of only two teams during the regular season to have defeated UT. It was an intriguing fact that no SEC team that had claimed the conference championship had gone on to win the national title in the same year. Almost as interesting were Auburn's and Tennessee's fates in the SEC tourney finals the last two seasons. The loser of the final had gone on to the NCAA championship game, Tennessee in 1987 and Auburn in '88.

In an uncannily psychic pre-SEC Tournament finals prediction, LSU head coach Sue Gunter said, "I wouldn't be surprised if what we see Monday will be the NCAA final. We could sit down and play checkers all day with Tennessee and Auburn, and one time Auburn would win and the next time Tennessee would win."

Mississippi coach Van Chancellor, having just suffered a bad taste of Tennessee the night before, suggested, "If UT plays like they did against us, it will be hard to beat them here or at the Final Four. They're both so deep it will come down to one stretch in the game. For five minutes one of them will take control, and whoever does will win the game."

The Lady Vols wisely elected to eliminate as much strain as possible. "We're not that pumped to play the final game," offered Frost. "Last year we came in here so fired up, and that lull afterward killed us. We're going in as the underdog, and I like it that way. We're not going to put any pressure on ourselves."

Even Pat Summitt was low-keying the Vols in the SEC finals. "We came down here to fine-tune our game. The biggest thing I'm seeing the last two weeks is our ability to attack both ends of the floor," she said.

So the curious backdrop to this tournament final essentially whittled down to this: Neither team particularly cared if it won the game or not.

Auburn again

In the you-take-it-I-don't-want-it-*you*-take-it finals of the SEC Tournament, Auburn's Lady Tigers (28–1) figured they wanted it less. In their lowest scoring output in six seasons, AU lost handily to Tennessee, 66–51, for the Lady Vols' second straight SEC Tournament title, before 4,508 at the Albany Civic Center.

Bridgette Gordon, the tournament's MVP, tallied 25 points and claimed eight rebounds, and Sheila Frost added 11 points and posted 10 rebounds to spark UT's second-half pull-away from the Lady Tigers. During a seven-minute run in the second period, Gordon hit 15 of the team's 19 points to boost Tennessee (30–2) to a 20-point lead with eight minutes remaining. Both were named to the all-tournament team. The pair's offensive output notwithstanding, it was the team's pressure defense and some expert foul shooting (80 percent) that made the difference in the outcome.

"We wanted to wear them down," said Frost, who came within one board of the team's all-time record for rebounds. "It was tiring. We worked for the whole thing. I looked up at the 20-point lead, and I was like, 'Oh my gosh!'"

Freshman point guard Dena Head, the midseason replacement for injured starter Tonya Edwards, scored 14 points, dished out three assists, and stole the ball four times. In the three tournament games, Head turned the ball over just five times. In addition, the SEC Freshman of the Year earned a spot on the All-SEC Tournament Team.

"She has the confidence now that she didn't have in the beginning," observed Head's teammate, Gordon. "I was just trying more or less to encourage her like the rest of the team has."

The level-headed Head, who speaks with a maturity belying her young years, said, "I wanted to keep my poise and play like we've been playing. This team has been working hard and playing together well. We took this game as the beginning of the postseason, and we fought for it."

For their effort, Tennessee was projected to be named the likely top seed in the upcoming NCAA East Regional at Bowling Green, Kentucky. Placing the SEC finals win in perspective, Lady Vols head coach Pat Summitt spoke of the just-completed struggle with Auburn.

"These were the two best defensive teams in the country—this was not an offensive game," she stated. "It was a defensive battle. Our defense influenced their offense, and their defense influenced our offense."

Even-keeled Auburn coach Joe Ciampi was complimentary of his archrival after the tussle. "Tennessee played a game that would be expected from a national championship team," he said. "They took us right out of our game offensively. When you shoot 29 percent, you don't deserve to win squat."

To the credit of Ciampi's Lady Tigers, UT didn't shoot much better, only 37 percent from the field, far off their seasonal 51 percent average. "I'm not upset at the loss," Ciampi added. "I'm upset with the execution. Tennessee is capable of playing great team defense. It's too bad they had to play it for 40 minutes tonight."

The Lady Vols began their quest for the NCAA East Regional title by hosting a second-round game on their home court against No. 18 La Salle, unbeaten at one point in the 1988–89 season but unrespected as well, as indicated by the pollsters' neglect of the team's play. In the week of January 16, the Explorers were 14–0 but failed to get consideration among the nation's Top 20 teams, most likely because of their unimposing non-conference schedule. Apparently it was justified. UT dispatched them 91–61, and it was on to Bowling Green.

Bowling Green

In Bowling Green you walk your own line
Kentucky sunshine makes the heart unfold
It warms the body
And I know it touches the soul

Pat Summitt, known more for her table-top dancing than her singing skills, might have sung in triumph this tune made famous by a pair of Kentuckians who found lasting fame in Tennessee, the Everly Brothers. Had she felt like it, the night of March 25, 1989, would have provided the perfect opportunity for her to have done so.

Two nights before, during the semifinals of the East Regional, UT had taken control of the women of Virginia, escorting them abruptly to the exit sign with an uncontested 80–47 win at E. A. Diddle Arena on the campus of Western Kentucky University.

But just as in the most diabolical of video games, when one vanquished foe is immediately replaced by another, even more dreadful enemy, who should lie in the Lady Vols' path but their formidable rival from the West Coast, those runnin', gunnin' 49ers of Long Beach State, whose key to victory rested with its two incomparable guards, Penny Toler and Traci Waites.

"Both Penny and Traci are outstanding players," admitted Pat Summitt before the clash. "They have explosiveness offensively and defensively because of their quickness. In all my years of coaching, I have never seen a more explosive backcourt."

A statement like that was not issued to bolster confidence in Tennessee's young freshman point guard, Dena Head, a mid-season replacement for injured standout veteran Tonya Edwards. But if the first-year player from Canton, Michigan, was anything before her meeting with the dynamic duo from Long Beach, she was her customary unflappable self.

"I can't say I know what it's like to be in the Final Four," Head confessed, "but the last two games have been exciting. This won't be any more pressure than I've felt before."

Old hand Sheila Frost surmised that UT, having won the previous two contests with the 49ers, including a Final Four semifinals matchup in the national championship season of 1986–87 and a December victory earlier in the current 1988–89 season, might encounter a revenge-minded Long Beach State in the East Regional finals.

"They probably feel like they have something to prove," said Frost before the match. "I would be out for revenge if I was them. It could help them, but we know how to stop Long Beach. We've done it before."

Niners head coach Joan Bonvicini, however, promised this wasn't the Long Beach State club of yore. "We may have the same personnel we had then," she remarked about the 14-point December loss at Thompson-Boling Arena, "but we're a very, very different team."

Frost felt like both clubs knew what to expect. "It will be a mental game more than anything," the senior center professed. "It will be who will outsmart the other. They'll be prepared more than they have ever been, but so will we."

Bonvicini countered. "When you play Long Beach you're never safe," she said. "It's hard to keep us from running."

Evidently the runnin' 49ers didn't run enough. In a continuation of Tennessee's dominance over its West Coast adversary, Summitt's crew laid the wood to Bonvicini's group, 94–80, to put the Lady Vols into The Show for the fourth straight year.

"I'm proud of everything," said the normally implacable Summitt. "I think we were working on both ends. We were clicking."

Behind a 41–31 control of the boards and a defense that curtailed Long Beach's two big shooters, UT seemed to answer every charge, silencing the Californians with effective post play, foul shooting, and on-court leadership.

"Bridgette went off," observed Bonvicini of the stalwart UT forward's 33-point, 14-rebound performance—both game highs. "She had a great game."

Nursing just a four-point lead at halftime, Tennessee's all-time leading scorer for both men and women took it upon herself to fire up some of her lethargic teammates, Frost in particular.

"I told Sheila, 'Sheila, you're stinking up the gym,'" schooled Gordon. "'Are you going to do something about it?'"

Frost, fortunately, did not react adversely to the slam. "Some might take that in a negative way," the senior center said. "I took it positively. Bridgette sparks this team."

"I know what it takes to get Sheila fired up," said Gordon, "and she knows what it takes to get me fired up."

With her pump primed, Frost went on to post 15 points and 11 rebounds, gaining all-tournament recognition for her substantive play. "Of any of the players I could pick from Tennessee to play for me," said Bonvicini, reiterating an earlier statement on her admiration of Frost made after the December loss to UT, "it would be Sheila. Bridgette is great . . . but she [Frost] comes to play in the big games."

Tennessee ruled from the foul line, taking advantage of 33 whistles and subsequently hitting 38 of 48 shots from the charity stripe. Conversely, Long Beach State went to the foul line just seven times, converting a paltry six of 13 shots. In addition, State's two big guns, Waites and Toler, were held to 25 points total, 22 under their combined average. Helping create that falloff was UT's steady backcourt senior, Melissa McCray, who supplied 11 points and five assists, but more importantly aided the freshman Head at the point. In the aftermath, Bonvicini, with perhaps just a touch of awe, was left to contemplate an 0–3 ledger for her efforts over the past three seasons against the Lady Vols.

"They had such a great height difference in the post," she said. "They have three great post players. And Bridgette plays smart. They make you foul them."

The game established yet another milestone for the productive Gordon, who became the all-time leading scorer in NCAA Tournament history, surpassing Southern California's legendary Cheryl Miller for the honor. Over her four years of postseason play, Gordon had thus far amassed 337 points, surpassing Miller's 333. Another record was set by the senior class of Lady Vols. Gordon, Frost, and McCray became the first seniors in NCAA annals to participate in four Final Fours.

"We're a different team from last year," noted Frost. "We

don't know we're going to win. Last year we knew we were
going to win just by showing up. We beat ourselves last year."

Terp time

With Maryland's upset of top seed Texas in the West
Regional final, a Final Four showdown for Tennessee loomed
with a team best described as having an element of the
unknown. The Terrapins, whom the Lady Vols hadn't played
since 1982, boasted All-America center Vicky Bullett, who, if
not well known to Summitt, was extremely familiar to UT's
Bridgette Gordon.

Both players had been teammates on the previous summer's United States women's Olympic basketball team that had
claimed a gold medal in Seoul. The two had bonded instantly,
becoming close over the 18 days in South Korea, and were the
only two active collegiate players remaining from that Olympic
squad. Gordon, however, did not anticipate any problem in
separating her feelings for her friend from the approaching
task at hand.

"Vicky and I know," said Gordon, "that when we go out on
the court, she has to play for Maryland and I have to play for
Tennessee."

With such an important match facing her and so little
practical info at her disposal on her opponent, Summitt hit the
trail to scout the Maryland-Texas West Regional final in
Austin, following UT's victory in the East, as a precautionary
measure should the Lady Terrapins advance. It was a good
plan. No. 5 Maryland (29–2) shocked the Lady Longhorns in
their own house, 79–71, and indeed would face the Lady Vols in
the Final Four semifinals.

"Maryland reminds me a lot of Auburn two years ago, when
I thought Auburn had the best team in the country," said Summitt of the Lady Tiger team that beat UT two out of three times
in Tennessee's 1986–87 national championship season. "There
is a difference in their starting five and what they bring off the
bench, whereas I think we have continuity bringing people in.
But I'm extremely impressed with Maryland's starting five—it's
as good as we've seen. I have to say they are the most balanced
offense we've seen this season."

So for the 10th time in her 15 seasons at the helm of the Lady Vols program, the unparalleled Summitt was taking her team onto the court of a Final Four. Unlike her postseason sojourn of two years ago that netted a national title with a predominantly sophomore and freshman lineup, Summitt was returning now with tested veterans. The Tennessee coach found it fun to compare a kind of before-and-after with her seasoned senior trio of Gordon, Frost, and McCray.

"Bridgette was not playing at the same tempo then as she does now," said Summitt of two-time All-American Gordon. "She didn't have that confidence. Melissa is so much better defensively and is playing with much more confidence. She and Sheila are just so much stronger."

In an almost spooky repetition of events, McCray wrote a note to freshman point guard Dena Head just before the Final Four that offered encouragement to the youngster, telling her to relax and believe in herself. It was all déjà vu to Summitt. The UT mentor then reminded McCray that, as a freshman guard in 1986, she, McCray, had received a similar note from senior point guard Shelley Sexton before the Final Four at Lexington. McCray had forgotten!

Of the four teams meeting in Tacoma, the Terrapins unquestionably took the label of Cinderella team. As such, anything they accomplished would be more than what people expected.

"So if we aren't supposed to win, we don't have anything to worry about," Maryland head coach Chris Weller logically surmised. "And the team that is supposed to win may be a little more nervous than us."

But underneath, the Lady Terrapin coach concealed a discernible layer of dread about her upcoming assignment. "The thing I remember about playing Tennessee in the past," admitted Weller, "is a feeling of terrible helplessness."

Summitt was matter of fact in her pregame forecast: "It comes down to 40 minutes and who arrives to play," she said. "Whether you've been here before doesn't count."

Weller's feeling of helplessness manifested, just as she feared. It came in the form of a 6-foot-4 woman in orange and white wearing No. 12. Sheila Frost went wild, apparently finding the feasting on Terrapins, a form of water turtle, much to her liking. The senior center scored 25 points and posted 13 rebounds to spur the Lady Vols to a 77–65 victory over Maryland before 9,030 at the Tacoma Dome, the same site a year ago of a forgettable nine-point loss to eventual champion Louisiana Tech in the Final Four semifinals.

"I didn't want to sit in the stands for the final like we did last year," said Frost, who that evening became the Lady Vols' second all-time leading scorer behind Gordon.

"Sheila Frost had one of, if not the best game of her college career," said a pleased Summitt. "She worked hard for the ball and did the job."

Following an off-tempo first half, in which Maryland slowed the pace and trailed by only two at halftime, Tennessee (34-2) put the game away during a three-minute span in the second half by scoring 12 unanswered points to claim a 53–42 lead, while holding the Lady Terrapins scoreless for nearly four minutes. Frost had six of the team's dozen points during that stretch, but UT's well-rounded game included a 43–36 rebounding edge and solid defense, especially during the second half.

"Their defense was unrelenting," said Weller. "They really shut down our passing lanes."

It wasn't just a one-man show by Frost offensively. Gordon recorded 24 points, 16 in the first half, during which she tallied 10 straight points, part of a 16–6 Lady Vols run. In all, Tennessee shot 44 percent from the field.

The victory set up an all-SEC final in the NCAA championship game. And yes, for the third time in the 1988-89 season, Summitt's group would face the redoubtable Lady Tigers of Auburn, a 76–71 winner over Louisiana Tech in the other Final Four semifinal. If meeting Auburn three times during the team's 1986-87 national championship season was the charm, then perhaps another NCAA crown awaited Tennessee.

Title in Tacoma

As they prepared for the final game of their college careers, the trio of Tennessee seniors knew that if they were going to leave Tacoma, Washington, with their second national championship in the past three years, one thing had better happen. They'd better make sure they got the ball to Bridgette Gordon.

"To stop her, you have to keep the ball out of her hands," said Auburn head coach Joe Ciampi of Gordon. "But to do that, you need a two-to-three player plan."

As it turned out, a 10-player plan wouldn't have contained the Lady Vol senior forward. Totaling 27 points and pulling down 11 rebounds, Gordon led a motivated Tennessee team to a decisive 76–60 victory over Auburn for the NCAA women's basketball title, earning the tournament's MVP award for her outstanding effort before a Tacoma Dome crowd of 9,758.

"Pat told me all year long that nobody will be able to stop Bridgette Gordon but Bridgette Gordon," said Gordon. "I had to put the ball in the hole."

The highly prized second ring for Gordon and her senior teammates, Sheila Frost and Melissa McCray, twice was in jeopardy during the contest, once in each half. Late in the opening period, the Lady Tigers cut it to two points, but UT answered with six straight points. Then AU came within three midway through the second half, before Gordon responded with three straight jumpers. Preceding Gordon's second-half point outburst, however, a little drama took place on the UT sidelines.

"I called a timeout," Summitt said of the event in her book, *Reach for the Summitt.* "I started talking, but I could see Bridgette was only half listening to me. She was glazed. She wasn't getting what I was saying at all. She had taken an elbow to her front teeth, and she was in pain. A lot of it. But I didn't know it. She had her hand over her mouth. But in that moment, on the floor, in all that noise and excitement with the game on the line, all I knew was that I had to find a way to reach her. She was our leading scorer, our go-to player. We needed her to take over the game.

"I got about three inches from her nose and started jawing right in her face. 'Bridgette, are you listening to me?' I demanded. She kind of nodded. I got even closer to her, ignoring the other four players.

"'Bridgette Gordon, what's wrong with you?' I snapped. She just shook her head. 'You can't tell me [Auburn star guard] Ruthie Bolton wants this more than you,' I said. Bridgette just shook her head again, wordlessly, with her hand over her mouth. I pulled her hand away.

"'Get your hand away from your mouth,' I said, my voice rising, 'and get back in there and *do* something. You mean to tell me you're not going to step up and make a play here? Don't you hide. You can't hide.'

"Bridgette nodded. She still wasn't exactly there, but she understood the message. After the timeout, Bridgette, dazed as she was, went back on the floor and sank three straight shots. By the time she was done, we were up by 18 points. She just looked over at me, with a hard look in her eye that said, 'Is *this* what you mean?'

"After the game, we got Bridgette to a dentist. That's when I realized her tooth had been knocked loose. As it turned out, she needed a root canal to save it."

Dentistry may have saved Gordon's tooth, but nothing could save Auburn.

"That showed me Bridgette had it in her heart," said McCray, who handled the point in the title game and registered 10 assists, tying the championship-game record. "She wanted to win so bad I could see it in her eyes. That's when I knew we would win. I knew Bridgette would take charge and wouldn't let us lose."

Gordon got superior support from her trusted frontline mate, Frost. UT buried the Lady Tigers on the boards, 45–30, and sank a convincing 20 of 26 shots from the foul line. Frost, named to the All-Final Four Tournament Team, took down a game-high 12 rebounds and tied an NCAA championship game record with five blocked shots.

"I can really appreciate this one more," she said. "It's more special in that not many seniors can say they won the title in their final game. We came in with a mission and played it calm. I never did have a doubt about it. It's very special."

Ciampi, whose Lady Tigers lost their second straight national championship game, as always was complimentary of his archrival. "That's a Who's Who roster," he said of the Lady Vols, before a tip of the cap to Summitt and her trio of seniors. "There are outstanding players there. But it takes leadership to mold them together."

Summitt herself concurred about her talented threesome. "They've done a lot for women's basketball and University of Tennessee basketball," said Summitt. "I've never had a class that did as much for the program."

The team that started out No. 1 ended No. 1. But the season was not without its trials and moments of grave concern. There was the exit of the team's best three-point shooter, Kris Durham, who quit the team in December. And Summitt confessed that she briefly thought the chance for a national title might have slipped away the night junior guard and floor leader Tonya Edwards went down with a torn ligament in her left knee in Texas. Easing those fears, though, was the rapid development and maturity of Edwards' replacement, freshman Dena Head, who scored 19 points, 15 in the second half, in the championship game victory.

"I think the last two months are going to be very special to me," said Head of her critical contribution to the championship run. "I had to grow up. I had no choice."

Summitt not only had Head back the following season but could look forward to the return of Edwards to form an imposing backcourt duo. "I think Tonya and Dena together can share the guard responsibilities. We'll find a place to play them."

Summitt paid a personal price for the title win. Her team had received a commitment from her that if the Lady Vols claimed the championship game, she would dance on a tabletop. That promise was fulfilled in a Seattle establishment the following night, with a little help from her friends.

"It's amazing what you can do when you surround yourself with a quality team," Summitt confessed. "When I got ready to dance, I had Carla McGhee on my left and Daedra Charles to my right. I've never danced better."

As happened after her championship win in '87, Summitt was again given the services of a Mercedes Benz by a Knoxville auto dealer for a year or until the Vols lost the title. A new red 560 SL convertible with a beige interior was wheeled out at a fan celebration when the team returned to Knoxville. Summitt had fun with the moment.

"After the game, people in the press room asked what I had said to the team during the timeout when Auburn had cut the lead to 50–47. I told them what I said didn't have a whole lot to do with X's and O's. What I really said to them was, 'If I don't get that Benz, it's your fault!'" The joke got a Letterman/Leno-type reaction.

The win, though, was no laughing matter to Auburn coach Ciampi, who, when asked his feelings on his second consecutive national championship game loss, commented, "Ever lose your dog? It's tough, real tough."

In one final salute to his nemesis Gordon, Ciampi left his immortal quote for the ages: "God bless her, graduate and get out of Tennessee."

"God Bless Her ..."

1988–89
(35–2, 8–1 SEC, 2nd)
Final AP Ranking: 1st
SEC Tournament Champions
NCAA East Regional Champions
NCAA NATIONAL CHAMPIONS

ROSTER

No.	Player	Yr.	Pos.	Ht.	Hometown
5	Regina Clark	Fr	G	5–8	Saginaw, MI
11	**Dena Head**	**Fr**	**G**	**5–10**	**Canton, MI**
12	**Sheila Frost**	**Sr**	**C**	**6–4**	**Pulaski, TN**
23	Kris Durham	So	G	5–8	Dunellen, NJ
24	**Carla McGhee**	**So**	**C/F**	**6–3**	**Peoria, IL**
30	**Bridgette Gordon**	**Sr**	**F**	**6–0**	**DeLand, FL**
32	Daedra Charles	So	C	6–3	Detroit, MI
33	Tonya Edwards	Jr	G	5–10	Flint, MI
34	Kelli Casteel	Fr	F	6–2	Maryville, TN
35	**Melissa McCray**	**Sr**	**G**	**5–10**	**Morristown, TN**
42	Pearl Moore	So	C	6–2	Harriman, TN
50	Debbie Scott	Fr	F	6–1	Gallatin, TN
52	Debbie Hawhee	Fr	F	6–1	Greeneville, TN

(starters in bold)

SEASON STATS

Player	PPG	RPG	FG-Pct.	FT-Pct.
Bridgette Gordon	20.4	7.0	.535	.697
Sheila Frost	13.7	6.7	.578	.678
Daedra Charles	9.8	6.7	.539	.567
Tonya Edwards	9.7	3.0	.452	.797
Dena Head	6.5	3.0	.443	.747
Melissa McCray	6.4	3.1	.413	.788
Carla McGhee	5.3	5.4	.528	.506
Regina Clark	5.2	2.2	.449	.682
Debbie Scott	4.5	1.8	.486	.565
Kelli Casteel	3.8	1.9	.698	.633
Debbie Hawhee	2.6	1.4	.404	.730

1988–89 UT POLL HISTORY

Starting position:	1st (11/21/88)
Highest 1988–89 ranking:	1st (11/21/88, 1/2/89, 3/13/89)
Lowest 1988–89 ranking:	3rd (2/13/89)
Final 1988–89 position:	1st (3/13/89)
NCAA Tournament finish:	NCAA CHAMPIONS

1988–89 SCHEDULE

Date	Rank	Site	W/L	Score	Opponent
11/21/88		H	W-ex	81–54	French Natl. Team
11/25/88	1/nr	N	W	81–50	Illinois
11/26/88	1/13	N	W	70–48	Washington
11/27/88	1/6	N	W	62–61 (OT)	Louisiana Tech
12/3/88	1/2	H	W	88–74	Long Beach State
12/6/88	1/17	H	W	102–69	Southern Cal
12/18/88	1/5	H	W	83–60	Stanford
12/20/88	1/nr	H	W	82–50	UCLA
12/29/88	1/nr	N	W	82–61	Wake Forest
12/30/88	1/10	A	W	93–53	Rutgers
1/1/89	1/nr	H	W	84–39	Western Michigan
1/4/89	1/nr	A	W	93–58	Old Dominion
1/7/89	1/3	A	L	59–67	Auburn
1/9/89	2/nr	A	W	97–62	Stetson
1/14/89	2/3	H	W	68–61	Mississippi
1/16/89	2/nr	H	W	79–54	Mississippi State
1/21/89	2/nr	H	W	101–57	Kentucky
1/23/89	2/nr	H	W	78–44	Southern Illinois
1/26/89	2/nr	A	W	80–60	Vanderbilt
1/29/89	2/5	H	W	78–64	Georgia
1/31/89	2/11	A	L	67–69	Texas
2/2/89	2/17	H	W	60–54	South Carolina
2/6/89	3/nr	H	W	85–50	Memphis State
2/10/89	3/18	A	W	89–65	Louisiana State
2/14/89	3/2	A	W	72–65	Louisiana Tech
2/15/89	3/nr	H	W	88–71	Georgia Tech
2/18/89	3/nr	A	W	85–52	Florida
2/20/89	2/nr	H	W	98–43	Notre Dame
2/24/89	2/nr	A	W	76–57	Western Kentucky
2/26/89	2/nr	A	W	81–65	Alabama

SEC TOURNAMENT (1st), Albany, Ga.

3/4/89	2/nr	N	W	89–61	Alabama
3/5/89	2/12	N	W	82–60	Mississippi
3/6/89	2/1	N	W	66–51	Auburn

NCAA SECOND ROUND, Knoxville, Tenn.

3/18/89	1/18	H	W	91–61	La Salle

NCAA EAST REGIONAL CHAMPIONSHIPS, Bowling Green, Ky.

3/23/89	1/nr	N	W	80–47	Virginia
3/25/89	1/7	N	W	94–80	Long Beach State

NCAA FINAL FOUR, Tacoma, Wash.

3/31/89	1/5	N	W	77–65	Maryland
4/2/89	1/2	N	W	76–60	Auburn

(rankings are for UT/opponent)

3

1990–91

Head of the Class

T HE YEAR THAT PAT SUMMITT dreaded—entering a season without her sensational seniors from 1988–89 and saddled with the knowledge that Knoxville would be the host site of the 1990 Final Four in a year when her Lady Vols' were still experiencing growing pains—came to pass. The Lady Vols, dumped in the '90 East Regional by Virginia, failed to even make the Final Four where they would have had home-court advantage.

"Anytime you come off a national championship, there is a motivational letdown," Summitt reminded her flock. "I think [the Final Four being held in Thompson-Boling Arena] was motivation, but I think it came too late. Motivation starts on October 15."

The setback, reminiscent of UT's Final Four disappointments in the past, seemed to make the spring and summer drag on endlessly.

"We had a very hard time handling that defeat," said the Lady Vols coach, in revisiting the painful loss to the Cavs, "because we had to live with it for a long time."

Now, in the fall of 1990, a team with underclassmen strength from juniors, sophomores, and two scholarship freshmen centered around a dominant 6-foot-3 senior center from Detroit, Michigan. Daedra Charles was a vital contributor to the 1988–89 NCAA championship team, and now she, along with junior guard Dena Head, stood in the spotlight as a preseason choice for All-America.

Charles had taken on the burden of senior leadership with gleaming qualifications, though in the beginning, the Lady Vols coaching staff had its doubts.

Charles had a somewhat lackadaisical attitude toward attending class. She figured that since she was now in college, as long as she did the work everything would be fine. What she didn't reckon with was Summitt's no-tolerance policy on skipping schoolwork: You attend class, you attend to your studies, you practice, you play, you graduate.

One day during her first year, Charles, academically ineligible her freshman year, skipped a class. Unbeknownst to her, Summitt is in contact with the university professors. If players miss class, the teachers are on the phone to the Lady Vols coach, reporting any absenteeism. Now Charles was being summoned to Summitt's office.

"I was on the phone when she got there. I smiled pleasantly, waved her to a chair, and said, 'Sit down,'" Summitt recollects of the incident in her book, *Reach for the Summitt*. "But as soon as I got off the phone, I started yelling. 'What gives you the right to skip class?' Daedra just sat there, stunned. I could literally see those words pass through her mind, *How does she know?*"

For the sins of the transgression, and with a teaching lesson in mind, Summitt made Charles hit the road at 5 a.m. to run up and down hills.

"Daedra never skipped class again," said Summitt. "She graduated in four years with a degree in child and family studies. Her team won two national championships in three years, while she became a two-time All-American, received the Wade Trophy awarded to the best player in college basketball, and became an Olympian in 1992. Daedra became the team's disciplinarian. I never had to say two boos to Daedra's teams. Whatever the problem was, Daedra took care of it."

There's not a teacher in the land who wouldn't enjoy experiencing the success of the Summitt-Charles interaction. Further proving that the lesson learned that day took root, Charles, three years later as a seasoned senior, figured prominently in the development of an underclassman. Her self-initiated role became that of intermediary. One of Summitt's freshman recruits, Peggy Evans, a 6-foot physical center from Charles's hometown of Detroit, was slow on the uptake effortwise as tournament time approached late in the 1990–91 season. As the wrath of Summitt was about to descend on the young player, Charles interjected, running across the floor to the pair.

"Pat, let me handle this," said Charles. Summitt's quick response was to the point.

"Okay, Dae, but you better straighten it out."

Charles defused the situation, finding just the right balance of communication skill and push to remotivate Evans, who went on to make a significant contribution to the Lady Vols' championship run.

The two Detroiters, along with former '89 freshmen holdovers Dena Head, Regina Clark, and Kelli Casteel, plus sophomores Jody Adams and Lisa Harrison, joined by bright freshman prospect Nikki Caldwell, formed the nucleus of the UT squad that would open the 1990–91 season against defending national champion Stanford.

Grounding the national champs

It was a strange payback of sorts. The Stanford Cardinal had won the national championship the preceding spring on Tennessee's home court at Thompson-Boling Arena. Tennessee, you see, was sitting in the stands, not having even made it to the Final Four.

So it was with pleasure that the Lady Volunteers opened the 1990–91 season on that same court with a convincing 95–80 victory over those incumbent national champion women from Palo Alto, California. Though it was just the opening game of the year, the win qualified as a small upset. Tennessee came into the contest ranked sixth nationally, while Stanford entered at No. 2.

The game had an improbable star, the aforementioned freshman center from Detroit, Peggy Evans. It seems the same lack of energy and concentration that caught the focus of Summitt's wrath late in the season was evident in Evans' preseason as well. During one lackluster practice, the coach even had Evans dismissed.

But there was no questioning the young Lady Vol's focus come game time against the Cardinal. Evans netted 20 points and ignited a crucial 18–5 UT run during the first half. With Tennessee up by only a single point halfway through the opening period, Evans took control of the game, hitting two free throws, followed by three consecutive baskets, another set of free throws, and a final five-foot jump shot to help Tennessee pull away to victory.

"I had a lot of questions about whether or not I could play basketball," said Evans following her uplifting start. "Now I know I can."

Senior Daedra Charles led the Lady Vols in points (24) and rebounds (10), while Evans' freshman teammate, Nikki McCray, a 5–10 guard from Oak Ridge, Tennessee, poured in 20 points in her collegiate debut, showing her outside shooting skills by ripping the nets with four three-pointers.

"Give the team credit for this victory, because I didn't have anything to do with it," said Summitt of UT's big win. "They worked hard, and they did it during the off-season."

The encouraging start lifted the Lady Vols' outlook. But the competition didn't get any less tough. It was off to Raleigh, North Carolina, for a matchup against the No. 7 Wolfpack from North Carolina State

Eaten alive

If the mood was decidedly upbeat after the impressive win over Stanford, it was the polar opposite upon leaving Raleigh a week later.

Before 7,340 at Reynolds Coliseum, N.C. State displayed a superior level of quickness, depth, and power in embarrassing Tennessee 90–77, outrebounding the Lady Vols 43–35 and roughing them up at the source of their greatest strength: down low, inside.

"We were whipped, really, in every aspect of the game," Summitt said after the pounding. "I was extremely impressed with N.C. State. I wish we could have given them and the crowd a better game. Hopefully we can learn a lot from a game like this. Their front line intimidated ours."

Make that annihilated, exterminated, obliterated. So overwhelming was the Wolfpack's play underneath that UT was eaten alive, as helpless as a newborn fawn devoured by circling wolves. The Pack led by as many as 26 points in the second half, and their trap defense unnerved Tennessee to the extent that the Knoxvillians were out of sync within a minute and a half of the opening tipoff. So stunningly complete was the consumption that Lady Vol star center Daedra Charles had more personal fouls (5) than points (4) or rebounds (1).

"They went after loose balls," Charles said candidly. "We *watched* loose balls."

There was no catching up. UT mustered 17 points from Dena Head, and the freshman Evans contributed another strong game, adding 16 points and a game-high 10 rebounds. "At times in the game, the team was either nervous or sometimes intimidated," observed Head.

The Lady Vols, routinely dictating the pace of so many of their games, played follow the leader in this one. "We talked about going out and setting a tempo," said Charles, "but we never set a tempo to the point where they had to follow us."

Wolfpack head coach Kay Yow conjectured that UT was clearly out of step: "I'm not sure Tennessee's best team showed up today," she suggested with a touch of diplomacy, a big hike in the national rankings now assured for her Wolfpack after the huge victory.

"N.C. State looked like a national championship team," Summitt replied graciously. "They were one of the best I've ever seen."

The Lady Vols could only quietly pack their gear and think of how they might begin to right their listing ship, as they trundled north to Blacksburg, Virginia, for a meeting with Virginia Tech 48 hours later.

"It will be frustrating," said a somber Charles, "if we don't learn from this."

Sour notes in Music City

Some measure of solace was taken in a 10-point win over the
Hokies, as the regrouping Lady Vols headed for Nashville for a
December 6 game against Vanderbilt, their third straight road
game of the young season.

However, the Lady Commodores, featuring a towering
front line of 6-4 All-America center Wendy Scholtens and 6-8
Heidi Gillingham, were as rude to the visiting Vols as North
Carolina State had been just five days earlier. Outrebounded
39-27, Tennessee got a fine 28-point performance from Daedra
Charles and little else, as UT fell to Vandy by a whopping 22
points, 88-66.

"For four years, one of my main goals has been to beat this
team" exulted Scholtens, who rang up 27 points to lead the
Lady 'Dores. "They had one player who was really on. We had
five or six."

Not halfway through the first period, VU assumed the lead
at 11-8 and was never headed. "We're at the top of the SEC
until January," said Vanderbilt head Coach Phil Lee, knowing
no more conference games were scheduled until after the New
Year. A Memorial Gym-record crowd for a women's game of
5,200 witnessed the Black and Gold victory, and Summitt
humorously quipped she was only too happy to help.

"Everywhere we go we set record crowds," she said. "I'm
glad we can do something positive for women's basketball
while we lose."

But Summitt had reason for concern. Her well-oiled UT
machine was clearly sputtering, and only four games into the
season was an uncustomary 2-2. The only known cure for losing is winning, and Tennessee for sure would find the W's
again—like the next 12 games in a row. Victory, it seems, is the
perfect tonic for what ails you.

Shooting down the Cardinal . . . again

Beginning with an 11-point home triumph over Maryland, the
Lady Vols' Final Four foe just two years earlier, Tennessee
began its trek to regain the high ground. Wins over Maine,
UCLA, and Illinois followed, with the 113-86 home victory
over the Uclans providing the team's high-water scoring mark

for the season. As New Year's approached, the seventh-ranked Lady Vols headed to the resort destination of Hilton Head Island, South Carolina, for a holiday tournament called the Super Shootout, where it handily disposed of Ohio State, 86–69, in the opening round.

In a rarity of return matchups, UT wound up facing No. 8 Stanford, the Lady Vols' season-opening opponent, in the championship round—the two teams' second confrontation in little more than a month.

Behind guard Dena Head's MVP performance, Tennessee, with balanced offensive and defensive play, pulled away from a 38–38 halftime deadlock to ease past the Cardinal 84–77.

"This was a really exciting win for us," said Pat Summitt. "I think the team surprised the coaching staff. I did not know if we were ready to play at this level and maintain the intensity for 40 minutes. We were able to take care of the basketball, and I was really pleased with that."

Head posted a season-high 21 points, with 18 coming in the second half, 11 during a critical run in which the Lady Vols ran away from a one-point lead to an eventual 70–58 advantage. The UT floor leader hit six of six from the foul line, where Tennessee shot 75 percent, converting 21 of 28.

"It was Dena's best game of the year on both ends of the floor," Summitt said of her star guard.

Ably assisting Head's effort were fellow guard Nikki Caldwell and senior center Daedra Charles. The freshman Caldwell scored 18, including a slicing bank shot near game's end after Stanford had cut the UT lead to five. Charles, working her usual strong game underneath, put in 12 points. Both joined Head on the all-tournament team.

The Lady Vols returned home for their second SEC game of the season, hosting Mississippi State on January 2. The 28-point blowout win over the Lady Bulldogs propelled UT down the road to four consecutive victories, topping Old Dominion, Alabama, Kentucky, and Richmond—all by no less than 10 points.

Pat Summitt's No. 4-ranked crew had found its footing, as it headed in mid-month to Gainesville for a conference game against Florida, where lax play, a dangerous flaw in Gator territory, nearly cost them.

Escaping the chomp

The Lady Vols stood together, awaiting their execution at the hands of the Florida firing squad. But Lady Luck must have been a UT fan. The Gators took aim at point-blank range but fired only blanks.

That was pretty much the case on January 16, when No. 2 Tennessee (13–2, 3–1), clinging to a narrow one-point lead, stood on either side of the paint waiting for Florida's Erika Lang to pull the trigger. All the Lady Gator center had to do was make both ends of a one-and-one and UT would be sent packing with its second conference loss of the season. But Lang missed, and Daedra Charles's second free throw, made an eternity ago, with 1:41 remaining, barely held up for an extremely fortunate 71–70 overtime victory for the Lady Vols.

In actuality, Lang committed double jeopardy. The identical situation that she found herself in during overtime occurred at the close of regulation as well. With 14 seconds to go, Lang missed the front end of that one-and-one, with the score tied at 65.

The Lady Vols had a glowing opportunity to win the game in regulation, having the ball with 11 seconds left, after Lang's miss. Incredibly, they failed to even get off a shot.

The play Summitt selected called for point guard Head to drive the lane and put the ball up, hopefully drawing a foul in the process. But Head was double-covered near the foul line and dumped the ball off to Lisa Harrison, the 6–0 sophomore forward from Louisville, Kentucky, near the left baseline. Harrison put the ball on the floor but was swarmed by Lady Gator defenders before she could shoot. The clock was now down to three seconds. Harrison quickly passed the ball to wing forward Nikki Caldwell, but time expired before the Vol freshman could take the shot.

"I understand what Dena was thinking," Summitt explained afterward. "But if we get in that situation again, I want her to shoot." The play brought to a close an exasperating final five and a half minutes for Tennessee, which couldn't buy a field goal in that time and only registered three foul shots.

In overtime, Head and Charles did the only scoring for the Lady Vols. Head, who was the team's top scorer with 16, hit two baskets early in the extra period to lead the triumph. Harrison hit four consecutive jumpers at one point in the second half and finished with 11, while Charles added 13. Freshman bulwark Peggy Evans left her mark underneath, pacing UT with 10 rebounds, but aside from her contribution, Tennessee's board work left Summitt far from impressed.

"We're just not rebounding and playing defense," the UT mentor said. "The commitment is not there."

If Gator fans felt their team's performance was commendable against such heavy hitters as the Lady Vols, it was lost on first-year Gators coach Carol Ross. "I'm not going to pat myself on the back for playing Tennessee close," she said. "It's no different than going to Georgia and losing by 21. All people know is you lost."

The thin win was the first overtime game for UT since the ill-fated overtime loss in the East Regional final to Virginia the previous March that abruptly ended Tennessee's season. "We can learn from this," said a reflective Summitt, before adding, "We sure better."

In the Tiger den

For only the third time in 15 meetings, Tennessee was heading to the "Loveliest Village on the Plains," which to Pat Summitt's Lady Vols probably felt more like the Lowliest Pilgrimage of the Insane, having lost each time they had visited the eastern Alabama hamlet. Second-ranked UT, riding a 12-game winning streak, was looking to continue its run, while Auburn, on a 59-game roll of its own at home, was just four wins shy of the Division I national record set by Louisiana Tech.

Tennessee took a three-point lead into the half, but then the Lady Tigers decided they wanted to hang around Lady Vol senior center Daedra Charles, not so much like a buddy but more like a chaperone. In keeping close tabs on the UT senior All-American, Auburn effectively denied Charles the ball and took control of the inside game, coming back from a five-point deficit midway through the second half to post a 70–65 victory.

"They were clamping down on me," remarked Charles after the game. "I've just got to prepare myself that that may happen." Though she pulled down a game-high eight rebounds,

Pat Summitt

Auburn won the battle of the boards, 33–29. Furthermore, AU held Charles, who totaled only eight points and attempted just three shots, in check on the scoreboard. Picking up the slack, guards Dena Head and Nikki Caldwell bucketed 15 and 14 points respectively, with Head canning a pair of treys in the final 43 seconds.

"The offensive rebounds are something we didn't do a very good job on," noted Summitt. "You have to credit them; Coach Ciampi's teams are always aggressive."

No. 10 Auburn (13–3, 1–1) got a wondrous performance from its senior guard, incumbent SEC Player of the Year Carolyn Jones, who logged a game-high 29 points despite playing on a bum ankle. Summitt dutifully tipped her cap to the Lady Tigers' star.

"Carolyn Jones is a great athlete and fierce competitor," acknowledged Summitt. "The fact she played so well did not surprise me. She just erased the ankle injury in her mind."

Poor shooting from the foul line also fueled Tennessee's demise, as just 12 of 25 free throws found their way to the net's bottom. Still, all of the above-mentioned elements notwithstanding, the Lady Vols (14–3, 4–2) found themselves carrying a five-point lead nearly halfway through the second period, when Jody Adams finished off a string of five straight points with a three-pointer. But then, it appeared that a bucket of ice water had been poured over the Lady Vols, who went without a field goal until Head's two three-pointers with less than 45 seconds left.

"Late in the game, Auburn had three seniors on the floor," said Summitt of AU's second-half stretch run. "That made a big, big difference, because they made good decisions and took care of the basketball. They played with poise under pressure, and we made costly mistakes."

The Lady Tigers upped their dominance over UT in regular-season play to 5–1, though Tennessee holds the edge where it counts, in postseason: 8–2. Auburn head coach Joe Ciampi added his own abstract assessment after the AU triumph: "You win through defense," he said. "Offense keeps you going. We had no magic plays. We only ran one play in the second half and that was to score."

There was little time to fret over the conference loss for UT. Another road game lay immediately in their sights, as the orange-and-white group safaried into yet another den of Lady Tigers, this time in Baton Rouge.

Battening down in Baton Rouge

Two uplifting developments arose from the Lady Vols' sojourn into central Louisiana:

1) They won.

2) Unlike their closing stretches in Gainesville and Auburn, they did not falter.

"More important than winning or losing is what happened," volunteered UT coach Pat Summitt, following Tennessee's come-from-behind 79–77 thriller in Bayou Country. "On Saturday at Auburn, we fell apart and Auburn came together. In this game, I think our team came together."

Actually, the game before the loss at AU, the overtime win at Florida, was nearly identical in form, with UT unable to continue momentum down the final stretch before backing into a one-point win.

From the start, though, there was every indication that LSU would blow the Lady Vols out of the water, as the Lady Tigers converted 14 of 15 first-half foul shots en route to a 13-point advantage just slightly more than three minutes before halftime. But UT went on a 9–0 spurt, cutting LSU's lead to four at the intermission. Tennessee continued its surge in the second half, with five Lady Vols ultimately winding up in double figures, led by Dena Head, who tallied 15.

Both of UT's big guns underneath fouled out, however— Daedra Charles, with a game-high 10 rebounds, sat down with 3:35 to go, and Peggy Evans, who scored 12 of the Lady Vols' first 20 second-half points, left halfway through the period, the victim of back-to-back fouls on consecutive plays, with Tennessee up by one, 55–54. The Lady Tigers hung tough, tying the game at 77 with 27 seconds to go on an NBA-range three-pointer by Dana "Pokey" Chatman. Tennessee, at the 18-second mark, then called a timeout to strategize what would become the game's big play.

"We wanted Dena to drive down the middle of the lane and

take the shot," said Jody Adams, the 5-foot-4 sophomore guard, echoing the exact plan that Summitt had desired at the close of regulation in the Florida game five days earlier. "But when she came off the screen, she wasn't open. I had the ball, and I thought it was best to drive and create a shot and possibly draw the foul. I felt confident and took what was open."

What was open was the game-winning shot, converted by Adams with just four seconds left. "I don't know if Jody could hear me," said Summitt of the play, "but I yelled, 'Take it!' It was a good decision because she had to keep the ball alive, and Dena was not open."

LSU, ranked 10th nationally before the game, saw its 10-game win streak, which included a victory over Auburn, halted. The No. 4 Lady Vols (15–3, 5–2), meanwhile, were only too happy to finally head home for a four-game stand, having survived the three-game road trip with two victories that had come by a grand total of three points.

Georgia on their mind

Back home again in the hospitable environs of Thompson-Boling Arena, the Lady Vols feasted on midstate Ohio Valley Conference opponent Tennessee Tech to post a 27-point win before hosting conference foe Mississippi, which fell by 10 to UT, 64–54. That set up one of the season's most eagerly anticipated matchups, with No. 4 Georgia. In a scheduling quirk, the game wrapped up Tennessee's SEC slate for the season—and it was only January.

Even back in 1991, an air of invincibility had begun to spring up around the standard-for-comparison program in Knoxville, Tennessee, that was establishing a market for women's basketball in America. There was no WNBA then, and only fledgling attempts at women's pro roundball were occasionally spotted, such as the Women's Professional Basketball League, which debuted in 1978 and lasted a surprising three seasons. Then there were the sexploitative "unitard"-wearing women of the Liberty Basketball Association who flickered for exactly one exhibition game in '91.

So it was that iconic status had gradually built up around the UT program headed by the No. 1 name in the sport, Pat Summitt. Wins were many and losses few for the Henrietta, Tennessee, native and her crew, and with each victory in the old Stokely Athletic Center or the current Thompson-Boling Arena, the legend grew almost as rapidly as the team's expanding fan base.

When a loss was experienced at home, it was big news. By the time Georgia had hit town for the January 29, 1991, encounter with the Lady Vols, UT was enjoying a 20-game home-winning streak that included 16 SEC games. More than that, Tennessee had lost only three games since the new arena had opened its doors in the early winter of 1987—to powers Louisiana Tech and Texas, with only one conference loss, Auburn. That sole SEC defeat to the Lady Tigers occurred three years previous, in 1988. On the other side of the ledger, UT had posted 49 home-court wins.

This, though, really wasn't much of a contest.

Like horses bolting from the gate, Georgia ran off 11 consecutive points early in the first half. Defensively, the Lady Vols, sporting a three-guard offense at times, coped poorly with the Lady Bulldogs' full-court pressure. But Tennessee's Head had a hot half herself, bagging 17 of her game-high 30 points—a new career high for the junior floor leader. With only three minutes till halftime, UGA lead by as much as 13. But UT patiently whittled away and went into the locker room at the half down by only five. In contrast to the productive Head, no other Lady Vol scored more than four points during the first 20 minutes.

"We did a great job, except on Head," commented Georgia coach Andy Landers. "She got the ball over and over again."

Her offensive output was the most by any Tennessee player to that point in the season. "I can't ask Dena Head to do much more," said Summitt. "I was so pleased with her effort. But I thought the other people didn't help her. Georgia was doubling up on Dena and forcing other people to handle the ball, and that really hurt."

But it seems those Georgia thoroughbreds weren't through running. Utilizing steals and fast breaks off the transition game plus marksman-like shooting from the field, the Lady Bulldogs went on a 9–0 tear in the second half that provided enough cushion until Head's dogged play helped cut the Bulldogs' lead to one with just 2:52 remaining. But UT had spent itself. Georgia closed with an 8–2 spurt and went back to Athens with a clear-cut 81–74 win.

"You have to give Georgia a lot of credit," said Summitt. "They forced us into a lot of mistakes. When we scored, Georgia just turned and attacked and sprinted down the floor. It's a mark of a great transition team. They ran it well after we scored and did a good job scoring off our mistakes. They are one of the quickest, most athletic teams we have ever played."

With the win, the Lady Bulldogs (17–2) remained undefeated in conference play, secure atop the SEC standings at 4–0. "It was a typical Tennessee-Georgia game: intense and aggressive," noted Landers in remarks after the encounter. "I would not want to be the officials for a Tennessee-Georgia game."

There was no way of knowing then, of course, but the Lady Vols, incredibly, would not suffer another home-court loss for *five years*, in the process creating a new women's NCAA record for consecutive wins at home, with 69.

TV in Texas

The month of February may have been cold and occasionally rainy in East Tennessee, but the action was hot on the hardwood. The Lady Vols cruised through the first five games, winning four of them by a whopping average of 38.25 points per game and edging old rival Louisiana Tech down in Ruston by three. The regular-season finale on February 23 was scheduled against powerful Texas down in Austin. The event would be played not only before a biased crowd of 8,225 in the Erwin Center but a national television audience on CBS, only the third time in the history of the women's sport that a regular-season game was carried by network TV.

UT women's athletic director Joan Cronan brought a pregame CBS Sports press conference to tears of laughter when she submitted that a certain someone connected with the Lady Vols basketball program just might be the No. 1 best-known woman in the Volunteer State.

"I tease Pat Summitt all the time about being the best-known female in the state of Tennessee—other than Dolly Parton," Cronan told the gathered press. "Pat can't help she is not built that way."

The showdown itself between the No. 4 Lady Vols and No. 15 Texas was almost as entertaining.

If the circus environment of the big game unnerved some, it failed to unglue Summitt and her charges. "Texas and Tennessee always play a very intense and emotional game," said Summitt. "I don't think our players are thinking about national TV. A win in Austin is what we are looking for."

Unquestionably it turned out to be the Lady Vols' finest road game of the year. Tennessee used its inside power and some sticky defense to maintain an upper hand throughout most of the contest, pulling away on a 20–10 run to close out the game at 64–55.

Center Daedra Charles was a force. As usual, she had her typically strong game under the boards, pulling down a game-high 12 rebounds, nine offensively, as the Lady Vols (23–4) collectively posted 11 offensive rebounds in the first half, scoring seven baskets on putbacks. Charles also led all scorers with 21 points, but Tennessee got a surprisingly stout contribution from forward Kelli Casteel, who put in 14.

"Kelli was very significant," remarked Charles. "She kept scoring for us."

Casteel, a junior, knew the worth of a strong finish. "I've been around here long enough to know the most important thing is how you end up the season," she said.

Contrasting the Lady Vols' offensive prowess, Texas shot just 36 percent for the game, dropping to 31 percent in the second half. The two teams left the court at halftime tied at 31.

"I don't know how much the national audience enjoys strong defense and post play," commented Summitt, "but in my eyes it was a great, great game."

Other Lady Vols left their marks. Point guard Jody Adams, who played all 40 minutes, stepped up when starter Dena Head got into early foul trouble. Adams put in eight points and made a critical three-pointer with 3:25 left that pushed Tennessee to its largest lead, at 62–49. Freshman guard Nikki

Caldwell, coming back from a two-game absence because of a stress fracture in her foot, also posted eight points, including a pair of treys that helped cue a 13-0 Lady Vols second-half run. Sophomore forward Lisa Harrison, challenged by Summitt at the half, responded with a pair of tricky, moving jumpers.

"We've been working a lot in practice on pressure situations," noted Charles of Tennessee's play. Summitt felt some satisfaction was in order.

"We're going to enjoy this one until Monday," she said, with the annual SEC Tournament looming. "Our players have worked very hard and have made a lot of improvement in the past three weeks [since the loss to Georgia]. They deserved it."

Later, Summitt offered a comparison of her '91 team with the previous year's squad that exited the NCAA Tournament in the East Regional finals. "We are a year older, and we realize what lack of leadership did last year," she said. "Dena and Daedra have really provided leadership. Last year when we won close games, I don't think we learned from that. I think this year's team has the attitude: 'We won tonight, and that was good, but we should have done this and that.'"

A week later, the steadily improving Lady Vols headed to Albany, Georgia, looking for their third conference tournament title in four years. Eagerly awaiting them in the opening round was the Vanderbilt team, led by 1990 Tennessee Sports Hall of Fame amateur athlete of the year Wendy Scholtens, that had blitzed them by 22 points back in early December. The formidable 6-4 Vandy center, a four-time All-SEC pick, was the impressive holder of 49 school records and VU's all-time leading scorer.

"A player like Wendy Scholtens is going to get her points," Summitt surmised. "Your best defense against her is to try and make her work as hard as you possibly can on both ends of the court." Summitt's ladies led the overall series with Vandy handily, at 14-3.

The conference tournament, in some coaches' minds, was a veritable three-day gauntlet; a test that called for more moxie than mid levels of the big tourney itself.

"I am firmly convinced that winning the SEC Tournament is more difficult than winning a regional in the NCAA

Tournament," said Auburn coach Joe Ciampi. "There is no rest for the weary in our conference format. You have to be 100 percent mentally and physically for three consecutive games. When you get to the NCAAs, there is a day of rest." Ciampi's Lady Tigers would be going after their fourth straight appearance in the NCAA championship game.

SEC Tournament

The answer to the question *Can our 6–3 girl beat your 6–4 and 6–8 girls?* is emphatically Yes!

Daedra Charles, the Lady Vols' senior 6–3 All-America center, went straight at Vanderbilt's strength—the gargantuan front line of Wendy Scholtens and Heidi Gillingham— and came out the winner, helping lead UT to a slim 62–60 victory over the Lady Commodores in the opening round of the conference tournament. For Vandy, it was their fourth straight opening-round loss in SEC tourney play. Charles, challenged early by Tennessee coach Pat Summitt to take it to VU's twin towers, lit it up for 27 points. She also posted a team-high 10 rebounds.

While Charles was doing her bionic woman thing underneath, her Lady Vol teammates were playing high-grade pressure defense on a level that Summitt felt won the game for Tennessee.

"Vanderbilt had a good plan," recounted Summitt. "They didn't deny us the pass inside. Instead, they denied us the outside shots and three-pointers. When we got inside, there was Gillingham. We had to win it with defense, and in the end our defense was what made the difference."

But it still came down to the very end, a game too close to call until UT's Nikki Caldwell made a steal and was fouled in the final 10 seconds, with Tennessee up by just one, 61–60. She hit the front end of two to post the final margin.

"I thought we played good enough to beat them," said a disappointed Scholtens, whose team scored only two points in the game's first seven minutes, as the Lady Vols streaked off to an 11–2 lead. "But that's what makes Tennessee the great team that it is. They played the game for a full 40 minutes, and we played in spurts."

There was plenty of drama throughout. Vanderbilt went on a 14-point run to take a 10-point lead early in the second half, after being down by three at the intermission. But UT came back to tie it at 45 midway through the period. The game was deadlocked on three occasions, and the two teams swapped the lead five times down the stretch.

Knock, knock. . . . Who's there? . . . Auburn.

Knock, and the door shall be opened. Ask, and it shall be given.

That's all Pat Summitt had to do before tipoff to wind up on top against perennial archrival Auburn in the second round of the SEC Tournament in Albany, Georgia.

"I asked this basketball team before the tournament to be playing on Monday night [the evening of the conference finals]," said Summitt. "That was my goal. Now that we are there, I have a lot of confidence we will be successful."

The No. 4 Lady Vols were a house afire from the field, bagging 65 percent of their shots in the second half and netting 53 percent overall. Auburn, fifth-ranked nationally, could only manage 38 percent shooting and dropped to 24–5 on the season. The 70–62 win set up a conference title game matchup between Tennessee and LSU, which upset top-seeded Georgia in the other semifinal.

It was a tiny 5–4 backcourt player who paved the way for the Lady Vols against Auburn. Jody Adams scored 19 points, hitting three of six three-pointers, including a trey that broke a 47–47 second-half tie. During two particularly productive stretches, with UT trailing each time by one, Adams put the Lady Vols in the lead, scoring eight of her team's 12 points in a first-half spurt and then eight straight points to fuel a second-half run.

"We had good ball movement, and that gave me the opportunity to get open," said Adams, who hit a game-high four of six three-pointers. "It was one of those days where I thought I could hit my shot."

Tennessee enjoyed a 38–29 rebounding edge, with the dependable Charles coming down with 10. But the big surprise under the boards was guard Dena Head's game- and career-high 12 rebounds. "Dena had to have a great rebounding game for us," declared Summitt about her starting point guard, whose marksmanship had tapered off since she sustained a sprained ankle two weeks earlier.

"I feel like my shot is not falling right now," said Head, who finished with 10 points on only 2-of-9 shooting from the field. "Regardless, I can work on other things. Rebounding and defense are two things I know I can do every night whether the shot goes in or not."

Head's teammate, Charles, added her own praise of the backcourt fireplug. "That's why we respect her so much," said the senior All-American. "Even when she is struggling offensively, she doesn't let it affect her."

Team defense ruled the day for the Lady Vols, with UT denying Auburn the ball and fighting off screens. And then Charles executed the play of the game with a minute and 15 seconds to go. With UT holding onto a four-point lead, the senior center flew from her defensive position on the wing, stole the ball near midcourt from Auburn's Carolyn Jones, and finished with a layup at the other end.

"I was stepping out from a screen," recounted Charles of the play, "and it just so happened the ball was right there. I wanted to get it. I went out and was able to get two points. Pat tells us our offense won't be on all the time, but we can still play good defense. Our team has learned that."

It was déjà vu for Summitt, who had witnessed the same action nine days ago in Austin. "Daedra did the same thing at Texas," she explained. "We really needed a big play at that time, and Daedra steps up and makes a steal. You do not expect that from a high-post player, but Daedra is our least conservative player."

The Lady Vols mentor beamed after her team's performance against an always-tough conference foe. "There were a lot of things we had to do differently to win this game," Summitt said. "I'm really proud of our team for coming ready to play, especially late in the game."

But the coach also issued a prophetic warning about her team's readiness for the upcoming SEC finals against Louisiana State. "If beating Auburn is the best we can do," she stated matter-of-factly, "LSU will be champion."

Like a soothsayer on a roll, Summitt pegged that exactly.

Before a largely Tennessee-flavored crowd at the Albany Civic Center, the No. 3 Lady Vols (25–5) bowed to Louisiana State 80–75 behind an utterly otherworldly performance by the Lady Tigers' Dana "Pokey" Chatman. The 5-foot-5 three-time All-SEC guard bombed in a tournament-high 30 points, including an extraordinary 16 points in a row on 9-of-10 shooting during a second-half stretch that brought LSU its first SEC Tournament crown. For that she was named tournament MVP.

"I'm disappointed, not so much that we lost," said UT's Summitt afterward, "but how we lost. I asked this team before the tournament to make a commitment defensively, and tonight I thought that was lacking at times. We can't afford not to influence the opposition."

Prior to the loss, Tennessee had claimed 14 consecutive victories over Louisiana State, dating back to 1979. It was Lady Tigers coach Sue Gunter's first win over UT in 12 tries.

Knock, knock. . . . Who's there? . . . Auburn again.

For the sixth time, two SEC teams would battle it out in a regional final.

Having disposed of Southwest Missouri State, after an error-laden, farcical opening 10 minutes, and surviving a less-than-Lady Vols level of play against Western Kentucky in the early NCAA rounds, Tennessee was facing oh-not-again Auburn for the third time in the '91 season for the Mideast Regional championship and the right to advance to the Final Four.

The Lady Tigers were administered an annoying slap in the face by the NCAA Tournament scheduling committee, when the group mysteriously overlooked No. 5 Auburn for placement among the tournament's top eight seeds, an egregious omission that miffed almost everyone, including Tennessee's Pat Summitt and AU's Joe Ciampi. As a result, the Lady Tigers wound up in the same Mideast Regional as UT, and only as the third seed there. This meant Auburn would face UT in the countdown regional showdown rather than later in the Final Four, where the Lady Vols had beaten AU two years earlier in the 1989 championship game.

"How do you pick the top four?" asked Ciampi aloud. "From what you do throughout the whole season, right? This way [the NCAA's questionable rankings], I don't understand. They need to explain it so I will know how to schedule. It's sad because it seems like both of us [Auburn and UT] are being penalized for playing well."

Tennessee benefited from having the famous "sixth man" advantage: the regional was being played on UT's own home court, at Thompson-Boling Arena, where it held a foreboding 17–0 mark in NCAA tournament games. And while Summitt expected a crowd of 7,000 to 10,000 orange-and-white well-wishers to raise the rafters behind her Lady Vols, she had to settle for a less-than-hoped-for 6,588 paying customers plus an ESPN TV audience.

Both teams sported deluxe individual stars: UT with its 6–3 All-America center Daedra Charles and Auburn with three-time SEC MVP guard Carolyn Jones. Defense was the measure of both team's excellence as well, Tennessee considered the nation's best at pressuring the ball in a half-court denial defense, while there were none better than the Lady Tigers at the full-court pressure game that compromised opponents' shot-making timetable within the constraints of the 30-second shot clock.

"This will be a game of great defense and adjustments," noted Ciampi, whose squad owned an ongoing NCAA Division I-record 67-game home winning streak. "The team that does those two the best will win."

Tennessee found out early that Auburn couldn't employ its terror-inflicting full-court pressure defense if it didn't score. With AU ice cold from the field from the opening tipoff, UT went on a 27–7 run until only seven and a half minutes remained in the first half. But the fighting Tigers clawed back, finding their range offensively and closing down the Lady Vols with their intense defense. Over the final five minutes of the half, Auburn held Tennessee scoreless while going on a 12–0 run and only trailed by six at halftime.

Daedra Charles played another outstanding overall game, totaling 15 points and pulling down 16 rebounds, twice as many as any other player in the game. As she did in the previous game against Auburn in the SEC semifinals only three weeks earlier, Charles made a critical steal in the final minute of the game. But on this day, the Lady Vols threw two less-likely players into the spotlight: Little Jody Adams and forward Kelli Casteel played consummate roles.

"Jody Adams has been a thorn in our side every time we play," said Ciampi of the UT playmaker who engineered a game-high 17 points on 6-of-7 shooting from the field that included three treys. "We're going to have to find a way to slow her down. If Jody played Auburn every game, she'd be an All-American."

The UT sophomore point guard simply has a fondness for the women of War Eagle Country. "I like to beat Auburn. I just like to beat Auburn," she explained. "They are at the top of my list. They get me fired up."

But Adams's *tour de force* was her game-ending step-up defensively. The crucial play's outcome sent Tennessee to New Orleans, site of the 1991 Final Four. With 18 seconds remaining and AU down by just two, the Lady Tigers inbounded the ball under the Tennessee goal. The ball came to their go-to player, Jones, and with the clock winding down to four seconds, Jones suddenly sliced from her right wing slot into the lane. UT's defense collapsed, with Adams firmly planting herself in front of the driving Jones.

Whistle. Offensive charge or defensive foul?

"I got you," Adams remembers thinking. And indeed, she had. The ref signaled charge on the Lady Tigers' Jones and Tennessee was bayou bound.

"I knew I was set," recalled Adams about the pivotal play. "I knew they were going to C. J. She came up the middle. I saw her and got as still as possible. A charge is a charge—that's part of the game. You have to be under control."

Summitt defended the vital closing call in addition to her young player's gumption. "I don't think it matters when it happens," she said. "If it happens, it should be called. You may think that's a gutsy call. I think it's pretty gutsy of Jody Adams."

Perhaps the biggest hero of all was Casteel, a surprise winner of Mideast Regional MVP honors. The junior forward repeatedly numbed Auburn with her turnaround jumpers from the right side of the lane, scoring 15 points. Two days earlier, in the regional semis, Casteel smoked the No. 10 Hilltoppers, with a season-high 13 rebounds plus 13 points. Charles, Adams, and Casteel were named to the all-regional tournament squad.

"When they called my name [as MVP], I can't explain it," said a euphoric Casteel. "I was at a total loss for words. I have to give credit to my teammates. They've pushed me really hard."

Summitt, whose team would now face No. 11 Stanford (26–5)—the West Regional victor over Georgia—for the third time during the 1990–91 season, complimented her conference rival's performance. "They never gave up," she said of Auburn. "They were never out of it for a minute."

For Charles, it was her last meeting against her worthy SEC adversary. She didn't want to be the only member of Tennessee's '91 team to end her collegiate career had the Lady Vols lost to Auburn.

"It's a great feeling," she said of the victory. "It's like being born again, like something new has come into your life. It's the way to go out in style. I knew there weren't any more tomorrows for me at Tennessee unless we won." There would be plenty of other tomorrows for Charles—interestingly, in orange and blue. Sixteen years later, Daedra Charles-Furlow, would be a Lady Tigers assistant coach.

Final Four: 3-for-3 against Stanford

It may have been noticeable to some that this 1991 edition of the Lady Vols appeared similar in some respects in throwback fashion to another former UT national championship team.

"This team is not like the 1989 team at all," said Summitt of her '91 Lady Vols. "We have some similarities with our 1987 team." No doubt she was reflecting on her first title squad's never-quit hustle. That team, too, had but one starting senior, guard Shelley Sexton. It was a young team, starting a freshman and two sophomores. In thinking of her '87 club, Summitt asked her '91 team to play with more emotion.

"I think we're in a position where we don't feel like we have to win the national championship or we're total failures," said Summitt before the semifinal with Stanford. "But I do feel like this is a tremendous opportunity for each and every person involved with our team. We want to come in and play our best basketball and make sure that we are focused."

Any normal pregame assessment of relative strengths and weaknesses was completely skewed because of Stanford's huge loss of the services of All-America center Trisha Stevens and leading Cardinal scorer Julie Zeilstra.

"You play with who is there," said Tara VanDerveer, Stanford's coach, hoping for the best. "But it's kind of like UNLV losing Larry Johnson." Johnson, a consensus All-America forward, led the Runnin' Rebels to the national title in 1990 and was the No. 1 overall pick of the NBA draft in 1991, going to the Charlotte Hornets.

VanDerveer had been discussed in some circles as Summitt-like. She, too, believed in thorough preparation and was considered a superb strategist able to adapt and make good adjustments. She even managed to get in a dig at Summitt at the expense of the UT coach's 6-month-old son, Tyler.

"I'm hoping Pat's new baby keeps her up all night and she doesn't have time to prepare for us," VanDerveer quipped.

Dena Head, the offensively embattled point guard-turned-defensive stopper had been counted on to carry a demanding load of responsibility, and now Summitt was relieving her of some of that weight, in hopes that less pressure would allow the talented star to concentrate on fewer things. Head said in some of the team's recent discussions of the previous year, when high expectations for Final Four home-court advantage created extra pressure resulting in a regional finals loss, that Summitt had been extremely helpful in alleviating the heat.

"Pat told us we don't have to feel any pressure, that she would love us if we win or lose," Head said. "Loosening up the pressure has really carried this team. That's the main reason we're here."

You wouldn't have known it from the game's start. Tennessee did its best impression of a classic fold, shooting a miserable 25.9 percent from the field and totaling just 21 first-half points.

Summitt may have done her best coaching of all time in

that intermission between periods, sequestered in their locker room at Lakefront Arena on the University of New Orleans campus. Her team flat, Summitt jumped on the Lady Vols, challenging them. "They're playing with more heart" and "Stanford wants it more," she baited them. With assistants Mickie DeMoss and Holly Warlick, Summitt zeroed in specifically on the riddle of UT's 6–3 two-time All-America center, who had a lame opening 20 minutes, netting just a pair of free throws and not one field goal.

"We all agreed that Daedra Charles needed to get the basketball," said Summitt, "and she might not be able to do it without some help, in terms of bringing her to the ball from screens and running some other options."

The skull session apparently worked. Charles came out and hit her first two shots of the second half. A three-pointer by Head followed and then a layup from Peggy Evans. Charles finished the run with two straight putbacks. Bingo, tie game at 40.

"I think everyone just buckled down a little harder," Charles commented later, after scoring 16 second-half points.

Head's game picked up after the break as well. The Canton, Michigan, native put in 11 of her 15 total points in the second half along with a team-high five assists. But her most outstanding stat was not committing a single turnover among the 14 that Tennessee registered for the game.

If one play were to be singled out that changed the balance of the contest, no vote would be required. Clearly it would be Evans's huge offensive rebound off a UT missed free throw with 4:38 remaining. She then converted it into a three-point play that gave the Lady Vols their first lead of the second half, at 56–54. They would not be headed again en route to their 68–60 victory, as Tennessee advanced to its fourth NCAA finals in hopes of becoming the first women's college basketball team to claim three NCAA crowns.

UT got excellent inside help from forward Lisa Harrison's game-high 12 rebounds, 11 of which were pulled off the defensive boards. Seven of Evans's eight boards were on the offensive end. No other player for either side had more than three. Three offensive rebounds came off missed Tennessee foul shots, including the big play mentioned above.

Not to be forgotten were Jody Adams's 14 points and hustle on defense. As she had done in taking a pair of game-saving charges in the two previous victories, Adams made another significant defensive stop against the Lady Cardinal when UT trailed 49–44, determinedly rushing back to break up a sure Stanford layup. Her overall improved play, ability to bring the ball upcourt against the press, and perimeter shooting skills had helped lessen Head's backcourt workload considerably.

Beyond Stanford waited Virginia, ranked No. 1 most of the season and considered the most talented team in women's basketball. As an extra incentive, the title-game matchup offered Tennessee a chance at sweet revenge for the loss inflicted by the women of Virginia in the previous year's East Regional championship game, a bitter loss that prevented the Lady Vols from hosting the Final Four on their home court.

Yes, Virginia, there is a UT

By now, people were beginning to figure out that there was an alternating-seasons/odd-numbered-years thing going on with UT and national championships, with the preceding 1987 and '89 titles and this being the close of the 1991 campaign. Even Summitt liked to imagine that it was so. "I'd sure like to think the odd years are ours," she said.

She got her third title, all right, but not before having to partake in one of the most thrilling games in NCAA Tournament history. Behind Dena Head's awesome athletic display that saw the Lady Vol floor leader score an NCAA championship game-record-tying 28 points, Tennessee (30–5) claimed an overtime cliffhanger, defeating their nemesis from a year ago, Virginia, 70–67.

It was the quintessential game of Head's sterling career, and it's a certainty that anything less than her inspirational performance would have allowed the Lady Cavaliers (31–3) to come away with the national crown. Time and again, Head was there to make the huge play offensively or defensively. Her two pressure-packed free throws, with an ice-attempting timeout called by Virginia between shots, with seven seconds remaining in regulation, earned the Lady Vols a trip to overtime with their foe, the first in the 10-year history of the women's NCAA Final Four.

In fact, a lifetime's worth of high drama still remained in the seven seconds of regulation. The Lady Cavs' All-America guard, consensus player of the year Dawn Staley, who also tied Head's championship game scoring mark with 28, suddenly was splitting the UT defense on a full-court dash and was releasing the potential game-winning shot, when Head caught up with Staley from behind and slightly deflected the ball just as it was leaving Staley's left hand.

"Dena Head did a great defensive job on the last shot," Staley said graciously. "She blocked it. It was a great defensive play. I think the officials did a tremendous job."

Once in OT, Head hit half of her team's 10 points—all foul shots. Peggy Evans's putback was the Lady Vols' only basket of the extra period. "Dena played the best game I ever saw her play," said Evans.

Head was not alone in the undoing of Virginia. Lisa Harrison pulled down a game-high 13 rebounds to go along with her eight points. The six-foot sophomore forward left an indelible image of her commitment, diving after a loose ball that resulted in loose teeth and a fat lip. "It all came down to desire," she said. And the reliable Daedra Charles was there, as always, grabbing 12 rebounds and bucketing 19 points.

"This is so sweet today," Summitt said. "This was a challenge, and we played with our hearts and heads and won the game. It feels great to win it, but you remember the others that did, too. This team reminds me a lot of the 1987 team," she said, alluding again to her first national championship team. "I felt like we were the underdogs in just about every game of every tournament."

The Lady Vols controlled the majority of the game's tempo, taking the Lady Cavaliers out of their set offense and using their superior strength and quickness to combat Virginia's taller front line. Only once did UT lose its way. Up 45–39 with a little more than 12 minutes left in the game, Tennessee was unable to halt an 18–8 Lady Cavs run and was down by five with only 1:25 remaining. That's when Head began to supply her dramatics, scoring UT's last five points in regulation, including a three-pointer.

"I felt the emotion was ours at the end," she said. "We were feeding off the emotions of our fans." In a cruel twist of timing, Head lost out to Staley for tournament MVP, because ballots were turned in with four minutes left in regulation.

With the championship game victory still reverberating around Lakefront Arena, what could only be described as a potential major bummer for Lady Vol fans was beginning to circulate in speculation involving the Tennessee head coach.

Long ago Pat Summitt had vowed to retire if she should ever gain her third national crown. With third title in hand, the moment was also at hand for a decision. "I always said if I got three national championships, I'd get out of coaching," said Summitt. "We've just signed probably the best [recruiting] class we've ever signed, for next year. I promised those kids that I would be at Tennessee four years. So I expect to be there . . . unless they run me off, and that's what I told them. They're going to have to run me off."

It didn't look like any ride-her-out-of-town-on-a-rail committee would be forming anytime soon. Summitt joined an elite echelon of working coaches with her title trifecta. Only then-Indiana coach Bobby Knight could match Summitt's superior achievement.

"We were a family that believed in each other," Summitt said in appreciation of her 1991 national champions.

And yes, the 1991 4-door 350 SD Turbo Mercedes was waiting.

1990–91
(30–5, 6–3 SEC, 3rd)
Final AP Ranking: 4th
NCAA Mideast Regional Champions
NCAA NATIONAL CHAMPIONS

ROSTER

No.	Player	Yr.	Pos.	Ht.	Hometown
3	**Jody Adams**	**So**	**G**	**5–4**	**Cleveland, TN**
5	Regina Clark	Jr	G	5–8	Saginaw, MI
11	**Dena Head**	**Jr**	**G**	**5–10**	**Canton, MI**
15	Marlene Jeter	So	C	6–0	Carlisle, SC
20	Peggy Evans	Fr	C	6–0	Detroit, MI
21	**Lisa Harrison**	**So**	**F**	**6–0**	**Louisville, KY**
32	**Daedra Charles**	**Sr**	**C**	**6–3**	**Detroit, MI**
33	Nikki Caldwell	Fr	G	5–10	Oak Ridge, TN
34	**Kelli Casteel**	**Jr**	**C**	**6–2**	**Maryville, TN**
50	Tamara Carver	Fr	G	5–6	Cosby, TN
52	Debbie Hawhee	Jr	F	6–1	Greeneville, TN

(starters in bold)

SEASON STATS

Player	PPG	RPG	FG-Pct.	FT-Pct.
Daedra Charles	17.3	9.2	.561	.585
Dena Head	13.1	5.7	.505	.713
Nikki Caldwell	8.6	1.6	.393	.657
Peggy Evans	8.5	5.7	.537	.744
Jody Adams	8.5	2.3	.460	.769
Kelli Casteel	7.9	4.1	.525	.672
Lisa Harrison	7.6	5.7	.397	.508
Marlene Jeter	3.7	2.4	.414	.606
Debbie Hawhee	3.0	1.9	.404	.548
Regina Clark	3.0	0.9	.390	.656
Tamara Carver	1.0	0.3	.500	.000

1990–91 UT POLL HISTORY

Starting position:	6th (11/19/90)
Highest 1990–91 ranking:	2nd (1/15/91)
Lowest 1990–91 ranking:	10th (12/11/90)
Final 1990–91 position:	4th (3/12/91)
NCAA Tournament finish:	NCAA CHAMPIONS

1990–91 SCHEDULE

Date	Rank	Site	W/L	Score	Opponent
11/21/90		H	W-ex	96–64	Athletes in Action
11/25/90	6/2	H	W	95–80	Stanford
12/1/90	3/7	A	L	77–90	N.C. State
12/3/90	6/nr	A	W	64–54	Virginia Tech
12/6/90	6/nr	A	L	66–80	Vanderbilt
12/9/90	6/23	H	W	82–71	Maryland
12/13/90	10/nr	A	W	77–64	Maine
12/16/90	10/nr	H	W	113–86	UCLA
12/21/90	9/nr	A	W	85–52	Illinois
12/29/90	7/nr	N	W	85–69	Ohio State
12/30/90	7/8	N	W	84–77	Stanford
1/2/91	5/nr	H	W	91–63	Mississippi State
1/6/91	5/nr	A	W	93–62	Old Dominion
1/9/91	4/nr	A	W	86–61	Alabama
1/12/91	4/nr	H	W	80–70	Kentucky
1/14/91	2/nr	H	W	80–54	Richmond
1/16/91	4/nr	A	W	71–70 (OT)	Florida
1/19/91	2/10	A	L	65–70	Auburn
1/21/91	4/10	A	W	79–77	Louisiana State
1/24/91	4/nr	H	W	77–61	South Carolina
1/26/91	4/15	H	W	64–54	Mississippi
1/28/91	3/4	H	L	74–81	Georgia
2/2/91	3/nr	H	W	94–67	Tennessee Tech
2/5/91	5/nr	A	W	77–74	Louisiana Tech
2/9/91	5/20	H	W	88–71	Notre Dame
2/13/91	4/nr	H	W	105–43	DePaul
2/21/91	4/nr	H	W	93–46	Memphis State
2/23/91	4/15	A	W	64–55	Texas

SEC TOURNAMENT (2nd), Albany, Ga.

Date	Rank	Site	W/L	Score	Opponent
3/2/91	4/nr	N	W	62–60	Vanderbilt
3/3/91	4/5	N	W	70–62	Auburn
3/4/91	3/10	N	L	75–80	Louisiana State

NCAA SECOND ROUND, Knoxville, Tenn.

Date	Rank	Site	W/L	Score	Opponent
3/17/91	4/nr	H	W	55–47	S.W. Missouri State

NCAA MIDEAST REGIONAL CHAMPIONSHIPS, Knoxville, Tenn.

Date	Rank	Site	W/L	Score	Opponent
3/21/91	4/10	H	W	68–61	Western Kentucky
3/23/91	4/6	H	W	69–65	Auburn

NCAA FINAL FOUR, New Orleans, La.

Date	Rank	Site	W/L	Score	Opponent
3/30/91	4/11	N	W	68–60	Stanford
3/31/91	4/2	N	W	70–67 (OT)	Virginia

4

1995–96

Chamique,
as in Unique-wah

F OR STARTERS, THE ODD-NUMBERED-YEARS thing went out
the window. The year 1993 not to mention 1995 came
and went, but no national championship string of what
had begun in 1987 and resurfaced every two years through '91
would continue.

And then there was the new kid on the block. A northern
usurper had taken up residence among the game's elite during
Tennessee's five-year interim between NCAA crowns. A legiti-
mate power, indeed the defending national champion, that had
risen like a rock star to the top of the ranks, a newcomer of
such immediate authority and ability that the country shifted
its focus to Storrs, Connecticut, as the apparent new seat of the
women's game.

But most of all the fall of 1995 brought the finest female
basketball player of the past century to Knoxville: A hoops
queen from Astoria, Queens, who would stand the game on its
ear for four straight years and bring to Tennessee a period of
supremacy unrivaled in women's athletics. Fortunately, Lady

Vols head coach Pat Summitt found out early what made Chamique Holdsclaw click.

"With Chamique, what makes her tick is a provocation," said Summitt in her *Reach for the Summit* tome. "You put the challenge in front of her, and if it's in her body, she's going to do it."

The coach found it difficult not to overpraise the talented youngster, who had led her Christ the King team to four straight high school championships. Holdsclaw's inspiration to others nearly matched her sheer athleticism, an element Summitt found simply amazing.

"When she steps on the floor, she is worth 20 more points to the team—not in what she herself scores, but in what she brings out in *other* people," said Summitt. "That's 20 points I wouldn't be able to get out of our team, no matter how long and hard I made them practice."

In addition to the acclaimed Holdsclaw, the 1995–96 Vols were paced by two senior guards, Michelle Marciniak and Latina Davis; a junior center, Pashen Thompson; a 6–3 junior forward, Abby Conklin; and an excellent sixth player off the bench, 6–4 sophomore center Tiffani Johnson.

Marciniak and Conklin had experienced highly publicized run-ins with their coach, but both regrouped to make out-standing contributions—Marciniak in this 1995–96 season, her last, and Conklin the following year.

Marciniak, a highly publicized backcourt star out of Macungie, Pennsylvania, by Summitt's own description, was "untamed, a freelancer; a 5-foot-9 young lady with a touch of glamour and a mane of blonde hair. . . . Trying to refine her game was a real challenge—and sometimes a battle. . . . My job was to convince her that she was going to be a better basket-ball player and enjoy more overall success within the team structure."

The contentious dynamic between the two once made a local Knoxville paper, with a photo showing Summitt collaring her guard during a timeout as she shouted instructions at her player. The caption beneath read, "Spinderella and her wicked stepmother." But Marciniak, a hard worker and certainly no rebel, eventually grasped the Summitt way. It paid off for both.

The name Abby Conklin can't be stated without connecting her to the infamous water cup-throwing incident that involved her and her coach during her senior campaign. But more on that in the next chapter.

By the time the Lady Vols entered the 1995–96 season, some followers felt that possibly the Lady Vols best days were behind them. True, UT never fell below No. 5 in the polls at anytime during those five, to some, barren campaigns (though during the championship season of 1995–96 they did fall to ninth for a week), but Tennessee still held sway in the ultra-competitive SEC, where it claimed three regular-season championships, two conference tournament titles, and an NCAA runner-up finish the previous year.

Since we're dealing only with the seven championship teams in this book, we can make the leap from title season to title season the same as calendar seasons blend from one to the next. And since we left UT closing out the 1990–91 season with an NCAA finals win over Virginia in overtime, who should come up against the hosting Lady Vols in the 1995–96 season opener but the Lady Cavs. The two had met only one time in the interim, with Tennessee taking an 11-point win in early December 1994.

Now, on November 19, 1995, a week after the team's 85–49 exhibition win over a traveling Lithuania team, the sixth-ranked Lady Vols debuted by controlling No. 3 Virginia, the key development in the game coming on a switch defensively from UT's customary setup to a matchup zone that confused the Lady Cavs.

"The matchup zone took them off-guard and surprised them," offered Marciniak, after Tennessee took an easy 78–51 win, in which the UT point guard came away with a game-high 16 points. "It gave us a different look, an opportunity to run the ball more."

Summitt summed it up. "We've traditionally been a man-to-man team," she explained. "But this year, with this team, you may see anything."

Still, the Lady Vols trailed by four with 7:30 remaining in the first half. Then Virginia went cold, going the rest of the period scoring only four points to fall behind by 10 at the break.

Tennessee dominated under the boards, hauling down nearly two for every one by Virginia (67–37, a whopping 30-board margin). Thompson grabbed a game-high 13 rebounds, followed by Davis's 12 boards, matching her 12 points. Chamique Holdsclaw, in her first college game, tallied 10 rebounds and 13 points.

"I was a little surprised [at the rebounding]," Summitt said. "I had said in practice this was the worst rebounding team of my coaching career. I was concerned with the lack of aggressiveness we had shown on the boards in the exhibition game against Lithuania."

Unbeknownst to both squads at the time, a late-March meeting lay down the line in the regional finals.

O how I want to be in Kailua-Kona

After the opening-day feast of Virginia, Tennessee further warmed up on some delectable appetizers. St. Joseph's, Texas Tech, and Alabama-Birmingham all fell to the Lady Vols, the latter two by an average of 36 points. Then it was off to Hawaii, where UT would take on No. 7 Purdue in the Kona Basketball Classic semifinals.

The Lady Boilermakers must have forgotten to shake the snow off their sneakers, going numb before Tennessee and the dazzling Holdsclaw, whose 27-point, 11-rebound performance—both game highs—led to an 81–63 pounding of Purdue. Summitt certainly couldn't argue that Holdsclaw's play wasn't exceptional, saying her young freshman "was a women among girls" at times during the game. Latina Davis posted 19 points to aid UT's effort, with Tiffani Johnson adding 10.

In another of those weird scheduling foibles, the two teams met just six days later in West Lafayette, Indiana, where the Boilermakers showed they had learned little from the previous week's experience against Tennessee, again getting trounced, 82–68, behind Michelle Marciniak's 21 points and Indiana native Abby Conklin's 15.

"We didn't play our best game," noted Summitt, "but, fortunately, we didn't have to." Her Purdue counterpart seemed somewhat deluded, maintaining that the licking wasn't as bad as before. "We didn't let them completely intimidate us like we did in Hawaii," said Lin Dunn.

Right. But back to the Kona Classic: In the tourney finals, No. 12 Penn State offered the opposition, and Summitt was impressed. "They're one of the best teams in the nation," she said. "They'll be playing in March."

The Lady Lions got their own firsthand look at Holdsclaw, who was named the Kona Classic MVP. The willowy forward downed 16 points and helped on the defensive end to preserve the Lady Vols' 79–67 victory. UT went on an 11-point run to take a 71–55 lead with 2:20 left in the game to provide a comfortable winning margin.

"Holdsclaw makes them such a good team," said Penn State coach Rene Portland. "She's an incredible dominator."

It wasn't all Chamique. Four other Lady Vols hit double figures: Marciniak, with 13, and Thompson and Conklin each with 10 supported the 16 apiece registered by Latina Davis and Holdsclaw, while Tiffani Johnson pulled down a game-high-tying 11 rebounds. The win put Tennessee (6-0) in the No. 2 spot nationally, jumping over Connecticut.

"Who knows," surmised Summitt about the Nittany Lions. "Maybe somewhere down the road we'll meet again." As it played out, there would be no further meeting between the two schools in that championship year. In fact, another six years would pass before the twain met again, when UT administered a 28-point whitewashing in the 2003 Mideast Regional semifinals in Knoxville en route to an NCAA runner-up finish to UConn.

Following the second victory over Purdue, the Lady Vols posted a win against Texas at home before absorbing their first defeat of the young season at Stanford. Victories over DePaul, Memphis, and Florida followed before the Lady Huskies of Connecticut arrived for their first appearance at Thompson-Boling Arena.

Here come the Huskies

Coach Geno Auriemma's No. 2-ranked troops had shown the Lady Vols nothing but the door in the schools' first two encounters, and Connecticut's January 6, 1996, visit proved no exception. In addition to posting a 59–53 win, the Lady Huskies pulled the rug out from under Tennessee's NCAA-record 69-game home-court winning streak, begun eons ago during the 1990–91 championship season in a conference loss to Georgia.

"It's hard to think about how special the streak was," Summitt reflected after the loss to UConn. "Records are made to be broken, and unfortunately, that is what happens. It was tough to lose today . . . and now we can start over."

The Lady Vols had a chance to win. With 6:40 remaining, UT held a 51–47 lead but then went scoreless until just 21 seconds were left on the clock. This despite committing just 14 turnovers, almost half as many as Connecticut (26).

"I'm trying to figure out how we won," said a miffed Auriemma afterward, whose team outrebounded Tennessee 42–31. "We had more turnovers than we had baskets [22]."

Summitt clearly sensed what fell apart with her team, in a seesaw game that produced 21 lead changes. "We didn't get a lot out of the turnovers, and we didn't get as much against their press as I thought we'd get," she said. "We didn't capitalize when we'd get a defensive board; we'd turn the ball over in the open court. We didn't come out of the dressing room ready to play the second half, and they came out very ready to play. It was apparent in what happened the first two minutes of the second half."

What transpired flew directly in the face of one of the Tennessee coach's greatest maxims: establish the upper hand when starting the second half. UConn, not UT, did the establishing—running off a 7–0 spurt that wiped out the Lady Vols' four-point halftime lead. Cool second-half shooting also hurt Tennessee, which hit just 28.1 percent from the field.

"What's tough for us and our team is that we lost to a team we lost to twice last year," said Summitt in summation. "We had them at our place, and we could not hang on and win this basketball game."

So the embryonic, one-year-old Connecticut-Tennessee rivalry was off to a sluggish start for UT: 0–3, including the 1995 NCAA championship game. But better days lay ahead for the Lady Vols in their confrontations with the women from Storrs.

Dawgged

Two nights later, with the sting of the Connecticut loss still burning within, UT traveled to Athens, Georgia, to take on the No. 7 Lady Bulldogs. As in the encounter 48 hours previously, two milestones occurred during the game, neither of them favorable to Tennessee.

While freshman sensation Chamique Holdsclaw racked up a game-high 21 points and UT walloped Georgia on the boards 63–30, with the omnipresent Holdsclaw pulling down 19 of those, another game high, the Lady Bulldogs (11–2), behind a pressing defense and effective three-point shooting, overcame an eight-point halftime deficit to take a 77–71 victory. For coach Andy Landers, the win included a milestone: his 400th coaching victory at Georgia, spanning 17 seasons.

Not so happy were the Lady Vols (11–3), who watched yet another of their streaks come to a close. Forty-four times in a row, Tennessee had beaten their formidable SEC opponents until running into the Lady Bulldogs. Another dubious mark was highlighted by the loss: UT had not lost twice in succession since the 1989–90 season, an incredible six-year run.

But the Lady Vols bounced back, rebounding against No. 15 Old Dominion—a future NCAA finals foe—and winning the next two after that, including a 12-point victory over No. 20 Arkansas, before hosting an imposing tandem: consecutive games against the No. 2 and No. 1 teams in the country, Vanderbilt and Louisiana Tech.

Pat, let's head out for a beer

Heading into the matchup with Vandy, both teams' coaches had time for some reflection and levity before meeting in a somewhat confusing non-conference affair. Confusing in that the game did not count in the SEC standings because the league at the time only recognized one true conference game per season between two teams, regardless of whether another was scheduled. In this case, the designated game was the February 25 meeting at Memorial Gym.

With the 1995–96 season nearing its midpoint, Summitt appraised her team to that point. "I'm an aggressive coach," she said to no one's surprise, "and this season we've got a passive team. We just haven't had the leadership we need. I always thought I'd coach as long as I was able to remain a national contender and the game was enjoyable. I expect my players to be as dedicated as I am."

That drive, so prevalent in the everyday workings of Pat Summitt, took root early, way back even beyond her high school playing days in rural Middle Tennessee, back to when she was able to hold her own in all sports with three older brothers. She was Patricia Sue Head then, daughter of Hazel and Richard Head, who showed such undying love for their athletically inclined daughter that they were willing to move from their farm in girls' basketball-less Montgomery County to neighboring Cheatham County, which did field a girls' team, so that Pat could play high school hoops.

The tenacious Head showed her toughness and leadership skills to the degree at Cheatham County High that seniors on the squad unmistakably knew the freshman was in charge. Even her high school coach, acknowledging his pupil's natural determination and comfortableness in assuming that leadership role, admitted years later that "knowing how driven she is, I'm glad I don't have to work for her."

Which by any assessment, including Summitt's, would be fair. She's even wondered about that herself. In the very first sentence of the very first chapter of her book, *Reach for the Summitt*, the UT coach candidly asks, "Could I play for me? The answer's not always yes."

On the other hand, Vanderbilt's Jim Foster seemed to be comparatively asleep in contrast to the wide-open running mechanism of his UT opposite number, whom he greatly respects, on and off the court.

"The competition has been great for both teams," said the VU mentor, then looking for his first-ever win in Knoxville. "It has stirred interest in women's basketball, and that's exactly what our sport needs."

Foster went on to describe his intrastate coaching foe. "She has a focus and a single-mindedness in the athletic arena that allows her to eliminate the external things and concentrate on her team and its effort. She doesn't get distracted easily, and that transfers to her team. When you play one of Pat's teams, you know what you're getting into."

Even the tough boss of the Lady Vols, though, has her soft side. "Pat has a great sense of humor and is a fun person to be around," Foster related, saying he had enjoyed the handful of occasions when it was possible to sit down informally with his UT equivalent. "I could have a beer with her."

Such pleasantries of course vanish come tipoff. Vandy blasted out to a 29–16 lead not eight minutes into the game, hitting 10 of its first 11 shots and gathering nine of the first 10 rebounds. Forward Sheri Sam bucketed 20 first-half points, and the Lady Commodores led by 11 at the intermission. But with VU's big inside twin towers—6-4 Mara Cunningham and 6-7 Angela Gorsica—both sitting for much of the second half, the Lady Vols patiently worked their way back, snagging 29 second-half rebounds to Vandy's 13.

"It was a different story without them in there," offered Lady Vol center Pashen Thompson, who scored the winning basket for Tennessee in the final seconds on an assist from versatile Latina Davis, who, in posting 15 points, eclipsed the 1,000-point mark for her career. Perhaps more importantly, Davis stepped up defensively, volunteering to guard the high-scoring Sam in the second half and limiting the VU sharp-shooter to just five points.

"I was calling for the ball," Davis confessed. "I was extremely tired and in a little pain [from a right-ankle sprain], but I knew we needed something. I didn't have time to worry about who was stepping up. I was just looking at the options."

Ably helping out Davis in the 85–82 victory, the other four Lady Vol starters all registered double figures: Holdsclaw (18), Conklin (14), Thompson (13), and Marciniak (10). Afterward, Summitt had nothing but praise for the successful program of UT's midstate foe.

"I admire and respect Vanderbilt," said Summitt. "They do things the right way."

And now for No. 1

Having put away the No. 2 team in the country, Tennessee went looking for bigger game. And who should provide it just three nights later but an old nemesis and the current No. 1 team in the land, Louisiana Tech.

If there was a turning point to the season, it unquestionably centered around these back-to-back games between the nation's two top-ranked teams.

"Before these last two games," said senior guard Latina Davis, we were trying to figure out just who we were."

They found out. Quickly.

Before a strong turnout of 11,188 fans at Thompson-Boling Arena, freshman Chamique Holdsclaw popped in 23 points and came away with 13 rebounds, both game highs, as the Lady Vols told Louisiana Tech and the entire women's basketball world who was really No. 1, downing the Lady Techsters 77–72. Oddly, the pollsters apparently didn't feel that beating the No. 1 and 2 teams consecutively merited anything higher than the same No. 4 ranking that UT possessed before heading into the game with Louisiana Tech.

Nonetheless, there was much to take away from the big win. "It's quite an accomplishment," added Davis. "I think this shows that we can beat any team that is put in front of us."

Most of the post-game attention, as it had been all season, was focused on the well-rounded athleticism of the phenomenal Holdsclaw. "It's really nice to have a freshman like that who wants the ball in tough situations," Summitt said, obviously ecstatic to have the consensus national high school player of the year wearing orange and white. Tech coach Leon Barmore couldn't resist dispensing an accolade or two himself.

"Holdsclaw reminds me of Cheryl Miller when she was in school," he said, citing the former USC standout and U.S. Olympian, before honoring the first-year UT player with higher commendation. "She's possibly the best freshman to ever play the game."

In typical Tech-Tennessee fashion, the game seesawed to the end, deadlocked at 63 with under four minutes to go. With Abby Conklin, scoring all 12 of her points in the second half, the Lady Vols picked a sweet time to insert a 6–0 run, topped off by Michelle Marciniak's 18-footer to give UT a six-point lead with a minute and a half remaining. Tennessee then salted the contest away, making its last eight free throws.

"We were the last ranked team that Louisiana Tech was going to play the rest of the regular season," Summitt noted. "I thought all the pressure was going to be on them."

The Lady Vols then prepared for three conference tilts in their next four games, defeating 18th-ranked Alabama by 12 before suffering their final loss of the year, 78–72 at Ole Miss, in the first of four straight road games. The team rebounded with wins at Wisconsin and Mississippi State, before heading to South Carolina, where it claimed the first of back-to-back overtime wins.

Consecutive OT games

Sometimes a game is so spectacular, you wish you were in the stands watching it instead of coaching in it. That was the feeling South Carolina coach Nancy Wilson conveyed after her team's brave but futile effort against No. 5 Tennessee, eventually losing to the Lady Vols in overtime, 79–73.

"It was a tremendous basketball game," said Wilson deferentially, even though she had to be fairly beside herself that her Gamecocks at one point had Tennessee clinging to the ropes and almost down for the count. That was after a first half, in which South Carolina roared out to a 36–20 advantage, mainly behind the deadeye shooting of guard Shannon Johnson, who scorched the nets for 35 points.

But as much a margin as the Gamecocks posted—16 points—in the first half, Tennessee returned the favor in the second, as Chamique Holdsclaw scored 16 of her 22 points and pulled down eight of her 11 rebounds after the break. UT pressed in the closing period and turned the tables on its opponent, outscoring South Carolina by 16 in the second half. With eight seconds to go, the Gamecocks' Johnson, who also recorded seven assists and eight rebounds, was at the line for the win. But she only hit the front end of two shots, and the game went to overtime. In the extra period of play, Michelle Marciniak poured in six of her 13 points, as the Lady Vols notched their 20th victory of the campaign.

Tennessee placed itself in double jeopardy three nights later at home against Auburn, returning to the same overtime scenario they had just come through against South Carolina.

Would the gods of OT shine favorably twice in succession? Were it not for the timing of Auburn forward Laticia Morris's fifth foul, the outcome may well have been different.

With 2:42 remaining in overtime, the Lady Tigers star fouled out, having scored 16 of Auburn's last 20 points, including a three-pointer that tied the game with just over 11 seconds remaining in regulation.

"She just controlled this game," said Holdsclaw, who had bolstered the Lady Vols with 19 points and 10 rebounds, both game highs, before fouling out with a little more than a minute left in overtime. "I was just happy [that Morris was gone]. But I was upset I wasn't out there to help our team."

It was already sewn up. Abby Conklin hit the three-pointer that gave Tennessee a 68–65 lead just before Holdsclaw exited. It proved enough as the Lady Vols claimed their second straight overtime game, 72–67.

"Abby had some threes and gave us some open looks at the basket," said Marciniak about her teammate, who logged 13 points including the trey.

One influencing element to the day's developments was the reinjury of senior guard Latina Davis. It was after Davis's departure with her impaired right ankle in the second half that Morris began her mad run, ending with 22 points.

"Her being out hurt us more defensively than offensively," said Summitt about Davis, who did not return after the injury. As always, Summitt saw a little more than others in what had just happened.

"Auburn's such a great defensive team," she said with admiration. "We struggled to get good looks. We don't have the great three-point shooters to extend a defense, so we have to hit them from 15 feet in. I think we beat one of the great defensive teams in the country."

Double-overtime jeopardy had turned into twice-is-nice W's. "The players seem to love overtime; I hate it," confessed Summitt. "We're struggling to play 40 minutes of good basketball; we don't need to try to play 45. But we were just in this situation, and I think they were comfortable because we had just been there and been successful."

It was the perfect attitude to hold heading into the postseason, which was the case after Tennessee disposed of Louisiana State and the real honest-to-goodness, on-the-road designated SEC rematch at No. 10 Vanderbilt, a tough 79–71 triumph but yet another victory on the Commodores' home court.

That brought the Lady Vols (23–4, 10–2) into Chattanooga, Tennessee, ground zero for the yearly conference carnage known as the SEC Tournament.

Topplin' the Tide

On March 2, 1996, the Lady Vols opened the three-day conference test by avenging an earlier loss to the last team, as it turned out, to beat UT during the 1995–96 season—Mississippi—with a convincing 73–51 victory. The following night, Tennessee took on Florida, getting a game-high 20 points from Chamique Holdsclaw. Even though the Lady Gators outrebounded them, Tennessee found enough ways to win, by 11, and ascend to its 11th SEC title game in 17 years, against Alabama.

"Tennessee came out aggressively and played like they know how to play," said Florida coach Carol Ross. "I felt like we were back on our heels. That's no way to win a championship."

The next night, Tennessee was forced to overcome the loss of its star player and regroup midway through the opening period of the tournament finals.

"When Chamique went down, it took a lot out of the team," said Summitt, who felt the gravity of seeing her fallen warrior on the court, incapacitated by a second-degree sprain of the medial collateral ligament in her right knee. To that point, Holdsclaw had hit all three of her shots from the field, pulled in a pair of rebounds, logged an assist, and helped push her team to a 19–8 lead. "Fortunately, we had halftime to reassure them. She's been a special player and a special person. When she went down, we hurt for her, not for us. We just told them, 'Chamique wants an SEC ring, let's go get it for her.'"

And that they did. Particularly picking up the slack was Latina Davis. The 5–6 senior guard from Winchester, Tennessee, put in 14 points, the sole Lady Vol with the ability to penetrate the Crimson Tide zone. Davis came up huge with the rebound of a missed Michelle Marciniak shot with under a minute to play that she converted into a three-point play.

"I knew it [Marciniak's shot] would come off pretty high," said Davis later. "I think I was going up when everybody else was coming down. When I got it, I knew I had to make the shot whether I was fouled or not."

The play left Tennessee holding a three-point lead with 54 seconds left. A 'Bama basket cut it to one, before Abby Conklin's pressure-packed three-pointer with just under eight seconds remaining closed it out at 64–60.

"We showed a lot of heart and character," said Summitt of her Holdsclaw-less troops. "We had wondered what we'd look like without her out there. Now we know: not very good."

But in fact, they *were* good. Playmaker Marciniak tallied a pair of buckets in the last five minutes to help UT open up a five-point lead, after Alabama had forged ahead 47–46 with just over eight minutes left in the game. Tiffani Johnson, at center, also played large, scoring nine points and controlling a game-high-tying 11 boards. Conklin made a trio of three-pointers.

Good news eventually surfaced surrounding Holdsclaw's injury, too. With rest and some rehab, it looked possible that the freshman phenom might be ready for NCAA Tournament play. Fortunately, there were 12 days before the subregionals opened.

East Regional

As was usually the case in the early NCAA rounds, Tennessee faced opposition easier than its regular-season slate that was traditionally chock full of challenging rivals. Such was evident against lowly Radford, which UT gobbled in stride by 41 points. A date with the Buckeyes of Ohio State then ensued, with the same result: a smashing 32-point margin of victory that sent Pat Summitt and her Lady Volunteers to Charlottesville, Virginia, site of the East Regional. There, they comfortably bested a Kansas team by 21, before hooking up with an old adversary, Virginia, on the Lady Cavs' home court.

The shoe was suddenly on the other foot for UT. They knew full well the tremendous advantage that a long home winning streak can mean momentum-wise, having set the national record earlier in the season of 69. Teams were clearly intimidated to come into the lair of the Lady Vols. Virginia knew that tune too. They had ended a run of 61 home victories earlier in the season, with a conference loss to Clemson, and were holders of an imposing 16 straight NCAA Tournament wins on their home court.

"The crowd, it will inspire Virginia," admitted Summitt before the game, before adding, "I think it will inspire *our* team. Our teams play better in a jam-packed arena."

Another noteworthy stat: of the nine previous times the two teams had met, seven were in postseason. "It's not a rivalry where we pull out the guns like the Hatfields and McCoys," said Lady Cavs coach Debbie Ryan. "There's a lot of respect."

Historically, it went down as the third-lowest scoring game in NCAA women's tournament annals. In reality, it was two games: a decisive winner in the first half and a likewise large marginal victor in the second.

Virginia's encompassing defense and uncompromising rebounding pushed them to a decisive 27–14 halftime lead. UT was stinking it up, scoring the game's first bucket then failing to lead again until less than two and a half minutes remained in the contest. From the field they shot a horrific 18.8 percent in the opening 20 minutes.

The second half was a different story, but things got worse before they got better. The Lady Vols fell behind 31–14 early, then made a 9–0 run to make it 31–23. Critically, Virginia lost its best defensive player, guard Jenny Boucek, to the bench for a large part of the half, when she committed her fourth foul with a little more than 13 minutes to play. That enabled the penetrating Latina Davis to pick it up for UT. Without Boucek in her face, Davis bombed in three straight jumpers. She totaled 12 points, all in the second half, was named East Regional MVP, and was selected to the all-tournament team along with mates Michelle Marciniak, who also had 12, and Chamique Holdsclaw (nine points, 10 rebounds).

In sharp contrast, the Lady Cavs froze over, scoring just three baskets down the last nine-minute stretch and registering a motley 21.2 percent from the floor. In all, they attempted 22

Michelle Marciniak

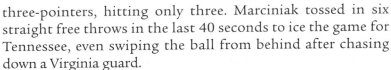

three-pointers, hitting only three. Marciniak tossed in six straight free throws in the last 40 seconds to ice the game for Tennessee, even swiping the ball from behind after chasing down a Virginia guard.

"We've never had a comeback in the postseason quite like our second-half comeback," said Summitt after the 52–46 win. "We had a lot of different people make big plays. It was one of the gutsiest performances I've ever been associated with in March Madness. I certainly will remember it."

We're going to Charlotte

No championship, no crown, no title carries true weight unless the victor walks through fire to get there.

For the ninth time, a Pat Summitt-led team of Lady Vols was headed for the Final Four, in Charlotte, North Carolina. But barring the immediate door was the new seemingly unbeatable rival from the North. Yes to grasp the gold, you must navigate through the dragon's den, overcome your biggest fear, climb your highest mountain, beat the team you have yet to beat, which defeated you for the national title a year ago.

Connecticut had doused Vanderbilt in the Mideast Regional final to advance, and the UT-UConn pairing in the semifinals had the early look of an instant classic. Yet Tennessee was in an unfamiliar role, a position it had experienced very few times in its illustrious past.

"Basically, for the first time since I've been here," forward Abby Conklin stated, "we're an underdog."

With this opponent, understandably. Connecticut had captured the upper hand all three times they had previously played the Lady Vols, including the 1995 NCAA championship game. Still, Tennessee remained unbowed.

"I think our attitude this year is the same as last year. And that's, 'We're going to go out and pretty much kick butt,'" said Latina Davis, entering her second and last Final Four. "I don't know what Connecticut's attitude is, but it's probably pretty much the same."

Huskies coach Geno Auriemma sounded like he was doing his best Rodney Dangerfield impersonation: "We came in here 33-0 last year and we weren't the favorite," he said, getting no respect from the NCAA selection committee. "Why should we be the favorite this year?" (UConn entered the Tennessee game at 34–3.)

Summitt was even-keeled about the enormity of the looming match. "The pressure is not on Tennessee unless we put it there," she affirmed.

Meanwhile, it was officially announced that Chamique Holdsclaw had been named to the 1996 10-player Kodak All-America Team, the sixth freshman ever selected to the prestigious squad. "It's very exciting," she said. "It shows that my hard work has paid off."

A Eulogy for UConn

In one of the epic battles in sports history, before 23,291 at the Charlotte Coliseum, the Lady Vols won a heroic struggle against their arch adversary from Storrs, Connecticut, in just the second overtime game in Final Four history.

The contest had a what-do-we-have-to-do-to-win air about it for UT, which outshot, outrebounded, and committed fewer turnovers than the Huskies, only to gain a tie at the end of regulation. Jumping off to a rapid start, Tennessee maneuvered out of its traditional man-to-man defense to a zone, taking an 11-point lead and hurting UConn inside by getting its 6–7 center Kara Wolters in early foul trouble. The Huskies eventually came back to tie it at 47 before the Lady Vols rattled off a 21–10 string in the second half that gave them a 10-point cushion at 72–62.

While all five Lady Vol starters scoring in double figures, it was senior guard Michelle Marciniak, with 21, who took the game in her hands in the final four minutes of regulation, hitting four foul shots and banking a left-hander off the glass over Wolters to guide UT down to the wire. With just 12 seconds to go, after a late 8–1 Connecticut surge, Marciniak's two free throws put Tennessee up 75–72. But the floor leader known as Spinderella for her long blonde mane, in the joy of converting her free throws, painfully overran hot-shooting UConn guard Nykesha Sales at the other end. Sales pulled up and buried a deflating three-pointer with just 4.2 seconds left. It was at that point that Pat Summitt achieved a major breakthrough as a head coach.

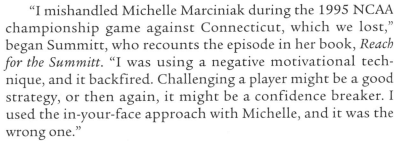

"I mishandled Michelle Marciniak during the 1995 NCAA championship game against Connecticut, which we lost," began Summitt, who recounts the episode in her book, *Reach for the Summitt*. "I was using a negative motivational technique, and it backfired. Challenging a player might be a good strategy, or then again, it might be a confidence breaker. I used the in-your-face approach with Michelle, and it was the wrong one."

With her junior guard pressing too hard, Summitt sat the UT floor leader after climbing in her grill. "That pushed Michelle further into the tank," recalled Summitt. "After I stalked away, she just sat there, staring off into space, not moving. Assistant coach Mickie DeMoss looked down the bench and knew we'd lost her."

In the off-season, Summitt had to reforge her relationship with Marciniak, coming back to The Hill for her senior campaign. "I told her how much I valued her," said Summitt. "I said, 'If I could choose any player in the country to run this team, I'd choose you. I don't want any other player. I want you on my side.'"

Now facing the identical situation with her backcourt star that she had confronted a year ago, Summitt huddled with her team at the break preceding the extra period. This time, the coach wisely changed tactics.

"My instinct was to go straight at Michelle and overreact again," said Summitt. "But I didn't say a word to her. I talked calmly, and I let Michelle regain her composure."

The approach worked. A remotivated Marciniak pushed a frenetic pace in helping lead the Vol overtime charge. But the thriller, which changed leads an astronomical 18 times and was tied 10 times, didn't end until center Tiffani Johnson, who scored 13 points and grabbed nine rebounds in a sterling inside performance, blocked Husky Jennifer Rizzotti's game-tying three-point attempt with just three seconds left.

"We just kept telling each other, 'Take it to 'em, take it to 'em,'" said Johnson after the titanic 88–83 tussle. Fellow center Pashen Thompson played no less an important role. The 6-1 junior from Philadelphia, Mississippi, bucketed four of seven second-half shots and collapsed effectively against Wolters in the paint. "I started thinking this could be our last game," Thompson said. "I didn't want it to end with a loss."

For Marciniak, it was redemption at last. "I was going to keep attacking," said the senior leader, who pulled down seven rebounds and recorded six assists, in addition to her team-high 21 points. "Going into overtime, we talked about how our team all year long had played together. And now we were going to go into overtime and win this game together."

The massive victory put the Lady Vols into the NCAA championship game against fellow-SEC power Georgia, which had clipped UT in early January in Athens. For the 14th time in 15 Final Fours, the SEC had placed a team in the NCAA semis. For only the second time, it was an all-SEC final, the Lady Vols having vanquished Auburn for the title in 1989. The Lady Bulldogs had made it to the championship game one other time and lost, to Old Dominion in 1985. Tennessee, on the other hand, was a seasoned veteran of the NCAA wars, making its second title appearance in succession and visiting the finals for the sixth time. Three times they had cut down the cords.

Longtime Georgia head coach Andy Landers would claim his 500th career coaching victory, including 82 wins collected at Roane State, should the Lady Bulldogs come out on top in the finals. One other noteworthy bulletin had been served before the game: NCAA officials would have their ears on the UT pep band, for it was uncovered that the Tennessee musicians had unleashed "Rocky Top" onto an unsuspecting public 19 times during the Connecticut game.

That's a lot of "home sweet home" for anyone.

"Tennessee played the way Tennessee plays."

Andy Landers has a knack for saying the perfect thing at just the right time. In this instance, he might rather have not uttered the above quote, as it meant the short end for him and his Lady Bulldogs in the championship round.

But my, doesn't Tennessee play the way Tennessee plays.

It couldn't have been expressed any better following the Lady Vols impressive 83–65 triumph over Georgia in the 1996 NCAA championship game that brought an unprecedented fourth national title to Pat Summitt and Tennessee women's basketball.

Tennessee, all of Tennessee, played and played well. Chamique Holdsclaw and Tiffani Johnson led the way with 16 points apiece, while three other Lady Vols posted double figures, including Final Four Most Outstanding Player Michelle Marciniak, who recorded 10 points, four rebounds, five assists, and two steals, in spearheading UT's title conquest. In addition to outrebounding Georgia 54–39, Tennessee shut down national player of the year Saudia Roundtree. The Lady Bulldog ace was held to just eight points, only hitting a dismal three of 14 shots from the field and turning the ball over five times in the first half.

Georgia had matched its star guard against Holdsclaw, and the outcome was surprisingly telling. Holdsclaw, using her seven-inch height advantage, schooled Roundtree with, first, a basket down low before moving outside and hitting a 17-footer.

"I went out there and played like a Tennessee player," said Holdsclaw proudly, after her solid performance that also included 14 rebounds, "because I wanted to win a national championship."

Just as they had done in the early going against Connecticut, Tennessee switched to a zone, throwing off the Lady Bulldogs, who went into a quick four-straight-missed-shots swoon. Still, three consecutive jumpers by Georgia's star this night—guard La'Keshia Frett—kept it close. Only Tiffani Johnson's two late jump hooks enabled UT to come away with a small five-point margin at the break. The Lady Vols sprinted out to an 11–2 run to start the second period and never looked back.

Johnson pulled in five boards to go with her 16 points and was named to the all-tournament team along with Holdsclaw and Marciniak. "I had the attitude, 'Give me the ball. I want to score,'" the former Charlotte high school All-American said.

As in the UConn game, Pashen Thompson again played huge, dictating muscle in the middle with her 12 points and 11 rebounds in addition to Johnson's compelling night. It made for a dominant performance. Combining both games in the

Final Four series, the pair collectively bagged 49 points and snagged 31 rebounds.

"They stepped out on the court tonight and they had an in-your-face attitude," said forward Abby Conklin, who netted 14 points including four treys, of Johnson and Thompson. "They took the ball right at people's noses."

Conklin talked of a running theme throughout the course of the campaign that defined the team's toughness. "People kept telling us we couldn't do it, and we kept doing it," she said.

Summitt initiated some perspective on the season that made it apparent even she had doubts her women could do it. "I told this team in the fall that they would have to over-achieve," she said. "They set the goals. I let them do their thing. I told them I wasn't sure they could reach them, but I'd do what I could to help them." Evidently good things happen to those who help themselves. "We felt no pressure to win the national championship. We felt excitement to play for one."

The game was a hit on TV too, pulling a 3.7 rating (2.52 million households) for the highest rating and the most-watched game in women's basketball history.

And then there was the MOP, what we once in other cultures and times called the MVP. Marciniak.

"I'm sleeping with it tonight," she said of the national championship trophy. In a fairytale ending of her own, Spinderella had been claimed; the glass slipper fit like a glove; and the pumpkin coach was genuine grade-A gourd.

The senior floor leader from eastern Pennsylvania enjoyed an uncommon relationship with her coach, one that only fate and circumstance can create. In the early '90s, Summitt and Tennessee assistant coach Mickie DeMoss had headed to Marciniak's hometown of Macungie to attempt to sign the national high school star. Turns out it also happened to be the day that Summitt would go into labor with her and husband R. B.'s child, their son Tyler. A snappy but less-than-focused pitch was made before the Marciniak family for the hoops services of their talented daughter. It didn't take long before everyone figured out that the guest of honor was in labor.

Wanting the baby born in Tennessee, Summitt was ushered through a wild adventure to get her back to the blue-green hills of East Tennessee before birthing. Marciniak became involved in the drama of getting her future head coach back to her plane and airborne for a two- to three-hour flight home. The incident bonded the two women in a way that bypassed the normal coach-athlete recruiting relationship. Summitt even called Marciniak after the baby was born to tell her that she and the new one were fine.

After a false start to her collegiate career, in which the blonde backcourt prospect initially signed with Notre Dame before transferring a year later to UT, Marciniak had now reached the heights. It was, well, Cinderella-like. If anyone ever truly wished upon a star and it somehow amazingly came true, tonight was the night, and Tennessee's No. 3 was the worthy recipient.

"Ever since I was a little girl," the MOP revealed, "I had that dream of cutting down the nets at a national championship game. I can't believe it's come true."

While Marciniak enjoyed the magical ride in her pumpkin-turned-coach-and-six for the evening, Summitt had to content herself with, yes, another Benz waiting back in Knoxville.

1995–96
(32–4, 9–2 SEC, 2nd)
Final AP Ranking: 4th
SEC Champions
NCAA NATIONAL CHAMPIONS

ROSTER

No.	Player	Yr	Pos.	Ht.	Hometown
3	**Michelle Marciniak**	**Sr**	**G**	**5–9**	**Macungie, PA**
4	Tiffani Johnson	So	C	6–4	Charlotte, NC
5	**Latina Davis**	**Sr**	**G**	**5–6**	**Winchester, TN**
10	Kim Smallwood	Fr	F/C	5–10	Richmond, TX
11	Laurie Milligan	So	G	5–8	Tigard, OR
13	Misty Greene	Fr	G/F	5–9	Decatur, TN
14	Kellie Jolly	Fr	G	5–10	Sparta, TN
23	**Chamique Holdsclaw**	**Fr**	**F/C**	**6–2**	**Astoria, NY**
31	Brynae Laxton	Fr	F	6–0	Oneida, TN
44	**Pashen Thompson**	**Jr**	**C**	**6–1**	**Philadelphia, MS**
52	**Abby Conklin**	**Jr**	**F**	**6–3**	**Charlestown, IN**

(starters in bold)

SEASON STATS

Player	PPG	RPG	FG-Pct.	FT-Pct.
Chamique Holdsclaw	16.2	9.1	.468	.713
Latina Davis	12.5	4.9	.499	.709
Michelle Marciniak	11.6	3.0	.439	.795
Abby Conklin	11.6	5.5	.453	.712
Pashen Thompson	9.1	7.2	.527	.711
Tiffani Johnson	7.5	6.3	.487	.618
Brynae Laxton	4.2	2.6	.359	.704
Kellie Jolly	4.2	1.2	.431	.694
Kim Smallwood	2.1	1.4	.432	.550
Laurie Milligan	1.7	0.7	.375	.640
Misty Greene	0.9	0.5	.192	.000

1995–96 UT POLL HISTORY

Starting position:	6th (11/19/95)
Highest 1995–96 ranking:	2nd (twice)
Lowest 1995–96 ranking:	9th
Final 1995–96 position:	4th (3/11/96)
NCAA Tournament finish:	NCAA CHAMPIONS

1995–96 SCHEDULE

Date	Rank	Site	W/L	Score	Opponent
11/11/95		H	W-ex	85–49	Lithuania
11/19/95	6/3	H	W	78–51	Virginia
11/22/95		H	L-ex	58–82	U.S. Natl. Team
11/25/95	4/nr	H	W	75–54	St. Joseph's
11/27/95	3/10	H	W	81–44	Texas Tech
12/1/95	3/nr	N	W	77–42	Ala.-Birmingham
12/2/95	3/7	N	W	81–63	Purdue
12/3/95	2/12	N	W	79–67	Penn State
12/8/95	2/10	N	W	82–68	Purdue
12/10/95	2/nr	H	W	83–67	Texas
12/16/95	2/9	A	L	72–90	Stanford
12/20/95	4/nr	A	W	76–68	DePaul
12/31/95	5/nr	A	W	84–63	Memphis
1/2/96	4/21	H	W	87–67	Florida
1/6/96	4/2	H	L	53–59	Connecticut
1/8/96	4/7	A	L	71–77	Georgia
1/11/96	4/15	H	W	69–47	Old Dominion
1/14/96	4/nr	A	W	60–45	Kentucky
1/17/96	6/20	H	W	78–66	Arkansas
1/19/96	6/2	H	W	85–82	Vanderbilt
1/22/96	4/1	H	W	77–72	Louisiana Tech
1/28/96	4/18	H	W	81–69	Alabama
2/4/96	3/20	A	L	72–78	Mississippi
2/8/96	9/8	A	W	72–61	Wisconsin
2/10/96	6/nr	A	W	92–76	Mississippi State
2/15/96	5/nr	A	W	79–73 (OT)	South Carolina
2/18/96	5/20	H	W	72–67 (OT)	Auburn
2/22/96	5/nr	H	W	88–75	Louisiana State
2/25/96	5/10	A	W	79–71	Vanderbilt

SEC TOURNAMENT (1st), Chattanooga, Tenn.

Date	Rank	Site	W/L	Score	Opponent
3/2/96	5/23	N	W	73–51	Mississippi
3/3/96	5/18	N	W	74–63	Florida
3/4/96	4/10	N	W	64–60	Alabama

NCAA SUBREGIONAL, Knoxville, Tenn.

Date	Rank	Site	W/L	Score	Opponent
3/16/96	4/nr	H	W	97–56	Radford
3/18/96	4/nr	H	W	97–65	Ohio State

NCAA EAST REGIONAL CHAMPIONSHIPS, Charlottesville, Va.

Date	Rank	Site	W/L	Score	Opponent
3/23/96	4/20	N	W	92–71	Kansas
3/25/96	4/11	A2	W	52–46	Virginia

NCAA FINAL FOUR, Charlotte, N.C.

Date	Rank	Site	W/L	Score	Opponent
3/29/96	4/2	N	W	88–83 (OT)	Connecticut
3/31/96	4/5	N	W	83–65	Georgia

(rankings are for UT/opponent)

5

1996–97

R-E-S-P-E-C-T

THE DEBUT OF THE GREATEST women's basketball player of the 20th century began like a book starting out on the *New York Times* best-seller list at No. 1. Chamique Holdsclaw was the real deal, and Tennessee had her.

While expectations were understandably high for Holdsclaw's sophomore season, a gaping hole widened in the UT backcourt, where floor leader Michelle Marciniak and penetrating guard Latina Davis had both exited. Head coach Pat Summitt had a right to be concerned not only with replacing her backcourt but how to ease the pressure off the talented Holdsclaw, who would be targeted by opposing defenses. The Lady Vols' top scoring threat wouldn't be sneaking up on anybody this year.

But an undercurrent of unsettling disrespect also hovered around the surface of the 1996–97 Lady Vols, a dilemma that would try Pat Summitt and her assistants. Junior center Tiffani Johnson, a repeat violator of team curfews, was suspended; developments after the season would result in her dismissal. And then there was the mystery of Abby Conklin.

Ya got trouble, right here in River City

Pat Summitt has undoubtedly had her share of recruits who failed to either understand or incorporate her system to the coach's strict liking. She has developed a keen ability to read her players and at times has displayed the skills of a trained psychologist in delving to the core of an issue or in getting a specific player to respond in a particular way. She's played part drill sergeant, part den mother, part big sorority sister. One way or another, though, she's going to find out what makes you tick.

But early into her senior season at Tennessee, the 6-3 Conklin still remained an unsolved riddle for Summitt. At the core of the problem was the forward's intractable demeanor that occasionally came off as appearing disrespectful. After a deflating defeat to Stanford in mid-December at Thompson-Boling Arena, in which Conklin had completely abandoned her role in the game plan, Summitt vented her frustration, calling the forward out in front of her teammates. Conklin contested her. Making matters worse, the whole incident was being filmed by HBO for a documentary on women's basketball. Summitt could not afford to lose control of her team nor have her authority challenged. A celebrated incident occurred not long after, in which a livid Summitt tossed a cup full of water across a room against a wall, spraying Conklin and Summitt's two assistant coaches.

The 1996–97 season certainly had the look of a roller-coaster ride for the Lady Vols.

Though the team won seven of its first eight games to open the campaign, only one victory was against a ranked team, Kansas. Their one loss was to Louisiana Tech, a narrow two-pointer on the road. It was in the midst of the next stretch that Summitt's problems with her unresponsive team escalated. Incredibly, Tennessee would lose five of its next eight games, beginning with an overtime home loss to Georgia, whom UT had vanquished in the previous spring's NCAA championship game.

In that affair with the Lady Bulldogs, Chamique Holdsclaw went nuts in the final two and a half minutes of regulation plus the five-minute overtime period, scoring 30 of her career high 34 points in that span.

"Chamique was phenomenal," said Summitt. "I keep challenging our team to step up and help her."

While Conklin aided the cause with 18 points, it was still a case of all Holdsclaw and little else for Tennessee. After taking a one-point lead at the half, UT forged ahead 53–44 with 12 minutes remaining in the contest. That's when the bottom fell out for the Lady Vols. In the span of three minutes, Georgia went on a 17–1 run to go up 61–54, and further increased its lead to 72–61 with 2:50 left. That's the point at which Holdsclaw put on an amazing one-woman display. In just a minute and 35 seconds, Holdsclaw hit a jumper, a three-pointer, assisted on a trey by Conklin, and sank another trey.

"Holdsclaw doesn't need the WNBA," quipped Lady Bulldogs coach Andy Landers. "She needs the NBA, and she should go hardship. What a fantastic display."

It just wasn't enough, however. Her three-pointer in overtime, with just 25 seconds to go, gave Tennessee the lead at 91–89, but Georgia came back with a three and a pair of free throws to win the dramatic duel 94–93.

OT for two

A week later, UT was hosting the infamous blowout by Stanford—the worst home loss for the Lady Vols in 10 years—in which Conklin triggered Summitt's wrath with her departure from company orders on the court. The senior forward was benched for the following game in Lubbock, Texas, against Texas Tech but, remotivated, came off the pine to register a career-high 26 points, including a school-record six treys, in the 79–71 win.

Three nights later, the women were in Austin for another round of pleasantries with old rival Texas, before 9,036 gathered in the Erwin Center. As with Georgia, UT was stretched the entire 40 minutes, coming away deadlocked and heading into overtime for the second time in two weeks. Making matters tougher was the fact that Tennessee had beaten the Lady Longhorns the last eight times in a row.

True to recent form, UT appeared headed for consecutive victory No. 9 over Texas, easing out to a 10-point lead with just over four minutes remaining to play. But with eight seconds left the Lady Longhorns tied it at 59 on a driving layup, and the extra period was called for. Chamique Holdsclaw chipped in with a pair of baskets in OT, but two missed free throws left the door open for the Lady Longhorns, who, trailing by one, watched their center's five-foot baseline turnaround clank off the rim in the final second, as Tennessee escaped 68–65.

"We may win ugly at times," noted a relieved Summitt, "but at least we found a way to win."

By statistical measure, it should have been all Lady Vols. Tennessee commandeered the boards, 58–37, and the magnificent Holdsclaw established game highs in scoring (24) and rebounding (16), along with team highs in assists (5), blocked shots (tied, with 3), and steals (tied, with 2).

The victory, sweet as it was, however, was short-lived. Storm clouds began to gather on the Lady Vols' horizon, as the team headed unknowingly into a dark stretch. Three of UT's next four games would result in losses and create further questions about this team that, according to Summitt, lacked personality.

"They were too quiet, they were listless, they had no attitude," Summitt said of her punchless posse prior to the start of the '97 season. Compounding matters was the loss of point guard-in-waiting Kellie Jolly, out with an anterior cruciate ligament tear even before fall practice began. It appeared that a patch-and-fix backcourt was in order and that Summitt would have her work cut out in unifying the group.

The road swing through Texas now in the rearview mirror, Tennessee reassembled after Christmas for a conference game at Arkansas. The Razorback women, a Top 25 team, held little holiday merriment for the Lady Vols, bah-humbugging UT in a two-point, 77–75, victory. Three losses in five games.

Timeout for an accolade

Oddly, at one of the low points in her fabulous coaching career, Summitt was named Tennessean of the Year by the *Nashville Tennessean*. The honor saluted her as the "standard-bearer of women's sports," and regardless of the way this particular season was progressing, there was little doubt that Summitt was THE person most responsible for elevating the stature of women sports in America. Title IX had cracked open the door, but Summitt kicked it wide open.

"Very early on, Pat got her sport treated with the respect that it deserved," noted Vanderbilt University women's basketball coach Jim Foster. "And that was at a time when it was not an easy thing to do. Tennessee was years ahead of others in its treatment of women's basketball. You have to respect her accomplishments."

Summitt's record, 947–180 through the 2006–07 season, speaks for itself. Never has she experienced a losing season in 33 years of coaching on The Hill, the closest coming way back in 1974–75, her first year at the UT helm, when the team went 16–8.

"Back then it was different," Summitt reflected. "I had to wear a lot of different hats. I was a graduate assistant. I was training myself. We didn't sell tickets. We didn't have scholarships. We didn't have games on TV or get written about in the newspaper. We were in our own world."

While her style and success have been compared to the dynasties of Kentucky's Adolph Rupp and Bob Knight at Indiana, longtime Tennessee athletics department figure Gus Manning sees more of a resemblance to one of Tennessee's old legends.

"She reminds me very much of Gen. Neyland, because she's so organized, such a great student of the game, a disciplinarian like he was," said Manning. "She's a great teacher. Watching one of her practice sessions, it's unbelievable how organized she is. When she speaks, everyone listens."

Former Lady Vol player and longtime assistant coach Holly Warlick says Summitt's contributions extend beyond the court. "She has shown you don't have to be a male to be in a leadership role," said Warlick. "She has shown that a woman can show leadership and still be caring. She has shown that it's okay to be aggressive, to be intense. But she doesn't carry that off the court."

Coaching rival Jody Conradt of Texas says her sport and the name Pat Summitt are synonymous. "As you trace the infancy of women's basketball, you can't say a word or have visions of the game without thinking about Pat," said Conradt, on news of Summitt's prestigious award. "And that's the case when I think about the state of Tennessee. I think of Pat."

Ya got trouble (reprise)

Tennessee rang in the New Year in Philadelphia against St. Joseph's, and again, mystifying courtside behavior by Conklin earned her yet another trip into Summitt's doghouse. A towel had become the object of a skirmish between Conklin and center Pashen Thompson, both sitting on the bench at the time. The it's-mine-no-it's-mine tug and pull netted Conklin another reprimand. Summitt was beside herself. With UT down by 14 with just seven minutes remaining, this was not the kind of leadership she envisioned from a senior.

UT rallied and won that evening, but later Summitt and her vexing young charge talked deep into the night in an attempt to arrive at some accord. The coach conveyed her exasperation to Conklin about how she had been counting on her, how she wanted her senior forward to lead. Conklin replied that she wasn't sure she knew how. Fortunately, each came away with a better understanding of the other. Several days later, in a fortuitous suggestion by Summitt, Conklin was placed in touch with graduated senior Michelle Marciniak, the feeling being that Conklin could benefit from Marciniak's feedback on the differences that rise between player and coach. The former playmaker of the 1996 championship squad had been Summitt's favorite whipping post for four years.

"It's hard to name a player I chewed out more," admitted Summitt of her eternal chastisement of Marciniak during her playing days.

Yet Marciniak understood precisely what Conklin was experiencing. Who better to help than a fellow former card-carrying member of the Summitt doghouse? The two chatted in depth about life under the watchful, critical eye of Pat Summitt. The wisdom that now pervaded Marciniak had been hard earned, but the ex-Lady Vol guard was infallibly certain of one thing.

"What you have to understand," Marciniak told Conklin, "is that's how Pat shows that she has confidence in you. By yelling. When she doesn't talk to you, that's when you know something is wrong."

The message clicked with Conklin. A dedication to the urgent task at hand of reunifying the team was gained, and Conklin would go on to have an outstanding second half of the season and in the process convert Summitt into a believer.

Hurting in Hartford

Three days later, Tennessee was in the Hartford Civic Center for a match with No. 1 Connecticut. Though the Lady Vols got the best of it the last time the two teams had met—in the 1996 Final Four—UConn still led the series, 4–1. Alas, the Huskies were not the team to face while attempting to right a listing ship. Matters continued to disintegrate for the downward-spiraling Lady Vols, who got smacked by 15 points in a 72–57 loss, shooting a horrendous 30.7 percent—a season low—from the field.

"We lost to a better team, and how we lost really disappointed us, as a team and as a staff," said Summitt afterward with her customary analytical skill. "We felt we had to take away easy baskets, and we were disappointed in our ball handling and lack of commitment to defending one-on-one penetration." Leading by one in spite of 2-of-13 shooting, UT committed seven consecutive turnovers to propel UConn on a 12–0 run. Embarrassed, Tennessee showed a paltry 16 points at the half for its efforts.

"Those seven straight turnovers really broke our momentum and took away from our offense, confidence-wise," remarked Chamique Holdsclaw, who despite her team's poor performance, posted 23 points and 12 rebounds.

Reserve guard Laurie Milligan spoke of another contributing factor to the defeat. "The mental pressure is what we really put on ourselves," she said. "We got scared by their press and didn't respond."

With three quarters of the second half still to go, UT was down by 23 points. There would be no typical Lady Vols comeback this time.

"When you play for the University of Tennessee, there's a lot of tradition and you want to uphold that, not go out and be the team that sets all these bad records," noted Holdsclaw. "This is about pride and the program."

It was the fifth loss to a ranked team for UT in the young season, more losses than any Lady Vols team had absorbed since the 1991 championship year. Still, in the wreckage following the debilitating defeat, and with No. 2-ranked Old Dominion immediately ahead, also on the road, Summitt found an opening to give her club a little lift.

"I knew the schedule was going to be very difficult for such a young team," said Summitt, "and I'm not going to give up on them. But we haven't matured to the point where we can play against really good teams. We have potential, but I hope we're not talking potential in March."

Confab at Old Dominion

Forty-eight hours after weathering a humiliating blow from the nation's No. 1 team, the No. 9 Lady Vols were in Norfolk, Virginia, to face second-ranked Old Dominion. A year ago, UT engaged the top two teams in back-to-back encounters, beating both No. 2 Vanderbilt and No. 1 Louisiana Tech. Now Tennessee hoped to salvage a victory in 1997's similarly quirky scheduling happenstance.

"They are well-respected nationally," said Ticha Penicheiro, the Lady Monarchs' record-setting playmaker. "Everybody knows who plays for Tennessee. We have to respect them, but they have to fear us, too."

And with good reason. Behind Penicheiro's career-high 25 points, Old Dominion dominated, posting 12 consecutive points early in the second half to take the lead permanently and securing a sizable advantage in rebounding, 40–24. Though UT's Holdsclaw did her thing offensively, scoring 27 points, ODU was never headed.

"I'm disappointed in our inside play," said Summitt of her team's performance. "Their post people beat us all night. That was the big difference, because you look at the boards, and we are not accustomed to seeing that difference in the paint."

Five losses in eight games.

But they say each cloud has a silver lining, and if there was a turning point to the 1996–97 team's season, it occurred behind closed doors, not on the court. En route to the ODU game, changing planes in Washington, D.C., a dejected and exhausted Summitt, still wrung out from the UConn defeat, had run into North Carolina women's basketball coach Sylvia Hatchell passing with her team through the airport. The coaching compatriot inquired of Summitt's well-being, wishing her well and telling her to "hang in there till next year." The UT mentor realized then that almost everybody had written off her Lady Vols. Even HBO, which had been following the team around for its documentary, was told to pull off Tennessee because it wasn't winning.

The next day, before the game against the Lady Monarchs, Summitt held a five-hour, no-holds-barred meeting with her team. Plenty was vented, but more was gained in a session that would change the tone for the remainder of the season. Even though they lost to Old Dominion, Summitt saw enough new heart in her troops to hold onto the possibility that good things might still be in store for her squad. With her women taking the ODU loss hard, the coach stepped forward in the gloomy locker room and asked for their attention.

"Get your heads up," she told them. "If you fight like this, I'm telling you, I'm *promising* you, we'll be there in March."

But the effects of this strange new thing called losing, though met head on by Summitt and her staff, was no comfort to Lady Vol fans and acquaintances and was downright head-scratching to opponents used to eyeing UT as a superior powerhouse. All were shocked to see Tennessee struggling.

"We have lots of friends who are players at other places, and every time we lose, there are phone calls," said Abby Conklin. "People are like, 'What's going on with y'all?' It's been a tough season, a very frustrating season."

Summitt knew the troubling experience could inflict possible psychological damage. "We live in a fishbowl," she said. "We've created a monster at Tennessee. There has been a lot of talk about what negative records our team could set."

Now that's a fish out of water.

Catfight at Vandy

Back home in Knoxville after six straight road games and a less-than-impressive 10–6 record, the Lady Vols entertained the SEC's bottom-dwelling Kentucky Wildcats, easily cruising to a

23-point victory. Five days later, the Lady Boilermakers of Purdue fell at Thompson-Boling Arena, victims of a 12-point Tennessee triumph. Then it was load the bus and head west on I-40 for three hours. The intrastate rivalry with the Lady Commodores was center stage in Nashville, January 19, 1997, and 12,417 patrons were on hand to witness the resurgent No. 9 Lady Vols against No. 7 Vanderbilt.

Mild intrigue again involved the enigmatic Conklin, a questionable starter after trying to break up a catfight in her apartment two days before the game. In attempting to separate two clawing felines, the Lady Vol forward jammed her foot into a sofa leg, fracturing the baby toe on her left foot.

"I came to Nashville thinking she wouldn't play," acknowledged Summitt of her senior shotmaker. "Even at game time I wasn't sure she would play and defend."

But Conklin gamely played, freezing the toe before the game and at the half. As it turned out, the game went into overtime, catching her and the UT trainer without an opportunity to refreeze the appendage.

"I was fine until overtime," said Conklin. "Then it began thawing out."

Neither the toe nor accompanying pain could stop the Lady Vol sharpshooter from coming up big at game's end. Three times Conklin hit field goals in the final five minutes, her two-pointer from the top of the key tying the game with 1:22 left in regulation. "She showed a lot of heart out there," added Summitt.

Vandy kept it close throughout the entire first 40 minutes, staying in the contest despite rugged athleticism from UT's powerful inside game headed by Tiffani Johnson and Pashen Thompson. Johnson was a terror from the get-go, making every shot she put up except her final one at the buzzer, for a 24-point aggregate on 8-of-9 shooting. The UT center's 11 rebounds also topped her team's total on the boards, where Tennessee registered a 45–36 edge.

Yet Johnson's near-perfect scoring performance yielded the Lady Vols nothing but a tie after regulation had expired. In overtime it was a different story. UT kicked it into gear, soaring off to a 21–8 advantage in the five-minute extra period and handily taking the contest 92–79.

"We just kind of laid back and accepted the fact that we were in overtime with Tennessee and happy to be there," said Paige Redman of Vanderbilt, who knotted the score at 71 at the close of regulation on a three-pointer with 13 seconds left.

"It was great that we could step up and have such a big overtime," said the toe-thawed Conklin. "That's a lot of points to have in five minutes. It showed a lot of heart and desire for our team, because we didn't give up even though they had hit that three-pointer to put it in overtime."

As for her fractured toe, Conklin could salve it with the knowledge of a big win and a game well played under trying physical circumstances. "It will definitely throb on the way home on the bus," suggested Summitt of Conklin's injury. "But she has this win to think about. It will help."

The scintillating Lady Vols committed zero turnovers in the extra period and scored on every possession down the floor except two.

"They outscored us by a lot of points," VU coach Jim Foster pointed out after the loss. "Their inside offensive rebounding was superior, and our press lost its luster in the last five or six minutes of the game and the overtime. They've always had big, strong kids, a nice mix of players. They win basketball games."

Chamique Holdsclaw got into early foul trouble and didn't score her first bucket until four minutes into the second half. But she soon made up for lost time, tallying 14 points in the final 22 minutes and stealing three balls.

"A lot of teams come into the game focusing on Chamique and tend to forget about the rest of us," said Johnson, whose physical inside play set the tone for the tilt.

From summit to plummet

The Lady Vols, up to 13–6 with an even 2–2 SEC mark, headed next for Gainesville, but the fighting Lady Gators nailed them with yet another defeat. Five nights later, on January 26, Tennessee journeyed to Tuscaloosa, looking to recover from the Florida loss. No. 4 Alabama was second in the SEC and had a deep ongoing score to settle with the Lady Vols: the Crimson Tide women had lost 16 straight games to UT. (The streak, by

the way, through the 2006–07 season, is still intact, with
Alabama now on the losing end of 30 straight games to Tennessee, dating back to March 3, 1984!) If that wasn't enough
motivation, the Tide had a school-record 14-game home winning streak in progress. But the Lady Vols came with a little
inspiration of their own.

"We want 20 wins this year," said Summitt, "I've promised
them, and I'm going to get them. We want to be alive in March
and do some damage."

Alabama broke out strong, leading throughout the opening half and carrying a five-point advantage into intermission.
That lead was augmented after halftime, the Tide upping it to
41–32 with nearly 17:30 left to play. But then UT, behind
Chamique Holdsclaw and its powerful inside game, began
reversing the Tide. A Holdsclaw jumper at 5:30 lifted Tennessee to a one-point, 52–51, lead. After one more lead
exchange, the Lady Vols slowly pulled away behind Tiffani
Johnson's jumper, Abby Conklin's three-pointer, and Holdsclaw's jumper to win 63–60. Holdsclaw and Conklin led UT
with 22 and 16 points respectively.

"This is really a great win for this team, and it's a good
comeback after the loss in Gainesville," said a pleased Summitt.
"We did it today against one of the most impressive front lines
in the country."

Alabama guard Brittney Ezell was crestfallen. The Tide had
missed an excellent shot at breaking the vice-like hold Tennessee owned on the series. "It's a very disappointing loss for
us," said Ezell. "It broke our winning streak and it broke our
hearts."

The victory in Tuscaloosa triggered an eight-game Lady Vols
win streak, with conference foes Mississippi, Mississippi State,
South Carolina, Auburn, Vanderbilt again, and Louisiana State
all falling along the way. The 104–39 walloping of the Lady Bulldogs, on February 9, was off the chart, a 65-point annihilation
that defied logic and math, instilling the belief that typographi-
cal errors might somehow be involved instead.

The squad did not lose again until the final conference
game of the season, at Baton Rouge. In fact, UT's junket
through the Bayou State was a total washout, concluding its

Kellie Jolly

regular season—and invoking Summitt's wrath—with back-to-back losses to the Lady Tigers, and two nights later on February 24, to Louisiana Tech by 18.

The Tech loss completely irked Summitt. "That perform-ance was an embarrassment," she said, simmering before the press, "and I *promise* you it will never happen again."

The double loss to the Louisiana schools was not Sum-mitt's idea of gaining momentum for the postseason. At a point when her team should have been getting stronger men-tally and physically, the Lady Vols were lacking confidence and seemed headed in the opposite direction. Summitt refused to even talk to her team after being smoked by the Lady Techsters.

"They didn't need to hear another negative speech from me," she said. "They were feeling humiliated enough. We were setting all those records for losing. We were seeing it, and we were hearing about it on every newsstand and TV channel. We were the only Tennessee team in 23 years to have back-to-back home losses."

Ousted in Choo-Choo land

Not the ideal script to be entering the annual conference tour-nament, this time held in Chattanooga, Tennessee. After dis-patching South Carolina in the opening round, the Lady Vols had their brightest moment of the tournament, taking on and beating Louisiana State in overtime to avenge their late regular-season loss to the Lady Tigers.

The nail-biter was made possible by the comprehensive play of Holdsclaw, who scored 24 points, six in overtime, and totaled five rebounds to bolster the Lady Vols, who had three players, including Holdsclaw, foul out in the 100–99 tourna-ment quarterfinals victory.

Tennessee lead from the start and held a 17-point halftime edge, before the Lady Tigers gave chase in the second half, finally taking their first lead with just 53 seconds left to play. Holdsclaw's jumper tied it with little more than a half minute to go. In OT Holdsclaw excelled, registering six points before exiting with her fifth personal. In the end, the ball and the game were in the hands of UT freshman guard Kyra Elzy, a

55.3 percent free-throw shooter, who stepped to the line and made the first of two foul shots to give the Lady Vols the one-point win.

"I couldn't watch it," admitted Holdsclaw, on the bench for the young player's tension-filled moment. "But we made great plays and stuck together as a team. Everybody was into it. I think that's why we pulled it out."

Summitt had to call upon some resourcefulness when three-fifths of her starting lineup got into early foul trouble. "We were running out of options," she said. "Foul trouble definitely affected what we wanted to do. We had to change our perimeter attack. We kept trying to think of ways to stay aggressive offensively and keep defensive matchups in mind."

The two teams totaled a hefty 199 points, an SEC Tournament record for combined score. It was also the first overtime game in the conference tourney since 1990. While the exulting win lifted UT, their bubble burst the following evening in the semifinals against Auburn, falling by two to the Lady Tigers.

A random encounter in a hotel hallway later that night between Abby Conklin and her coach may have delivered the national championship to the Lady Vols, according to Summitt.

Conklin had had a poor SEC tournament and was buried deep in a shooting slump. During their corridor run-in, Summitt assured her player that she would help her get out of the shooting doldrums. The show of support humbled Conklin, and true to her word, Summitt worked hard with her ace three-point shooter in practice, eventually eliminating the nosedive.

One thing the UT coach had learned from prior mistakes in handling her past teams: You don't beat a dead dog. Summitt gave her team three days off after the unceremonious exit from Chattanooga to refresh and regroup. When the team reconvened, Summitt, looking Conklin straight in the eye, asked her Lady Volunteers: "What do you want to do?"

The NCAA tournament loomed, with the Final Four that year held in southern Ohio along the banks of the Ohio River. Unflinchingly, Conklin replied, "We want to go to Cincinnati."

Trip to La-la Land

A two-week respite after the SEC tourney afforded the Lady Vols much-needed time to avidly prepare for the upcoming NCAA Tournament. As usual, Tennessee ground up the competition in the subregional rounds conducted at Thompson-Boling Arena, flattening Grambling and Oregon en route to the Midwest Regional, where it dumped No. 18 Colorado 75–67, behind Chamique Holdsclaw's 20 points, at Carver-Hawkeye Arena in Iowa City, Iowa.

Much fun was made at Holdsclaw's expense in the postgame locker room celebration by the two-time All-American's teammates, who mimicked her departure from the game with a leg cramp by falling down and sticking their legs straight up in the air. She was asked by her fellow Lady Vols to yell "cramp!" the next time it occurred, rather than leave the team panicked that a more serious injury could be taking place.

Colorado coach Ceal Barry, who watched a season's worth of video on UT in preparation for the matchup, noticed the Lady Vols' defense had gotten more aggressive as the season wore on. In particular, she singled out Tiffani Johnson's play at center as pivotal in Tennessee's overall development.

"Their intensity level is much different now, much greater," said Barry. "They're big and strong. You can't move them."

The victory set up the most eagerly anticipated rematch of the 1996–97 season: Connecticut vs. Tennessee, together again, in the Midwest Regional final. The matchup was the first regional battle between two previous national titlists in NCAA women's annals.

It would be the teams' sixth meeting in the last three seasons, the Huskies holding a palpable 4–1 edge, defeating the Lady Vols 70–64 for the national championship in 1995 to complete an undefeated season (33–0). The following year, the pair had met in the 1996 Final Four, with Tennessee taking a classic win in overtime. That game was so outstanding it rated nomination for an ESPY award. Overall Connecticut had fashioned a 132–7 worksheet over the previous four seasons, an amazing compilation. In contrast, Tennessee was in the throes of its worst season in 11 years, weathering 10 losses.

"Connecticut hasn't lost that many games in five years," Summitt remarked in comparison of the two programs. Nonetheless, here was UT once again in the postseason, playing in its third successive regional final and the 13th in the school's 16 straight seasons of NCAA play. That's a lot of tradition to carry forward.

"I think a lot of what we do is just pride," said Conklin before the big game. "Pat does a good job of reminding us where the program has come from and that we have to maintain what Tennessee basketball means."

Fortunately, the Lady Vols would catch a break. Sharp-shooting Husky guard Shea Ralph was out following knee surgery, but a frightening tandem of UConn power awaited inside, where 6–7 All-American Kara Wolters and 6–5 freshman Paige Sauer lurked. Tennessee would need to find scoring support for Holdsclaw, who found the nets for 23 points in UT's dismal loss at Hartford back in January but was mostly alone in producing the team's offense.

"We know we're supposed to win but we play like we're not sure we're the best," remarked Husky coach Geno Auriemma before taking the floor. "There isn't a whole lot to say. I think everyone is anxious to play."

But once the ball was put in play, it looked like it would be no game at all. Tennessee dashed off to a 15-point lead, hitting nine of 14 from the field at a dizzying 64 percent clip and looking like they might blow UConn out of Carver-Hawkeye Arena. They maintained a comfortable lead throughout the first half, leading by 12 at halftime, then extending the margin early in the second period to 47–33 before the Huskies made their own 19–6 run to come within one, at 53–52, with just over 12 minutes left. But the swarming UT defense and courage of multiply injured Kellie Jolly were too much for Auriemma's bunch this time. Holdsclaw made a crucial steal and basket that propelled a seven-point run by Tennessee, and the lead was quickly back to 10.

Jolly's heroics were laudable. Shelved in preseason with a torn knee ligament that required surgery and rehab, the blonde sophomore point guard was considered to be about 80 percent healthy for the UConn game. But in addition to the knee, Jolly had badly sprained an ankle in the win over Grambling a week and a half earlier. Yet she played tenaciously in the Midwest Regional final, inspiring teammates with her gritty determination and performance. Jolly hit two timely three-pointers after Connecticut's second-half run that aided in further defusing the Husky attack.

"Kellie Jolly made huge shot after shot," praised Auriemma after his team's 91–81 loss. "That's the reason they're going to the Final Four and we're not. I have a lot of respect for her personally. I know how hard she had to work to get this chance."

Lady Vol assistant coach Mickie DeMoss concurred with Auriemma. "She gives this team so much heart," she said of Jolly, who missed playing in the earlier loss to Connecticut in January. "I think the players feed off it. She's like an iron woman. She's sacrificed her body. She deserves a Purple Heart."

The upset pushed Tennessee into its 10th Final Four appearance in a repeat matchup with Notre Dame, which the Lady Vols had vanquished by 12 in the NIT back in mid-November. Tennessee, with its 27–10 season record, now became the losingest team ever to make the Final Four.

"So many teams were kicking us when we were down," said DeMoss. "We got back up and came back swinging."

Clearly Tennessee benefited from the fruits of being the underdog that evening. "Obviously, the pressure was on Connecticut," said Summitt following one of her program's biggest non-championship game victories ever. "I've been in that situation and gone home because of having had teams motivated to play against us. It's tough."

The Huskies noted that this was very much a different game than the beating they administered to UT in Hartford back in early January. "They were physically stronger," said UConn guard Amy Duran of the Lady Vols' intense play. "Every time we had a good stretch, they found some way to stop it. We played differently than a couple of months ago. We're the same team, better than we were, but we didn't take it to them. We didn't do it for 40 minutes like we needed to."

Holdsclaw, named the Midwest Regional's most outstanding player, topped Tennessee's offensive display, with 21 points, and along with Tiffani Johnson, shared team honors for rebounds, each with 11.

"I think they were scared for once," Holdsclaw conjectured of the former No. 1 team in the country. "I'd never played against a UConn team that looked like it was scared."

"They did things against us that no one else did," marveled Auriemma. "I definitely have to give them credit."

Both Jolly and center Pashen Thompson joined Holdsclaw on the All-Midwest Regional Tournament Team. "This is the best, because nobody expected us to be here," said Thompson, a senior who poured in 15 points and helped contain UConn's high-scoring Wolters. "I'm still in La-la Land right now."

Avoiding spring break

Abby Conklin's wish for her and her team, expressed in a moment-of-truth challenge from their head coach after failing in the SEC Tournament only a month ago, had come true. Tennessee was going to Cincinnati.

Waiting for the Lady Vols at Riverfront Coliseum was a Notre Dame team that UT had handled without concern in the budding days of the 1996–97 season. If previous encounters were any indication, then Notre Dame's chances appeared slim to none in the Final Four semifinal, having never beaten Tennessee in 12 previous contests. In addition N.D.'s playoff experience was limited, competing in just eight postseason games in its history compared to UT's 64.

But the Fighting Irish had a one-two senior scoring punch in 6–3 center Katryna Gaither and forward Beth Morgan, the latter of whom was averaging 47.5 percent from the field in the NCAA Tournament. Pat Summitt, looking to shut down Morgan, challenged her two-time All-American, Chamique Holdsclaw, to do the job. The UT sophomore forward responded, holding Notre Dame's sharpshooter to just three first-half points and 18 in all, while totaling 31 points herself, as well as contributing four steals and five rebounds.

Holdsclaw received little scoring support in the opening period. Though Conklin hit a pair of three-pointers, she exited the game early with three fouls. Jolly, the gutsy star of the UConn upset, was 0-for-6 in the first 20 minutes. The centers,

Tiffani Johnson and Pashen Thompson, delivered just four first-half points, with Johnson getting those.

Notre Dame took the early lead on Gaither's strong inside showing. The Irish center posted 12 of her 28 points in the first half, and Notre Dame's matchup zone befuddled UT. In addition, Notre Dame was outrebounding the Lady Vols, 11–9. But with Holdsclaw shining on defense, as well as contributing 12 points, Tennessee managed to come away with a one-point lead at halftime.

In the second period, UT established control from the start. Notre Dame turned the ball over on its first five possessions, with Tennessee guard Kyra Elzy stepping up, her long arms intercepting passes and pilfering steals to get quick points off transition. She would post 14 points, five steals, and most surprisingly, nine rebounds—joining Pashen Thompson for team honors on the boards—as the Lady Vols flew into the NCAA finals 80–66.

"On defense, we had a lot of intensity," said a happy Summitt afterward. "It's a team effort, but I have to single out one player. Kyra Elzy's defense was great."

As great as Elzy's contributions were to the Vols' victory, Holdsclaw again was indispensable. "I can't say enough for what Chamique has done for this team," praised teammate Johnson. "When she scores and shows a little emotion, I think that gets the rest of the team pumped up."

Then again Holdsclaw may have had her own special motivation. "You don't want Coach Summitt screaming down your neck," said the Tennessee star. "My coach put up a challenge for me to stop Beth Morgan. I didn't want to let the team down. We just want to leave here with a national championship."

Asked where the Lady Vols would be without Holdsclaw, Conklin, who finished with 11 points, three of them three-pointers, said, "Spring break."

Fifth in the SEC, No. 1 in the country

The improbable became fact. Against all odds and an army of doubters throughout the long season, Tennessee, with the worst record of any contestant in Final Four history, won its fifth women's NCAA basketball championship. It was yet another first for the Lady Vols, who claimed back-to-back national crowns for the first time in their storied history.

With the persistence of a nagging shrew, Tennessee just wouldn't go away and ceased to be quieted. Against Old Dominion in the finals, Pat Summitt unleashed a furious pair of freshman defenders at the Lady Monarchs' star guard, in a defensive strategy that won plaudits from the ODU coach. But riding comfortably with a 16-point second-half lead, UT suddenly went into a swan dive, allowing Old Dominion back in the game and even yielding a two-point lead to the Lady Monarchs, before righting itself and pulling away for a nine-point, 68–59, victory.

"Of all of our runs to a national championship, this one is the most unexpected," said a jubilant Summitt after the final buzzer.

"Awesome, it's absolutely awesome," added Abby Conklin, the often-under-siege senior forward. "If you had asked me about a possible national championship after we played Old Dominion the first time [a nine-point loss at Norfolk, Virginia, in early January], I'd have said you're crazy."

If everyone else had given up on the Lady Vols, Summitt and her assistants hung in with their own private belief, though barely so. The temptation to look ahead to the 1997–98 campaign, with four absurdly talented incoming freshmen, was overwhelming but in the end resisted.

"We couldn't focus on next year," said assistant coach Mickie DeMoss. "It wouldn't be fair to these kids."

In front of 16,714 at Riverfront Coliseum in Cincinnati, UT opened the game with three straight Chamique Holdsclaw baskets, while defensively setting to work on Lady Monarch guard Ticha Penicheiro. Summitt deployed first Kyra Elzy then reserve Niya Butts into pressuring the All-American into 11 turnovers and just 10 points overall, shutting Penicheiro out in the first half. Butts, in only eight minutes of play, contributed eight points as well.

"Pat's plan to work over Ticha was magnificent," admitted Old Dominion coach Wendy Larry. "She was fatigued. She never makes 11 turnovers." Penicheiro had bombed Tennessee for 25 points in their regular-season encounter.

Though the Lady Monarchs outrebounded UT 34–29 and each team turned the ball over 26 times, the big stat that placed Tennessee atop the champion's pedestal was the team's sizzling 59.2 field-goal percentage—16 points above its season average. As usual, Holdsclaw powered the offense with her game-high 24 points, complemented by seven rebounds. The Final Four MVP was brilliant in her floor work following ODU's collaring of the Lady Vols in the second half. The Lady Monarchs erased a 16-point first-half Tennessee lead with nine minutes remaining in the game and eased ahead by a basket, 49–47. After tying the contest with a baseline jumper, Holdsclaw followed with two assists on baskets by Tiffani Johnson and Pashen Thompson, before reeling off three straight buckets to push the game out of reach.

"It's phenomenal what she did," confessed Larry of Holdsclaw. "We were unable to do much defensively to keep her from scoring."

As Conklin, the only other UT player in double figures (12), put it, the Lady Vols know they have an ace up their collective sleeves at all times and under all manner of adversity. "We have Chamique Holdsclaw," she said. "We can handle it."

Point guard Kellie Jolly, who had scorched UConn in the Final Four semifinal with 19 points on an ankle with torn ligaments, set an NCAA Final Four record for most assists, 11, in the title-game win. Summitt called her the "heartbeat" of the Lady Vols.

"She [Summitt] has players who have been here before," said Larry of the Tennessee lineup. "That's a great plus. She took a group of experienced players and brought along her young ones."

DeMoss reflected on the arduous journey of the 1996–97 Lady Vols, who completed the year at 29–10. "We were seasoned for the postseason," she said of the up-and-down turmoil and rugged regular-season schedule that had the team in near collapse after consecutive losses at UConn and Old Dominion in early January. "Once we got into the NCAA Tournament, there was light at the end of the tunnel. We could see where we were headed. There were no more road blocks. We were so much more active on defense. Chamique, Kyra, and Niya elevated their defensive games. It allowed our post people to get in front of people."

Holdsclaw, savoring her award and looking back on the incredible swing of the 1996–97 season that enabled Tennessee to register back-to-back national titles and the school's fifth crown in 10 years, said, "Right now, we have our place in history."

The team would welcome four sensational freshmen—many claiming it to be the best class of prospects ever to hit The Hill—the following year. But as current frosh Butts noted, this season and this improbable championship belonged to *this* group. "We got tired of hearing about next year."

A spent Summitt offered one last bit of perspective on the just-concluded, emotionally draining campaign: "Fifth in the SEC and No. 1 in the country—doesn't that sum up what this team just accomplished!"

1996–97
(29–10, 8–4 SEC, 5th)
Final AP Ranking: 10th
NCAA NATIONAL CHAMPIONS

ROSTER

No.	Player	Yr.	Pos.	Ht.	Hometown
3	Niya Butts	Fr	G	6–0	Americus, GA
4	Tiffani Johnson	Jr	C	6–4	Charlotte, NC
5	**Kyra Elzy**	**Fr**	**G/F**	**6–1**	**LaGrange, KY**
11	Laurie Milligan	Jr	G	5–8	Tigard, OR
13	Misty Greene	So	G/F	5–9	Decatur, TN
14	**Kellie Jolly**	**So**	**G**	**5–10**	**Sparta, TN**
23	**Chamique Holdsclaw**	**So**	**F**	**6–2**	**Astoria, NY**
31	Brynae Laxton	So	F	6–0	Oneida, TN
34	LaShonda Stephens	Fr	C	6–3	Woodstock, GA
44	**Pashen Thompson**	**Sr**	**C**	**6–1**	**Philadelphia, MS**
52	**Abby Conklin**	**Sr**	**F**	**6–3**	**Charlestown, IN**

(starters in bold)

SEASON STATS

Player	PPG	RPG	FG-Pct.	FT-Pct.
Chamique Holdsclaw	16.2	9.4	.498	.667
Abby Conklin	11.7	4.8	.439	.835
Tiffani Johnson	10.0	7.4	.532	.705
Kellie Jolly	8.4	1.9	.409	.750
Laurie Milligan	8.3	2.3	.359	.868
Pashen Thompson	8.1	6.5	.522	.758
Kyra Elzy	5.8	3.5	.363	.569
Misty Greene	5.8	1.4	.385	.839
Brynae Laxton	2.9	2.1	.344	.526
Niya Butts	2.5	1.3	.406	.676
LaShonda Stephens	2.4	1.5	.380	.696

1996–97 UT POLL HISTORY

Starting position:	4th (11/11/96)
Highest 1996–97 ranking:	3rd (11/18/96)
Lowest 1996–97 ranking:	11th (3/3/97)
Final 1996–97 position:	10th (3/10/97)
NCAA Tournament finish:	NCAA CHAMPIONS

1996–97 SCHEDULE

Date	Rank	Site	W/L	Score	Opponent
11/15/96	4/nr	H	W	80–59	Austin Peay
11/17/96	4/12	H	W	79–60	Kansas
11/19/96	3/nr	N	W	72–59	Notre Dame
11/20/96	3/11	N	L	64–66	Louisiana Tech
11/23/96	3/nr	N	W	83–68	Marquette
11/24/96	3/nr	A	W	87–58	Vermont
11/26/96	5/nr	H	W	71–36	Wis.-Green Bay
12/3/96	4/nr	H	W	79–63	Memphis
12/8/96	4/5	H	L	93–94 (OT)	Georgia
12/15/96	5/1	H	L	65–82	Stanford
12/18/96	6/11	A	W	79–71	Texas Tech
12/21/96	6/13	A	W	68–65 (OT)	Texas
12/29/96	6/22	A	L	75–77	Arkansas
1/2/97	8/nr	A	W	64–52	St. Joseph's
1/5/97	8/1	A	L	57–72	Connecticut
1/7/97	9/2	A	L	72–83	Old Dominion
1/12/97	9/nr	H	W	84–61	Kentucky
1/17/97	8/nr	H	W	72–60	Purdue
1/19/97	9/7	A	W	92–79 (OT)	Vanderbilt
1/21/97	8/19	A	L	62–71	Florida
1/26/97	8/4	A	W	63–60	Alabama
1/28/97	9/nr	H	W	94–83	DePaul
2/2/97	9/nr	H	W	74–72	Mississippi
2/4/97	9/23	H	W	78–74	Wisconsin
2/9/97	9/nr	H	W	104–39	Mississippi State
2/11/97	8/nr	H	W	90–59	South Carolina
2/15/97	8/nr	A	W	76–63	Auburn
2/17/97	8/15	H	W	64–59	Vanderbilt
2/22/97	8/13	A	L	78–83	Louisiana State
2/24/97	8/6	A	L	80–98	Louisiana Tech

SEC TOURNAMENT, Chattanooga, Tenn.

Date	Rank	Site	W/L	Score	Opponent
2/28/97	8/nr	N	W	75–48	South Carolina
3/1/97	8/9	N	W	100–99 (OT)	Louisiana State
3/2/97	8/nr	N	L	59–61	Auburn

NCAA SUBREGIONAL, Knoxville, Tenn.

Date	Rank	Site	W/L	Score	Opponent
3/15/97	10/nr	H	W	91–54	Grambling State
3/17/97	10/nr	H	W	76–59	Oregon

NCAA MIDWEST REGIONAL CHAMPIONSHIPS, Iowa City, Iowa

Date	Rank	Site	W/L	Score	Opponent
3/22/97	10/18	N	W	75–67	Colorado
3/24/97	10/1	N	W	91–81	Connecticut

NCAA FINAL FOUR (1st), Cincinnati, Ohio

Date	Rank	Site	W/L	Score	Opponent
3/28/97	10/15	N	W	80–66	Notre Dame
3/30/97	10/2	N	W	68–59	Old Dominion

(rankings are for UT/opponent)

6

1997–98

Perfect

A FULL-FLEDGED DYNASTY WAS FLOURISHING. Back-to-back national titles will do that for a program. Now for a third. A three-peat. Interestingly, the personnel makeup for each of the 1996, '97, and '98 teams presented only one common thread: Chamique Holdsclaw. The two-time All-American, the Lady Vols' cornerstone nonpareil, had watched a changing cast of support players come and go into her junior season. Gone were the hustling guard tandem of Michelle Marciniak and Latina Davis, along with three-point bombing forward Abby Conklin. Gone, too, were centers Pashen Thompson and Tiffani Johnson, the former lost to graduation, the latter dismissed from the team for disciplinary reasons.

Johnson, a 6-4 senior-to-be power presence under the basket, at first glance looked to be a huge loss. With the departure of Thompson, the job at center was hers to lose going into the 1997–98 season, before Summitt kicked her off the squad for violating team rules.

"I had no choice," Summitt said of the discharge of Johnson, the inside core of her back-to-back national championship squads. "I call upon our seniors to be the most disciplined, responsible members of the team. Everyone else on the team was living up to their responsibilities, and it wouldn't have been fair to them to have a separate standard for T. J. Much as it hurt to cut her, it would have hurt the team more to keep her. Especially with four freshmen coming in."

Ah, the four freshmen. Not the vocal group from the 1950s, but the best crop of recruits Pat Summitt and her staff had assembled in the 24 years that the five-time NCAA coach of the year had been at the helm of the Lady Vols basketball program. Lacing up their sneakers for the first time in orange and white were backcourt passing/scoring wizard Kristen "Ace" Clement, from Broomall, Pennsylvania; Teresa "Tree" Geter, a shot-blocking rebounding talent in the post, from Columbus, Georgia; energetic guard defender/scorer Semeka Randall, from Cleveland, Ohio; and Tamika Catchings, hailed as the next Chamique Holdsclaw, from Duncanville, Texas. Though it had been more than 30 years since the world was subjected to the mania of the original Fab Four, women's basketball at Tennessee immediately found new life in the old handle. It is not known if Paul, George, or Ringo voiced any objection.

Tipping Tech

What does a back-to-back national champ do for an encore? Try, try, try again. The "three-peat" challenge to the Lady Vols was being heard everywhere. The gauntlet had been thrown down. Even Summitt herself would experience the unknown. Never before in her long tenure at UT had the iconic coach prepared to mentor such a young team. In addition, she had never coached a Tennessee squad that did not have a proven post game.

After a season-opening 92–54 wipeout of Ole Miss at home, No. 1-ranked Tennessee raised its 1997 national championship banner on the night of November 21, 1997, before 16,490 howling faithful at Thompson-Boling Arena, during a square-off against perennial rival, No. 2 Louisiana Tech.

The rafters shook as UT took off on a 12–0 run midway through the second period, after trailing the Lady Techsters by one at halftime. As had occurred for nearly every game over the previous two seasons, Chamique Holdsclaw copped game-high scoring and rebounding honors, with 24 and 11 respectively, adding three assists and two steals.

"She may be the best player ever," said Louisiana Tech coach Leon Barmore, in high praise of the Astoria (Queens), New York City product. "She does what she wants whenever she wants to."

But it was a unit minus the star—with the four freshmen and sophomore Kyra Elzy—that produced the 12–0 run, while Holdsclaw sat for a breather. Key to the skein was Tree Geter's 10 points and five blocked shots, the latter defensive swats bringing the courtside Lady Vols, players and staff, to their feet. Coupled with Geter's heroics UT went wall-to-wall with full-court defensive pressure, eventually forcing the Lady Techsters to cave.

"It looked like Tennessee was the team with five starters back," marveled Barmore, whose Lady Techster powerhouse was a preseason favorite to win the national crown in many quarters. "In 21 years of coaching, this was my worst coaching job. We just didn't get it done. We got hammered on the boards."

At halftime, Summitt prescribed control of the boards and defensive pressure as her formula for victory, should the Lady Vols wish to accept it. They took the challenge, playing shut-down defense and taking the overall battle in rebounding, 51–42.

For the veteran Tennessee coach, the 75–61 victory was almost euphoric. Clearly her new contingent offered encouraging possibilities. "You don't have to motivate this group," Summitt said. "But the crowd certainly excited us. I've worked 24 years to see a team this exciting and a crowd that enthusiastic."

New freshman starter Tamika Catchings posted 17 points, including a key three-pointer to open the big second-half run. She grabbed nine rebounds as well, the second highest total in the game. Her freshmen mates, Geter and Semeka Randall, each scored 11, with Elzy putting in 10, for UT's first win over Tech since a 1996 home game. Injured first-year point guard Ace Clement directed the team smoothly in her 11 minutes of action, showing natural poise, leadership, and hustle.

The Lady Vols next visited Summitt's old school, UT-Martin in West Tennessee, which was dedicating the gym floor in their old star's honor. But Summitt didn't show her appreciation by letting up any on her alma mater, burning them by 50 points. Ditto the same two days later against visiting Vermont, a 40-point victim of the Vols.

Standing up to Stanford

The West Coast beckoned for one of the two games that Pat Summitt felt her young team could lose in the early going. Stanford had turned extremely formidable since Tennessee had its way with the Californians, beating them three times back in the 1990–91 national championship season. This version of the Cardinal had forged the longest active home winning streak in women's Division I basketball, 49—a stretch that ran over three years, dating back to a 1994 loss to Purdue. Even though this contest would be played at the San Jose Arena, several miles down the road from the campus in Palo Alto, it was considered a home game for the Cardinal women.

Stanford blistered the cords from the beginning, shooting a hot 57 percent in the first half, while UT, in Summitt's mind, was soft on defense, exposing the vulnerable underbelly of its undeveloped post game, as the Cardinal had its way underneath. Only equal outstanding shooting by the Lady Vols enabled the Tennesseans to keep pace, trailing at the half by just one.

In the locker room, the UT coach scolded her youthful charges for their lackadaisical defense. "It's a 40-minute game," Summitt admonished, in an account related in her book, *Raise the Roof*. "The mentally tougher team will win. We've never been able to beat this team in a shooting contest. So you better defend them."

The diatribe worked. In the second half, UT exploded, with its guards, particularly Kyra Elzy and her tentacle-like arms, hassling Stanford unmercifully. The action produced the desired result for Summitt: horrendous 17 percent shooting by the Cardinal in the final 20 minutes, a cold five of 29 from the floor. On the offensive end, Tennessee roared out, scoring 14 straight points behind the Three Meeksketeers, or "the Meeks" as they were called—Chamique (Holdsclaw), Tamika (Catchings), and Semeka (Randall) all shared the same-sounding middle syllable in their first names. They flat tore up the court, Holdsclaw netting 25 points, followed by Catchings's 20 and Randall's 17. Randall also secured 11 rebounds, the game high.

"I knew our players had the ability to play one-on-one defense like they did in the second half," offered Summitt, "but not to the extent of holding Stanford to 25 points. I'm pleased we could go on the road with this young team and do this well. Right now, our team is better than I thought it would be."

Rebounding, a Lady Vols staple, paved the way for UT, which logged a 53–34 board advantage. In addition, Elzy contributed two blocked shots and nine points in the 88–70 win—Tennessee's first over the Cardinal since a 105–89 victory in 1994.

"They're definitely better than they were last year, talent-wise," noted Stanford guard Vanessa Nygaard. "They had an awesome spurt in the second half." Actually two. In addition to the aforementioned 14–0 run to start the second period, Holdsclaw opened and closed an 8–0 run with baskets, after Stanford had pulled to within nine with 10:15 left to play. The victory upped the series lead to 9–4 in favor of Tennessee.

The Lady Vols were now 5–0; a young team had hatched, hitting the ground running.

By New Year's Day, they would be 14–0, the notches on their belt including wins over Portland—significant in that it was one of only two regular-season appearances made all year by gritty senior guard Laurie Milligan, whose career was acutely curtailed by degenerative knee issues—and a Manhattan College team that they beat by 50, but more impressively, held to 28 points. They dumped an old rival, Texas, by 34. And there was the Illinois game that pitted sister against sister, Tamika Catchings versus older sister Tauja.

The game was a duel, with Tennessee down 17 at the half. Summitt's staff never stopped encouraging them, urging more. With 12:32 remaining and the Illini up by 11, Elzy noticed that Illinois seemed out of breath. *Now's the hour; now's the time!* she thought. And then Kellie Jolly's "steal and score" dash delivered five straight points off Illinois turnovers. In just 10 seconds, Jolly had cut the deficit to six. The roll continued until, with 32 seconds left, Ace Clement threaded a no-look pass to Hold-sclaw for an easy layup, and the Lady Vols came away with a hard-earned 10-point, 78–68, win. The sisters hugged afterward and exchanged sisterly words. Tamika had had a big night. Not only did her team come out a winner, she had scored 20 points and recorded 13 rebounds.

Then it was north to Alaska, to the wilds of an Arctic winter, where the Lady Vols rode in dogsleds before participating in the Northern Lights Invitational in Anchorage. There they defeated Akron by 35 before blasting Texas A&M 105–81, with the Meeks credited with 76 of the team's points against the Aggies. Tennessee then added No. 9 Wisconsin to its victory string, now at 13, in the holiday tournament finals. Back in the Lower 48, they celebrated the first of the year with a 30-point victory over Arkansas, a team that would surprisingly resurface at season's end.

With the holidays over, things turned serious again. Business was at hand. Time once more for Tennessee's annual blood-letting war with its modern-era rival from Storrs, Connecticut.

Hunting down UConn

The blue and white vs. orange and white rivalry had escalated in just three short years to become the nation's top matchup in women's hoops. It was cross-cultural north vs. south and then some. The Huskies held a mysterious hold over the Lady Vols, winning the first three matchups, including the 1995 NCAA championship game. But when Tennessee exacted its revenge, it leveled UConn at the neck, eliminating coach Geno Auriemma's women twice in succession in the NCAA playoffs, most recently the year before, in 1997, when the two met in the Midwest Regional final. The youthful rivalry had grown, as Pat Summitt once described it with author Sally Jenkins, "with the rapidity of a brushfire."

"It has been good for us and good for Tennessee," acknowledged Auriemma. "It's good for the fans and the game of basketball."

As January 3, the encounter date, neared, Summitt became increasingly edgy, wondering who among her troops would and could defend the explosive All-America Connecticut guard

AP IMAGES

Chamique Holdsclaw

Nykesha Sales. She decided it had to be Chamique Holdsclaw. But the problem was that Holdsclaw—having carried the burden of the team's scoring and rebounding load throughout her career—hadn't been consistent enough on defense for Summitt's liking. The UT coach issued her superstar a challenge.

"Coach sat down with me and said, 'If somebody asked me to name the best offensive player in the country, I would say you,'" reiterated Holdsclaw of the conversation with Summitt. "'But if somebody was to ask me about the best defensive player, I might not say you.'"

Videotapes compiled by assistant coach Al Brown, showing lackadaisical effort by Holdsclaw on defense, were then wheeled out. Holdsclaw got the message and translated the findings into the game, helping shut down the high-scoring Husky sharpshooter, who didn't hit double figures until the final minute. Sales's game total was a mere 12 points.

"I just responded," Holdsclaw imparted afterward.

The game opened before 24,597 Tennessee partisans at Thompson-Boling Arena with a rock concert aura—the largest crowd ever to witness a game in the history of women's college basketball, breaking the mark set by the Texas-Tennessee contest back in 1987. At the urging of the NCAA Rules Committee, the game was conducted as a test-tube experiment of sorts, being played in four 10-minute quarters as opposed to two 20-minute halves.

UT roared out of the gate, rolling up a quick 10–0 lead that escalated to 17 points, with Kyra Elzy fueling the run with all nine of her points scored in the first half. But Connecticut began a comeback that finally cut it to one, 49–48, with two minutes left in the third period. Holdsclaw then ignited a 7–0 run, which turned into a 12–2 spurt with the ruthless defensive pressure of Semeka Randall, who nailed a three-pointer following a pair of steals to propel UT's hot fourth-quarter run. The freshman dervish tallied 16 of her 25 points in the final quarter to push Tennessee to a 15-point victory over its northern nemesis, 84–69. Holdsclaw totaled 25 points and was hailed for her defense against Sales, while Tamika Catchings's 17 points and nine rebounds showed a solid game underneath. But on this afternoon, it was the freshman Randall who played the catalyst.

Her 10 boards were a game high and keyed the Lady Vols' sizable 41–28 rebounding advantage.

"That's where we dominated, on the boards," remarked Catchings. "And that helped us win the game."

The victory stopped Connecticut's regular-season winning streak at 52 and pushed UT to 15–0. The Huskies' inside might had been minimized. "This was a game of our quickness against their power," said Holdsclaw, who nailed seven free throws down the stretch, as did Catchings.

"Tennessee is certainly everything it was advertised to be," Auriemma stated. "There just seems to be very little you can do, because they put such tremendous pressure on you. . . . And they had a lot of assistant coaches up in the stands, too. It's hard to beat all of that."

In the end, all Auriemma could do was shake his head and think of what might have been, with regard to the vastly talented Randall, a onetime UConn recruit. Randall recalled telling him of her choice to wear orange and white rather than blue and white.

"When I made my final decision to go to Tennessee, Geno said, 'I'm going to have to put the whammy on you when we play,'" recounted the freshman sensation. "I think Connecticut about ran off the floor they were so scared."

The latter comment stirred a controversy the next day when it appeared in the press. Randall had meant that the crowd was so intimidating that it had to unnerve the Huskies, but Auriemma took his own dig back at Tennessee. The first inklings of genuine discord between the two schools had officially surfaced.

Summitt, eternally cautious regarding the placement of praise with her players, warned that a deeper look at the game would be required by her squad to attain full benefit from the victory. "We have to learn from this and not walk away thinking we played a great game," she said. "If we did not take and learn from it, the only team that will benefit from it is UConn."

Both coaches delivered comments regarding the awesome nature of the burgeoning rivalry and its glowing future. People were even saying it had become the women's equivalent of Duke–North Carolina.

"When they compare you to the men's game, it's progress. Hopefully this matchup can continue to have a positive impact," noted Summitt. "It's been great for exposure. Hopefully we can keep this matchup alive for several years."

Oddly, Summitt's words would be a harbinger of a shocking and curious development a decade later. Even back then, in 1998, the effects for the losing team were devastating. Both squads were letting the poison of a loss to the other affect their outlook on the remainder of a season. The feeling had become entrenched in Knoxville and Storrs that the year was basically tanked if it included a loss to the other team.

Summitt and Tennessee would rock the world of women's sports in the spring of 2007, when the school abruptly pulled out of its regular-season series with Connecticut, offering no reason for its action. Even a personal intervention by the head of ESPN programming couldn't alter Summitt from her controversial decision. Here was the premier matchup in all of women's basketball, a vessel that continued to carry the torch for and bring new fans to the women's game, suddenly silenced. Worse, no explanation was given.

But that letdown of untold proportions wasn't even a distant cloud on the horizon in 1998. Fifteen more meetings still lay ahead for the two teams.

In the next two weeks, the Lady Vols reeled off four straight conference wins over South Carolina, Florida, Georgia, and Kentucky—none of the victories by less than 25 points. They followed that run, on January 20, with their most awe-inspiring display of the season (on the scoreboard, at least), trouncing a hapless DePaul unit by the astronomical score of 125–46, a numbing 79-point margin in which the four freshmen totaled 82 points! Five days later, they played host to Vanderbilt, the ninth-ranked women's team in the country, their seventh meeting of the season with a ranked team in the Top 20.

The new women's game

After the DePaul massacre, Tennessee was at the 20-win plateau. Long ago Pat Summitt had given up her hope that the young squad might experience defeat as a learning tool for further development. Instead, she wondered what wondrous thing her charges might do next. In front of her, the culmination of a life's ambition was at work. As she said, she had waited 24 years to coach a team like this one.

Her dream team, after a competitive first half against Vanderbilt, smoked the Lady 'Dores to begin the second period, charging out on a 20-0 run that resolved the contest right there.

"If I wasn't on the bench, I'd pay money to see these kids play," an ebullient Summitt said. "They can do things I haven't seen many collegiate teams do, just the pace they play at."

Vandy outrebounded UT and easily broke the Lady Vols' full-court pressure defense in the first half to keep it close. But Summitt made an adjustment at the intermission, switching Kyra Elzy to forward and placing Semeka Randall at guard. The result was the explosive 20-0 spurt keyed by Elzy's three straight baskets and Randall's four points that came in transition after a pair of VU turnovers. Holdsclaw totaled the game high in points scored, with 24, while Elzy grabbed nine boards to lead both teams. Randall and Tamika Catchings made it another honorable showing by the Meeks, as each posted 22 points and Randall copped four steals.

"When the Chicago Bulls get in a zone, you're like, 'Gosh, they're unstoppable.'" Randall pointed out after the 86-54 shellacking. "We want to get to that same level where it's hard to stop us. It's hard to shut everybody down on this team when everybody's working together and flowing the right way."

Summitt, upon review of the stats, was disgruntled to see a 37-31 edge on the boards by Vandy, but there was truthfully little to quarrel about. Her racehorse runaway fillies were tearing up the schedule, leaving a wake of the defeated with no doubters in sight.

"They're dynamic athletically and have dimensions, in some respects, that are almost new to the women's game," said an impressed Jim Foster, Vanderbilt's coach, after the debacle.

And that new team with the new game kept cranking it up a notch. Three nights later at home against Georgia, UT gutted the Lady Bulldogs by 59 points in a tumultuous 102-43 whitewash. Alabama followed, offering the sternest test of the regular season, losing by only seven in Knoxville. Ole Miss then went down for the second time, scoring 46 less points than its conqueror. Now at 24–0, on February 7, Tennessee was facing the team it challenged for the NCAA crown the previous year. Old Dominion entered Thompson-Boling Arena ranked No. 3.

Dominating Old Dominion

If ever a team had motivation to squeeze the living orange out of Tennessee, other than Alabama, it might be Old Dominion. The Lady Monarchs had lost 16 of their previous 17 meetings with UT, including the national title game the preceding March. But as with most any team she chose to up her level of play against, Chamique Holdsclaw would have a big say in it.

Before a crowd announced at 20,495, Holdsclaw scored on her patented glide moves off the dribble and Jordanesque-hangtime shots, posting 33 by evening's end. But ODU, with an effective zone defense early on, was not allowing UT good looks at the basket, including Holdsclaw in the beginning.

"Even the baskets I made, it seemed like three people were on me when I shot," she said.

Tennessee led by 12 at the half and was up 48–30 with 16:22 remaining. But then, as it had in the 1997 national championship game, ODU came back, five times cutting the deficit to nine points. Each time, Holdsclaw would answer, her final move a dandy as she took a pass on the baseline, dribbled between her legs and then from side to side, before hitting a 20-foot three-pointer. UT's two-time All-American rattled 24 points through the rim in the second half and added a game-high 12 rebounds to go along with a pair of steals and two blocked shots.

"Chamique Holdsclaw made big plays when we needed baskets," said Pat Summitt after the 85–61 win, the worst defeat suffered by the Lady Monarchs in four years. "That's why I think she's the best player in the game."

As in the '97 national championship game, Old Dominion's Ticha Penicheiro was hounded relentlessly. The Lady Vols forced the All-America guard into nine turnovers. She committed 11 in the title game. "I was really tired," she said. "That's a lot of turnovers for a guard."

Missing from the UT lineup was Kyra Elzy, whose clinging defense was missed. The embattled sophomore guard, who dealt with a stalker for much of the season, was now out for the rest of the campaign with a blown right knee suffered in the first half of the Alabama game from an awkward fall. Elzy was the defensive leader, the hustler that instilled inspiration with her willingness to take on the tougher tasks, like the role of defensive stopper. Picking up the slack, Semeka Randall helped force mistake after mistake from ODU's Penicheiro and added 18 points, along with her game-high six steals.

"She's relentless on defense," said Summitt of her young freshman dynamo. Down the stretch, Randall's two steals and Holdsclaw's remarkable aim produced a 23–8 run that sealed the game for the Lady Vols. Tamika Catchings added a strong presence to the tilt, pulling down 11 rebounds and putting in 16 points, while getting three steals.

The streak of perfection was intact. Holdsclaw, dubious of an undefeated season at the outset because of UT's tough schedule, commented after the team's 25th straight victory of the season, "It's pretty remarkable. We know if we continue to improve, we could go undefeated, but it's not something we talk about. This team really hasn't played its best basketball yet. When we play our best basketball, we're going to be pretty scary."

Romper room

The Lady Vols continued to roll it up, taking the next three games against Mississippi State, Memphis, and Auburn by a combined 21.3-point margin, before facing Vanderbilt for the second time in the regular season. But the long campaign was becoming eternal for the exhausted Lady Vols, the price paid for no-let-up, all-out play.

The Lady Commodores rushed off to a fast start before the third-largest crowd in Memorial Gym history for a women's game—14,848—opening the game at 16–7 and creating a defensive tempo that did not allow Tennessee to find its game in the early going. But then UT burst off on a 17–0 run, returning a strangling defense of its own that held Vandy to an anemic field goal during one eight-minute stretch. That stifling crush defensively forced VU point guard Ashley Smith into a career-high 10 turnovers.

Jimmy Davy, a veteran writer for the *Nashville Tennessean*, eloquently chronicled the Lady Vols' killer D after witnessing UT's awesome defensive swarm: "The attacking, suffocating defense of the Tennessee women's basketball team is a thing of beauty—like a Bengal tiger," wrote Davy. "It swarms, contesting every pass. Quick hands flip away careless attempts by the opposition to put the ball on the floor. And quicker feet arrive to contest shots, when just a split second before, the shooter was wide open. Mental fatigue often sets in before bone-weary fatigue for the Big Orange opposition. Coach Pat Summitt is the master of nose-to-nose, physical defense."

Tennessee took a nine-point lead into halftime then finished off the Lady Commodores with a relentless second half, in which they outscored VU by 22. At the helm as points leader once again was Chamique Holdsclaw, holing 28 points and snagging seven boards.

"If you want to beat them, you've got to find a way to keep Holdsclaw from being able to do whatever it is she wants to do," assessed Vandy coach Jim Foster after the 91–60 carnage. "She's just a great, great player. She is one of those once-in-a-decade players, and you've got to try and make her human."

She was not without help. Combined, the three Meeks totaled 73 of the team's 91 points. The rattled 'Dores, meanwhile, shot just 36.9 percent for the game and labored under their 24 turnovers, as Tennessee pilfered the ball 15 times. The Lady Vols' super team was becoming an unbridled powerhouse, a ladies' version of UCLA or Duke. "Defensively, UT is unique to the women's game," Foster added. "They remind me of Kentucky's men's team two years ago, which won the NCAA championship and was loaded with NBA players. They have a lot of dimensions, a lot of talent. To beat that team, you're going to have to play an almost perfect game. I'm not sure they can get much better."

Summitt couldn't realistically argue. "We love defense and pressing. It gets us going," she said. When asked to evaluate the reasons for the team's defensive success, Summitt readily pointed out: "They just play it quicker. And they play it for 40 minutes."

The Lady Vols, now 29–0, were just one win away from achieving a women's collegiate milestone. "No Division I women's team has won 30 games in a regular season," Summitt emphasized. Here was yet another gauntlet thrown down for her magnificent young assassins. The chance to extend that perfection would come a week later in the regular-season finale against Louisiana State.

Here's looking at you, 30–0

The war-weary Lady Vols were banged up and limped into their final game, attempting to make history with one more win. In a practice before the LSU game, Tamika Catchings broke her nose going up for a rebound. Another gauntlet thrown down.

Summitt regained the services of oft-injured Ace Clement, and the freshman, though creaky and mistake-prone at first, began to consistently display her enormous talent. In addition, Laurie Milligan, mentioned earlier, the only senior and playing in just her second game of the season, had been promised a start by Summitt for her loyal participation despite limited physical ability to perform. She played the first three and a half minutes, lame legs and all, registering two assists and two steals in her brief but inspirational appearance.

It didn't take much time for the Lady Vols to shake off the nagging hurts and stiffness. Within the first eight minutes, UT forced Louisiana State to turn the ball over 15 times and allowed them just six shots, as Tennessee vaulted off to a 30–8 lead and a whopping 54–23 margin by the half. In fact, so dominant were the Lady Vols in the first 20 minutes that they scored more points off turnovers, 26, than LSU did total (23). Catchings played with a splint over her broken nose, but it failed to alter her play in the slightest, as she led all scorers with 21. The Fab Four totaled 65 of the team's outlay in the 90–58 romp. The tenacious UT defense recorded 27 steals, the second highest single-game total in Lady Vols history. By game's end, the Lady Tigers had committed 36 turnovers.

"Right now, I don't see anybody in the country that's going to touch Tennessee," said LSU coach Sue Gunter. "The strange thing is that they're not as good as they're going to get. Next year, they will be untouchable."

Summitt and her team had their 30th win and their place in women's college basketball annals secured. "This was really special," Summitt admitted. "It's fitting this record came today. This team has been so exciting, scored more points, drawn more fans and been talked about more than any other team we've had."

With the SEC Tournament in Columbus, Georgia, not scheduled to begin for another week, the Lady Vols could rest their worn out legs and look forward to a first-round bye.

SEC Tournament

It seemed incongruous that the Columbus Civic Center should be the host of a major function to which the giant of the industry had been invited when only a relative handful of people showed up. That's what the four-digit attendance figures seemed to indicate for the women's conference tournament. Tennessee appeared to do its part. The nation's No. 1 team had much of its core fan base in attendance for the school's tourney games, but few supporters of other programs were visible.

In the tournament finals, a sparse crowd of only 7,603 was on hand, nearly a thousand under the facility's capacity. As much as Pat Summitt had done to escalate interest in the women's game over her lengthy and sterling career at Tennessee, could it be that the sport was really only a draw around the epicenters of women's basketball—Knoxville, Storrs, Austin, and Palo Alto? The Columbus foray had been a bust financially. The following year the SEC Tournament would move back to Chattanooga, which had hosted the event the previous five years. The failure at the box office, however, had little to do with the quality of play on the court.

After dismissing Mississippi State 88–60 in the tourney's second round, UT turned its attention for the third time that season to the Lady Commodores of Vanderbilt, the nation's 14th-ranked team, whom Tennessee had stifled by 32 and 31 points in late January and mid-February. Now, in the conference tournament semifinals, Vandy was to experience a fury unknown in its women's basketball history.

Not unlike the LSU affair, UT broke from the starting gate with unimagined fierceness, forcing VU into five turnovers in the first five minutes and surging to a 17–6 lead. The hungry Lady Vols were everywhere, hard after every shot, pass, and drive to the hoop. By the end of the first half, the score was a motley 61–29, and it only got worse. The Lady 'Dores did not record their second field goal of the second half until just 5:58 remained in the game, making just one of their first 26 shots in the final 20 minutes, for a pathetic second-half shooting percentage of 18.4. Another perspective on the pounding: from just under three minutes left in the first half to midway through the final half, UT mounted an unfathomable 43–4 run.

"It was difficult just to complete a pass at times," said a beleaguered Jim Foster, Vandy coach, after the slaughter. "They have three of the best athletes I've seen in my 20 years of coaching, and they're all playing on the same team."

The Meeks, of course, were at it again, with Chamique Holdsclaw totaling 25 points and 10 rebounds and Semeka Randall finishing with 16 points. Tamika Catchings had a milestone day. In addition to her 20 points and 10 rebounds, Catchings, for the second straight game, had achieved a double-double in the first half. On a larger scale, she surpassed Holdsclaw's school freshman scoring record.

"We can still pick it up from here," said Catchings, after the 106–45 annihilation. "And when that comes, it will be awesome."

The 61-point thrashing was the worst loss in Vanderbilt women's basketball history. "It kind of killed us and was embarrassing," confessed Vanderbilt senior forward Lisa Ostrom, "but they are a great team. Even greater than they were [earlier in the season]. They're getting better and better, that's what is scary. They play so well together. When you attack one thing and you think you have it, then they come at you with something else. They just have so many weapons."

Even Summitt herself conceded that the game had been a fine display of Tennessee Lady Vols basketball, though deferring to the plight of the Lady Commodores. "We've probably played as well in a few other games," she said, "but Vanderbilt didn't shoot well."

Holdsclaw, the junior superstar, knew that the rubber was now finally hitting the road for Tennessee. "This is where it counts," she said. "This is where you're going to see if we're the best team ever. You can go 30–0, and it doesn't mean anything in the regular season."

And now Alabama stood between UT and the SEC Tournament championship, a team that had given the Lady Vols a physical battle and yielded UT its smallest margin of victory in 1998.

Prior to the tourney finals, it was announced that HBO was finally releasing its documentary on the Lady Vols recorded over the previous 1996–97 season. It had appeared that the show's producers had pulled back from the project after Tennessee's five-times-in-eight-games losing skein from December 1996 through early January '97, but Summitt needn't have worried about the cable giant losing interest. The up-and-down season only made for a better film. The 75-minute movie, *A Cinderella Season: The Lady Vols Fight Back*, even had a world premiere scheduled at the historic Tennessee Theater in Nashville the night before the Final Four would begin.

Close call

No season the likes of which Tennessee had assembled in 1997–98 comes without at least one close call. That near miss came in the SEC Tournament finals against No. 20 Alabama. Though all players were accounted for, a particular element of the well-honed Super Lady Vols machine was MIA: passion. The team's now-legendary defense was playing without the verve evident in such notable blowouts as the previous night's destruction of Vanderbilt. Shutdown guard Semeka Randall had just one steal and admitted to playing with fear when the game with the Crimson Tide got tight.

"Yes, during the major parts of the game," she said. "I didn't come out mentally ready. It was in my heart to play hard and defend to the best of my abilities, but evidently, I didn't do that."

Though Tennessee led 29–26 at the half, the Tide controlled the tempo of the game, utilizing the clock well and never letting the Lady Vols settle into their running game.

AP IMAGES

Pat Summitt

Early in the second half, UT's thin three-point lead expanded to 14, but Alabama came right back, muscling its way through a 17–8 run over the middle five minutes of the second half. Yet the Tide wound up falling just short, 67–63, as Tennessee claimed its eighth SEC Tournament title. Alabama could at least take solace in knowing that it was the only team thus far in the season to limit UT's victory margin to single digits, and they did it twice.

"I'm in awe of what they can do physically," said Tide senior guard Brittney Ezell. "There's no question that Tennessee's got the best athletes in the country. But you can't be scared of them."

In her usual, almost quiet, way, Chamique Holdsclaw posted 22 points and was selected tournament MVP, with the other two Meeks contributing 16 (Catchings) and 11 (Randall). Catchings pulled down a team-high nine rebounds, but Summitt was not happy that the Lady Vols lost the rebounding battle, albeit by one, and for the only time during the long season, displayed fear for an opponent.

"If this team plays scared like some of them did tonight, I don't think we can win a national championship," warned Summitt. "We can't be afraid to go out and win the game. We didn't handle their physical play. It affected our shot selection. We had people kicking the ball out instead of putting it back up." Then with a directive to her two young starters, Summitt employed one of her customary challenges: "Semeka and Tamika have to play like veterans."

The dream team with the dream season rolled on. The NCAAs loomed next, and UT had two weeks to prepare, before it reentered the fray of the ultimate quest.

Top seed in the Mideast

After hosting two subregional games on their home floor, comfortable wins over Liberty and Western Kentucky that brought their season record to 32–0, Tennessee moved on to Nashville, site of the Mideast Regional, where it assumed the top seed.

The Lady Vols tanked Rutgers with a 92–60 bullying in the regional semis, coasting into the regional title game against athletic and determined North Carolina. And what a final it was.

In a game in which Pat Summitt felt the crowd was worth 10 points, UT initially had to visit its worst nightmare before coming from behind like Seabiscuit down the backstretch to overcome a physical, hungry, and running North Carolina five. Summitt and her staff, frantically watching the club go through a cold, cold night of shooting in what had become a demandingly physical contest, were beside themselves to come up with a solution to the riddle of the Lady Tar Heels. Holdsclaw, who had pulled out so many games with her insuppressible talent, went the last 12 minutes of the first half without scoring a point. Somehow UT managed a 33–27 lead at the break. But UNC came out on a 7–0 run to start the final half that brought them a one-point lead, which quickly advanced to seven. Then finally to 12, at 61–49.

A television timeout stopped the clock with 7:19 remaining. The Lady Vols had made just four of 17 second-half shots; Holdsclaw had missed 12 of her last 13, going 16 long minutes without scoring. Kellie Jolly demanded the team run the court. "We've got to go *now*!"

Tennessee stepped back out onto the court. But this time it was as if they slipped through a thin veil separating past from present, good performance from bad; a transformation that Summitt had pleaded for all game long from her young troupe. The deciding moments were at hand. Out of instances like these champions were born.

But rubbing out a 12-point second-half deficit would take patience, focus, and a decided turn of fortune. That began to happen when Ace Clement fired a pass past a UNC defender just barely into the clutches of Tree Geter, who bounded to the hoop, made the shot, and was fouled. The huge Memorial Gym crowd howled at the three-pointer. Within the next four minutes, Tennessee doggedly went on a 17–3 sprint, pulling ahead by a single point, 68–67, with 2:48 to go. The Lady Vols increased it to five, before a Tar Heel trey made it a two-point ballgame with 21 seconds left. Kellie Jolly, the team's best free-throw shooter, was reinserted into the lineup and was immediately fouled. She canned both shots, and UT registered one of the biggest wins in school history. The Lady Vols had truly refused to lose.

"I didn't want to be a player who choked," Holdsclaw said about her personal motivation at the end, when all her teammates and Summitt, too, were looking to her to take over the game. She responded, primarily at the free-throw line, where she downed 13 of 14 foul shots, offsetting a bad night of shooting from the field (30.7 percent). Still, she wound up with 29 points and pulled down 13 rebounds, coming away with the regional MVP hardware as well.

Though it took time, the other players produced big performances. Semeka Randall came up especially huge, with eight boards and three steals supporting her 20 points. It was Randall's driving baseline bank shot that broke a 64-64 tie and gave Tennessee a lead it would not relinquish down the stretch. Catchings contributed 11 points, seven rebounds, and four big steals; Jolly chimed in with three assists and the two huge free throws that gave UT a four-point lead with 12 seconds left.

And then there was Tree Geter. The 6–3 freshman center from Columbia, South Carolina, scored 11 points—seven in the final seven minutes—and grabbed eight rebounds while altering several North Carolina shots. Her three-pointer to start the 17–3 run was the play that changed the game. During a time-out before the stretch run, assistant coaches wondered if Geter was emotionally into the game, her silence and staring eyes raising doubts that she was hearing the messages bombarding her from the coaches. But Geter was indeed thinking, her thoughts centering around a harrowing possibility: *I'm not ready to go home yet!*

"I've pretty much hid on our team all year," Geter admitted later. "I made up my mind that 'tonight was the night.'"

Jolly saw it as a blueprint for the future. "We've seen spurts of the great player she is going to be," said the blonde point guard. "She really made big plays for us."

Summitt had once said that the regional final was, of all the games in the NCAA Tournament, by far the toughest to win. The game offers far too easy a vantage point to look ahead down the yellow brick road to the Final Four. It had been a close shave, but her resilient team found meaning in the old adage that it's a 40-minute game, finally and heroically discovering something within themselves that keyed the way to victory.

"When your backs are to the wall, that's the true test of a competitor," said Lady Vol assistant coach Mickie DeMoss after the 76–70 heart-stopper. "Anyone can compete in a 30-point game when you're winning."

Goin' to "Kansas City." The old song classic never held more meaning for a reenergized group of orange-and-white women's basketball players.

Final Four

In the midst of the circus environment of the NCAA Final Four, taking place at Kansas City's Kemper Arena, it was awards time. For the third successive year, Chamique Holdsclaw was named to the Kodak All-America team. This year some friendly company joined her. Reminiscent of Holdsclaw's selection to the hallowed 10-woman team as a freshman, Tamika Catchings served notice of her substantial talent, gaining the accolade as a first-year player as well. Holdsclaw also took the coveted Naismith Award given annually by the Atlanta Tipoff Club to college basketball's player of the year.

And Pat Summitt, no stranger to honors, received the Associated Press Coach of the Year award and the Naismith Coach of the Year award to go along with her three previous Naismith selections (1987, '89, and '94) and her two Women's Basketball Coaches Association honors, copped in 1983 and '95. But, really, the Tennessee coach saw all the pomp as an unnecessary distraction at this time of the year.

"I've always said select the coach of the year, the player of the year, the All-American teams after the Final Four," Summitt stated logically.

The Lady Razorbacks were UT's foe in the semifinal, a team Tennessee had beaten handily by 30 points back on New Year's Day. But this latest edition of the Hogs was a much-changed club. No. 9-seeded Arkansas had stunned the world of women's basketball with its defeat of Duke in the West Regional final and, though the lowest-seeded team ever to advance to the Final Four, had a regular-season upset victory to its credit over the previous year's 1997 national champs—a game in which the

Lady Razorbacks held Holdsclaw to a career-low five points, on 1-of-11 shooting.

A noticeable addition to the Lady Vols pregame warm-ups was rehabbing guard Kyra Elzy, the 6-1 sophomore defensive anchor who had torn an anterior cruciate ligament in her right knee just two months earlier against Alabama. Her presence was a healing balm for both her and the team. "She might be the best defensive player in the country," saluted Arkansas coach Gary Blair.

On March 27, before a Kemper Arena crowd of 17,976, Arkansas stayed at close range during the first half, even mirroring an element of Tennessee's winning formula, as evidenced by its UT-like defensive tactics that dampened the Lady Vols' output. Still, the Hogs faired no better offensively, committing six turnovers in the game's first seven minutes, yet it required Kellie Jolly's three-pointer to give Summitt's troops a 39–28 lead at the break. Semeka Randall, as was customary, made herself large in many areas. The freshman sparkplug scored 14 of her 22 points in the opening 20 minutes, executed three steals, and perhaps biggest of all, grabbed five offensive rebounds.

As had also been the case of late, Holdsclaw started slow, not recording her first bucket until the game was almost nine minutes old. She warmed up considerably in the second half, ending with game highs in scoring (23) and rebounding (10). Tree Geter, as she had in the previous game against North Carolina, came to play, asserting herself in the middle with five blocked shots and seven rebounds. Catchings scored only 13 points but lent considerable assistance with two steals, four assists, and eight rebounds. Jolly canned five of seven from the field, including the first-half-ending trey, and dished five assists.

The 86–58 win nearly equaled the final score of the regular-season victory over Arkansas, shy by two points on UT's end, but it was still enough to set the record for largest victory margin in an NCAA Final Four semifinal and to send Tennessee to its fourth straight NCAA championship game.

Now a true test lay ahead for the perfect 38–0 team: longtime rival Louisiana Tech, which had overwhelmed North Carolina State by 19 points in the other semifinal. Both finalists were, safe to say, completely different teams than they had been when they faced each other in the second game of the season back in late November, a game the Lady Vols won by 14.

"We're more together as a team," said Louisiana Tech guard Tamicha Jackson. "We're a lot better prepared now." To which Tennessee's Catchings could only reply, on a level that included both competitors: "Obviously, anything can happen."

Talk was proliferating of a Tennessee dynasty, with the school's opportunity for a third successive championship undeniably a possibility. While Lady Techster coach Leon Barmore concurred that five or six championships in a row could very well happen for the Lady Vols, such an occurrence, he felt, might not be in the best interests of the sport overall. And of course, there were his personal reasons.

"I don't want her to win 10," Barmore said. "I'd like to win one or two myself."

Of concern was Louisiana Tech's postseason mastery of Tennessee. The Lady Techsters totally dominated UT in NCAA Tournament play, owning a 5–1 edge over the Lady Vols. But it was Louisiana Tech that provided the opposition in Tennessee's first NCAA championship, in 1987. That landmark victory opened the floodgates to the unparalleled modern-era success the Lady Vols' program has enjoyed. The Lady Techsters opened an 11–1 overall series lead when the two first began facing each other in the late 1970s. But by March 1996, UT had clawed back to respectability, the record standing at 13–16 in Louisiana Tech's favor.

"It could be ugly," cautioned Summitt. "You have two teams that are committed to defense and rebounding and, if necessary, grinding it out."

DeMoss, the energetic UT assistant coach who once starred as a Lady Techster during her collegiate playing days in the mid-1970s, noted, "It's going to be a battle of athleticism."

Tech star guard LaQuan Stallworth, Barmore's choice for his team's MVP, foresaw a titanic struggle defensively. "The defense is going to be there," she said before the game, "It's going to wear both of us out."

On the orange-and-white side, Summitt didn't envision a departure from what had gotten her Lady Vols to this point.

"We've been pressing and running through 38 games, and we're not going to change for No. 39."

At least one player was weary of all the pregame hype. "Me personally, I'm sick of hearing all this stuff about Tennessee," said Louisiana Tech forward Amanda Wilson. "I'm just ready to play the game."

39–0

Wire to wire. No. 1 to open the season, No. 1 to end it.

With the power, finesse, speed, and stamina that had carried them unblemished through an entire season into the finals of the national championship game, Tennessee completed its mission of perfection, claiming its third successive NCAA women's crown. Among the icing on the cake were records posted for most women's Division I wins in a season and most first-half points scored in an NCAA championship game (55). Louisiana Tech could only wonder what happened.

The Lady Techsters got the first score of the game but never led again. Before 17,976 at Kemper Arena, UT's display of dominance had the Lady Vols up 19–6 following an early 11-point run and leading at the half by 23. Shooting star of the night Kellie Jolly, the junior point guard, told by Summitt beforehand to be more aggressive offensively, hit her first five shots en route to a career-high 20 points that included four of five three-pointers, several from NBA range.

"I wanted to be an honorary Meek," said a joyous Jolly.

Midway through the second half, when Louisiana Tech made overtures at a run, cutting the Lady Vols' lead to 18, Jolly responded with back-to-back treys, pushing the advantage back to 24.

"Any hope we had, those two threes shut the door," said Barmore, acknowledging Jolly's superb performance in his team's 93–75 loss to Tennessee.

Tamika Catchings wound up leading all Ladies in points scored, with 27. She also paced both clubs in steals (4) and totaled seven rebounds. Tree Geter was a force defensively, blocking four shots and snagging seven boards.

Chamique Holdsclaw came away with Final Four MVP honors, as a result of balanced play, leading the team in assists, with six, and following Catchings in points scored, with 25. Her 18 first-half points, along with Catchings's 15, set the tone offensively, as Tennessee broke out to 25-point leads twice in the opening 20 minutes.

"For this final game, their blood was boiling," said assistant coach Mickie DeMoss.

Barmore cited his team's thin bench as a hindrance but was grimly realistic about the inevitable outcome. "If we'd had a little more depth, I think we probably could have made a run at them," the Louisiana Tech coach reasoned. "Beat them? Probably not."

Senior Laurie Milligan got in the game and in so doing became the first player in women's college basketball history to play in four straight championship games, dating back to the Lady Vols' loss to Connecticut in the 1995 title game.

With 39 seconds left, an emotional note was struck when Kyra Elzy took the floor. The returning floor leader, making her first appearance since the devastating knee injury on February 1, was serenaded with the biggest cheer of the night.

"I'm extremely proud of this team," said Summitt, warmly in the glow of her consummate moment. "The players and staff have combined for a tremendous chemistry." Perhaps she was smiling too because her franchise player, Holdsclaw, announced after the game that it was "firm and final" she would return to UT for her senior year. Holdsclaw, incredibly, still knew nothing but championships in her basketball career, having won four New York state titles in high school and now three at UT. The string even went all the way back to the eighth grade, where she also played on a title team.

In looking back, the Lady Vols had gone 15–0 against teams ranked in the final Top 25 and 22–0 against teams making it to the NCAAs. Their average margin of victory in SEC games was staggering—31.9 points.

"Every championship is special," said Summitt, reflecting. "It's about the relationship with the players."

But beyond the fulfilling interaction with her 1998 team, Summitt had enjoyed the rarest of coaching pleasures, the exceptional season, the campaign unequaled. 39–0. This group had carved an indelible niche into the consciousness of

American sports. Barmore capped it with an appreciative and respectful nod: "It's the greatest women's basketball team that I've personally ever seen."

Footnote

Though this book deals exclusively with the Lady Vols' seven national championship teams, a word about the Dream Year follow-up team: the 1999 aggregate.

Following the victory celebration after Tennessee's NCAA title game win over Louisiana Tech in '98, Chamique Holdsclaw was asked in a postgame news conference if this was the best team ever in women's collegiate basketball. She replied, "I think next year's team will be the best ever."

On paper, it certainly looked to be the case: Holdsclaw plus the Fab Four, but all of them one year older. But as Pat Summitt said, you have nowhere to go but down when you're perfect. That happened in just the second game of the season, when eventual national champion Purdue took a 10-point decision in Indiana. The Lady Vols rebounded as only they can, winning 24 straight games before losing the regular-season finale to LSU in Baton Rouge. UT regrouped and claimed the SEC Tournament but was ousted by Duke in the East Regional finals. Holdsclaw's dream of four straight NCAA championships was over.

But what a legacy she left on The Hill: three national championships, four-time Kodak All-American, two-time Naismith Player of the Year, Naismith Player of the Century, Sullivan Award winner, and the leading Lady Vol scorer and rebounder of all time. A pro career beckoned, and though Holdsclaw earned WNBA All-Star status six times, she never was on another winner the rest of her career. Sadly, she retired from the sport suddenly in the summer of 2007 without explanation, at age 29.

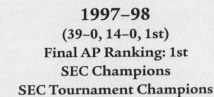

1997–98
(39–0, 14–0, 1st)
Final AP Ranking: 1st
SEC Champions
SEC Tournament Champions
NCAA NATIONAL CHAMPIONS

ROSTER

No.	Player	Yr	Pos.	Ht.	Hometown
3	Niya Butts	So	G	6–0	Americus, GA
5	Kyra Elzy	So	G/F	6–1	LaGrange, KY
11	Laurie Milligan	Sr	G	5–8	Tigard, OR
13	Misty Greene	Jr	G/F	5–9	Decatur, TN
14	**Kellie Jolly**	**Jr**	**G**	**5–10**	**Sparta, TN**
21	**Semeka Randall**	**Fr**	**G**	**5–10**	**Cleveland, OH**
23	**Chamique Holdsclaw**	**Jr**	**F**	**6–2**	**Astoria, NY**
24	**Tamika Catchings**	**Fr**	**F**	**6–1**	**Duncanville, TX**
31	Brynae Laxton	Jr	F	6–0	Oneida, TN
33	Kristen "Ace" Clement	Fr	G	5–11	Broomall, PA
34	**LaShonda Stephens**	**So**	**C**	**6–3**	**Woodstock, GA**
40	Teresa Geter	Fr	C	6–3	Columbia, SC

(starters in bold)

SEASON STATS

Player	PPG	RPG	FG-Pct.	FT-Pct.
Chamique Holdsclaw	23.5	8.4	.546	.765
Tamika Catchings	18.2	8.0	.537	.760
Semeka Randall	15.9	5.3	.487	.728
Kellie Jolly	7.6	2.3	.463	.843
Kyra Elzy	7.0	4.0	.408	.686
Teresa Geter	6.3	4.8	.547	.623
Kristen "Ace" Clement	5.6	2.2	.421	.644
LaShonda Stephens	4.0	3.4	.308	.587
Laurie Milligan	2.0	0.4	.429	.571
Misty Greene	2.0	1.2	.289	.857
Niya Butts	1.8	1.1	.415	.457
Brynae Laxton	1.2	1.9	.279	.400

1997–98 UT Poll History

Starting position:	1st (11–10–97)
Highest 1997–98 ranking:	1st (all 18 polls)
Lowest 1997–98 ranking:	1st (all 18 polls)
Final 1997–98 position:	1st (3–9–98)
NCAA Tournament finish:	NCAA CHAMPIONS

1997–98 SCHEDULE

Date	Rank	Site	W/L	Score	Opponent
11/4/97		H	W	ex 111–54	U.S. Armed Forces
11/18/97	1/nr	H	W	92–54	Mississippi
11/21/97	1/2	H	W	75–61	Louisiana Tech
11/23/97	1/nr	A	W	73–32	Tennessee-Martin
11/25/97	1/nr	H	W	92–52	Vermont
11/29/97	1/11	N	W	88–70	Stanford
11/30/97	1/nr	A	W	74–51	Portland
12/3/97	1/nr	H	W	98–64	Texas
12/6/97	1/nr	N	W	93–61	George Mason
12/7/97	1/nr	A	W	78–28	Manhattan
12/12/97	1/nr	H	W	78–68	Illinois
12/18/97	1/nr	N	W	98–63	Akron
12/19/97	1/nr	N	W	105–81	Texas A&M
12/20/97	1/9	N	W	87–66	Wisconsin
1/1/98	1/nr	H	W	88–58	Arkansas
1/3/98	1/3	H	W	84–69	Connecticut
1/6/98	1/nr	A	W	94–52	South Carolina
1/10/98	1/12	H	W	99–60	Florida
1/14/98	1/19	A	W	96–71	Georgia
1/18/98	1/nr	A	W	93–65	Kentucky
1/20/98	1/nr	A	W	125–46	DePaul
1/25/98	1/9	H	W	86–54	Vanderbilt
1/28/98	1/17	H	W	102–43	Georgia
2/1/98	1/nr	H	W	73–66	Alabama
2/4/98	1/nr	A	W	91–45	Mississippi
2/7/98	1/3	H	W	85–61	Old Dominion
2/9/98	1/nr	A	W	74–52	Mississippi State
2/12/98	1/nr	A	W	91–65	Memphis
2/14/98	1/nr	H	W	79–63	Auburn
2/16/98	1/14	A	W	91–60	Vanderbilt
2/22/98	1/nr	H	W	90–58	Louisiana State

SEC TOURNAMENT, Columbus, Ga.

2/27/98	1/nr	N	W	88–60	Mississippi State
2/28/98	1/14	N	W	106–45	Vanderbilt
3/1/98	1/20	N	W	67–63	Alabama

NCAA SUBREGIONAL, Knoxville, Tenn.

3/14/98	1/nr	H	W	102–58	Liberty
3/16/98	1/15	H	W	82–62	Western Kentucky

NCAA MIDEAST REGIONAL CHAMPIONSHIPS, Nashville, Tenn.

3/21/98	1/nr	N	W	92–60	Rutgers
3/23/98	1/7	N	W	76–70	North Carolina

NCAA FINAL FOUR, Kansas City, Mo.

3/27/98	1/nr	N	W	86–58	Arkansas
3/29/98	1/4	N	W	93–75	Louisiana Tech

(rankings are for UT/opponent)

7

2006–07

Lucky Seven

NOT A SINGLE SOUL WHO experienced the miraculous 1998 Tennessee season would ever have taken odds that nine long years would pass before the Lady Vols stood at center court and lifted another NCAA title trophy overhead. To think that premiere stars such as Michelle Snow, Kara Lawson, and Shanna Zolman went through the Lady Vols program during that span, never knowing the feeling of wearing a championship ring. Yet in the final analysis, not unlike when Chamique Holdsclaw hit Knoxville, it took the presence of a major player to vault that last step for UT. That person was Candace Parker.

Parker came from some fine hoops stock. A product of Naperville (Illinois) Central High School, her brother Anthony was a former first-round draft pick of the New Jersey Nets. Parker came to Knoxville as the most celebrated women's high school player in history. An athletic, 6–4 forward/center/guard, she had 27 inches of vertical leap that ultimately translated into six dunks heading into her junior season at UT. An accurate jumper from 15 feet in and her off-the-dribble explosions made her a threat to score from anywhere. And when she wanted, she could play intimidating, shutdown defense, altering opponents' shots with her condor-like wingspan. One of the school's first redshirt freshmen, after she missed the 2004–05 season with a pair of surgeries, she went on to earn SEC Freshman of the Year and All-SEC first-team accolades in 2006. In 2007, she just took over, becoming the major force in the women's game and gaining the Wade Trophy as player of the year in addition to All-America honors.

But this Lady Vols team wasn't just all Parker. It had a highly productive and effective point guard in little Shannon Bobbitt and the team's steals and assists leader at the other guard in Alexis Hornbuckle, along with rangy 6-4 Nicky Anosike at center—all juniors. Senior forward 6-3 Sidney Spencer rounded out a physical, highly athletic quintet.

Early challengers

After a 3–0 start at the front of November 2006, the Lady Vols entered a five-game mid-month stretch, in which they would play five ranked teams in succession. Arizona State, Stanford, Middle Tennessee State, Louisiana Tech, and North Carolina—the team that ousted the lady Vols in the 2006 Cleveland Regional finals—all were played within a fortnight around the Thanksgiving holiday, with three of the games on the road.

Following a nine-point win over the Sun Devils in the southwestern desert, in which Candace Parker posted 25 points, Tennessee headed home, on November 24, to take on No. 11 Stanford, a team that had succumbed to the Lady Vols 11 straight times dating back a decade to 1996. UT unleashed Parker on the fluttering Cardinal, humbling the West Coasters with an all-around performance that included her second straight 25-point game and leaving no skill unturned. Parker recorded nine rebounds, five blocked shots, four steals, and swished her first three-pointer of the season in the 77–60 victory. But it was one play nearly halfway through the opening period that brought the Thompson-Boling Arena crowd of 13,352 to its collective feet. That's when Parker, on a breakaway, slammed home her second dunk of the season.

"She had a lot of what I call valuable spurts throughout the game," commented Pat Summitt of Parker's play. "We would go for two or three possessions, and then it was like Candace would take over for two or three possessions."

The Lady Vols led by seven at the half then went on a 10–2 run shortly after the second half began, ultimately shooting 60.9 percent from the floor in the final 20 minutes to distance themselves from the Californians. UT also held a 19–8 second-half rebounding edge.

"I think shot selection played a big part in the second half," Tennessee junior guard Alexis Hornbuckle said. "We came out shooting a lot of outside jumpers, shooting a lot of quick shots, not really rotating the ball and getting great ball movement. Coach put a point of emphasis on that in the locker room—play together and kill them inside."

Forty-eight hours later, Tennessee played host again, this time to instate Middle Tennessee, clouting the team from Murfreesboro 88–64. It had been 22 years since the two had last met, in the 1984 NCAA Tournament, where the Blue Raiders lost by 18. In the interim, the MTSU women had elevated their program as witnessed by their No. 17 national ranking by season's end.

Four Lady Vols reached double figures against Middle Tennessee, led by Parker's and Sidney Spencer's 16 points apiece.

"We have a great offensive team," said Alexis Hornbuckle, who registered nine points. "Any individual person at any point in time can knock down a shot. We have faith in each other, whether it's a three or a two or somebody's driving. That's been a concern the past few years, when there's maybe six or seven people you can count on scoring. . . . This year, it's like everybody can do it at both ends of the court."

UT quickly made no game of it, rattling off runs of 10–0, 9–0, and 7–0 before taking a halftime lead of 49–27. In the second half, they led by as many as 35 points.

"Tennessee played great," said Middle Tennessee coach Rick Insell, who coached the Lady Vols' Alex Fuller at Shelbyville High School before taking the MTSU job. "They just flat took it to us and controlled every facet of the game. We played hard, we didn't quit, but they just happen to be six inches taller than us at every position."

Candace Parker

Two days later, who should trundle into Thompson-Boling but the Lady Techsters, UT's NCAA finals opponent from its last championship season of 1998. Since that meeting, the two clubs had met eight times, with Tennessee winning seven of them.

Halving your Tech, and eating it too

They had been on the receiving end of a perennial butt-kicking from this team for 10 years before the Lady Vols' first national championship. When UT went into that 1987 NCAA title game against Louisiana Tech, it was just 1–11 lifetime against the Lady Techsters. But now, in 2006, the Lady Vols had more than evened the score. *They* were now the butt kickers, leading the series 21–17. With the 1998 national championship game win over their rivals from Ruston, they also owned two NCAA titles at Tech's expense. On top of that, the Lady Vols had recorded the last six wins in a row in the two teams' fierce competition, four consecutively at the Thomas Assembly Center.

The tenor for the evening was established on Tech's first possession, when Candace Parker blocked a shot with authority. By the half, UT led by 27, and it was all over but the final statistics. In assessing the victory, it was clear that Tennessee had played a whale of a first half defensively, registering a phenomenal 15 steals in 20 minutes (22 in all). Louisiana Tech, normally averaging 18 turnovers a game, had 19 by the end of the first half. UT also held the Lady Techsters' shooting to a barely breathing 21.4 percent from the floor.

"I thought in the first half our defensive intensity was really strong," said Pat Summitt. "I thought it was very disruptive."

Disruptive? That Orange defense brought on something a tad more ferocious to be up 42–15 at the half.

Doing damage offensively for No. 4 Tennessee was little-heralded reserve Dominique Redding, a 6-foot-1 senior forward from Clearwater, Florida, one of the Lady Vols whom Summitt admits she hounds the most, who posted a career- and game-high-tying 13 points. And there were solid performances by Alberta Auguste, who put in 11 points but more impressively stole the ball eight times; Alexis Hornbuckle, who added six more steals; and Parker, who towered like a Goliath defensively, rejecting seven Louisiana Tech shots, a career best, in the 71–50 UT victory.

Though Tennessee had a poor-to-maudlin second half against the Techsters, it really didn't matter. Some said it was because North Carolina was looming in the on-deck circle, and that appeared valid since the Tar Heel women had inflicted a mortal wound to the Lady Vols the previous March in the finals of the 2006 NCAA Cleveland Regional. Now it was off to Chapel Hill for the early-season showdown.

Carolina blue

A sold-out crowd of 8,010 at Carmichael Auditorium anxiously awaited the battle of undefeated teams—No. 4 Tennessee versus No. 2 North Carolina. Actually, it wasn't much of a game at all, after UT's big gun, Candace Parker, got stuffed early in the game. The 6–4 All-American had intercepted an errant UNC pass and was headed for a layup at the other end, when the Tar Heels' LaToya Pringle, no peanut herself at 6–3, raced from behind, stuck with Parker through two spin moves, then stuffed the Naperville, Illinois, ace in an electrifying defensive play. The action triggered a shift in momentum and fortune for Tennessee, which never seemed to get back in sync.

"She made a great play," Parker said of Pringle. "That wasn't the dagger. It came from so many different places." It must have seemed that way to the Lady Vols, who went two stretches of 3:28 and 5:38 in the first half without scoring a single point. At that, it was miraculous UT was only down by five, 30–25, at the half. And then, the Volunteers even went on a 5–0 run to start the second period, tying the game at 30, before a North Carolina surge that built a 39–30 lead.

"They did a great job of making us play fast," noted guard Alexis Hornbuckle, who logged four steals, "faster than we'd like to."

The Lady Vols were outrebounded 43–33 and shot a season-worst 36.2 percent from the floor. And while Parker regrouped to score a game-high 27 points, there was little else for Tennessee to feel good about.

"We struggled to put the ball in the hole," acknowledged Summitt after the 70–57 defeat. "North Carolina had a lot to do with that, their physicality. We couldn't get the runs going. They did."

The loss dropped UT to 6–1, the only glitch in a record that marched forward with seven straight wins, including a 21-pointer over Texas in Austin and a 16-point victory over Old Dominion in Norfolk, before heading to Hartford to face perennial nemesis Connecticut on January 6, 2007.

Dunking UConn

Pat Summitt's 14–1 fourth-ranked Lady Vols had been making headway of late in the overall 8–13 series record against the formidable Huskies, with UT going for its third win in a row over the Storrs contingent and second consecutive victory before the usual hostile 16,294 at the Hartford Civic Center.

A mountainous performance by Candace Parker, who recorded a game-high 30 points and 12 boards, signaled to the Connecticut crowd that it would be Tennessee's day and a long afternoon for the Blue and White faithful. UT led by as much as 18 points early in the second half, which featured another highlight Parker moment—her fourth dunk of the season (sixth of her career), initiated by a steal and pass from Sidney Spencer. As with her previous three, Parker received extensive media coverage, the play recycled again and again throughout the remainder of the weekend on various sports highlight shows.

"I think it got attention because it was a bigger stage," said Parker of the play, delivered before a live CBS national television audience. "It was Connecticut versus Tennessee. It was just historical."

Parker, who has dunked five times on the open floor and once in the half court, has never been one to get swallowed up in the mysticism surrounding the celebrated aerial act. "It's not anything that goes through my mind," she said. "It's just like a layup. It's not anything serious."

Others, including former Lady Vols, give her a little more credit than that. "It's God-given ability," believes Michelle Marciniak, the sparkplug of the 1996 national champions. "She was blessed with the body and the talent and the skills to dunk the ball, and she's taken advantage of it."

Even Parker's coach knows there's something special going on out on the court when her gifted athlete climbs. "It's still new to this game," said Summitt. "There're not that many players that have dunked, much less to the extent that Candace has. It does bring national exposure. It brings exposure specifically to the women's game. I don't think it's been a distraction. It is what it is."

In truth, Parker is not all that wild about her game being solely attached to the dunking phenomenon. "Dunking has something to do with working hard in the weight room, but it has nothing to do with skill," she revealed. "People that don't even touch a basketball can dunk. There are volleyball players out there that can dunk. Honestly, I hope that doesn't define my game. I hope that it is defined by other things besides dunking."

Like a block and subsequent no-look pass to a cutting forward under the basket. That's the play Parker produced not long after her crowd-quieting dunk, when she blocked UConn high scorer Charde Houston's shot attempt, grabbed the ball in midair, then rifled a no-look pass to Nicky Anosike for an easy layup and a 47–29 Tennessee advantage with 17:55 remaining in the game.

That's when the motor started sputtering for the Lady Vols. Connecticut began a comeback that cut that 18-point lead in half in just three and a half minutes. In typical UConn fashion, they ate up the rest of the deficit, tying it at 49 on a three-pointer with 4:49 to go. If ever a house was rocking, it was the Civic Center, reverberating under a thundering roar from the partisan Husky crowd.

But that's when a big-time player stepped up for Tennessee. With Parker supplying an effective screen, Sidney Spencer drained a three-pointer at the 3:49 mark, and UT never lost the lead again.

"The only three they make in the second half was that one," Connecticut coach Geno Auriemma said, shaking his head, before courteously giving the 6-foot-3 Hoover, Alabama, native her due. "She's a senior, and she made a helluva shot."

Spencer, who logged 14 points and a career-high-tying nine rebounds, knew that the Huskies, the nation's leader in rebounding margin at plus-18.5, would present a tough inside front for her and her teammates. "We knew they had great rebounders on their team and we needed to box out and get second-chance points," said Spencer, who posted 10 points and six boards by halftime.

Though Connecticut claimed the battle underneath statistically, 44–40, one manifestation of the Lady Vols' intensity on second effort was exemplified by a Parker rebound put-in to close the first half, the fourth such attempt at the hole on the same possession.

"I think our team really pulled together," said Parker. "We knew it was crucial we needed stops and baskets. I credit everyone with coming together and keeping their composure."

Huskies guard Renee Montgomery, UConn's leading scorer on the season and the first sophomore in team history to be named a co-captain, had enough physical encounters with the bigger Lady Vols to have formed a sound opinion. "I definitely think they outplayed us," she said. "They made it tough on us. Tennessee's big and long, and they can do a lot with that."

In the end, though, it was Parker who left the Huskies babbling. Her four points in the final two minutes put the quietus on UConn's game-tying second-half run.

"It's kind of like when we had Diana Taurasi," Auriemma reminisced. "What's the answer [to containing Parker]? Individually, there was no answer."

Connecticut's defensive scheme was not to double- or triple-team Parker, but rather to silence the other Lady Vols on the court. It proved to be the wrong plan.

"As the game went on, she got better and better," Summitt said of her superstar forward, whose complete game included six blocked shots and four assists. "Candace is better under pressure. Look how assertive she was. She stepped up big for us."

Interestingly, Parker of late has even become a role model for the Tennessee Vols football team. During the summer of 2007, Vols head football coach Phil Fulmer happened to engage Summitt in some inter-athletic department dialogue. The Vols' grid mentor asked her what, in her estimation, had been the reason it had taken nine years for the Lady Vols to notch, in 2007, another national championship. Summitt replied with two weighty words: "Candace Parker." Every athletic program needs a bona fide superstar on which to hang its hat, she told Fulmer, who was hopeful that his quarterback, Erik Ainge, would "reach that Candace Parker level." Ainge witnessed firsthand Parker's take-charge attitude down the stretch that resulted in the Lady Vols' 2007 title. It impacted him, watching Parker rally teammates during crucial moments, urging them on in the way that a leader leads.

"She's special," Ainge remarked, before quipping, "She can probably take half the football team in basketball. She's a special player."

Before Parker's arrival at Tennessee, it had been seven long years since Chamique Holdsclaw had dominated women's college basketball in an orange-and-white uniform in much the same way Parker is currently doing. Fulmer's last national title, ironically, came in 1998—the same year the Lady Vols had won their last crown before the 2007 title.

So Parker, the reluctant dunker, and her fired-up shipmates now eased into deeper SEC waters, scuttling Florida and Georgia on the road before drowning Mississippi State by 29 points at home. That brought them to a certain doorstep in Durham for a showdown with the top women's team in America.

D-o-o-o-k

Tennessee's big matchup on Big Monday, January 22, 2007, with No. 1 Duke had the earmarks of a big-time classic before tipoff. In a show of festive support, UT men's basketball coach Bruce Pearl went with orange-painted bare chest to the match, making good on a commitment made prior to the game. The men's coach and several of his players were parked courtside behind a basket. On their orange chests the words "Go Vols," were spelled out.

But during the first six minutes somebody forgot to tell the Lady Vols the game was on. The Blue Devils ran off to a 19–0 lead, and though Tennessee eventually tied the score in the second half, they could not sustain their effort nor contain Duke's prolific scorers, as the North Carolinians came away with their No. 1 ranking intact, 74–70.

"It looked like we were almost overanxious early on," Summitt said. "That could've been. We hadn't been in a situation

AP IMAGES

Sidney Spencer

quite like that. We missed some easy shots. We played against a great basketball team. There's a reason they're the No. 1 team in the country."

Candace Parker completed a three-point play with just over 10 minutes to go, knotting the affair at 48, but the sophomore forward was a miserable one for seven from the foul line, missing free throws when UT needed them most. "That's my fault," Parker said. "If I would have made my free throws, we maybe would have won. I take full responsibility for that. It won't happen again."

The loss ended the Lady Vols' 11-game winning streak, but they were now 0–2 to the two powerhouses from the state of North Carolina, Tennessee's only two losses of the season to that point.

Voodoo in Vandyland

Little time was available to wallow in the aftermath of the Duke defeat. Three nights later the No. 4-ranked Tennessee women were in Memorial Gym on the Vanderbilt campus. The intrastate rivalry featuring two of the SEC's premier women's basketball powers, for all its possibilities, truly had been a dud over time. The Lady Vols held a commanding 47–6 series lead over VU, winning 25 of the previous 27 contests, including the last 11 in a row. Somehow, you'd have expected more, particularly since No. 15 Vanderbilt was a perennial Top 20 team. Tennessee simply worked its substantial mojo on the Lady Commodores time and again.

This game, on January 25, was to prove no different. Vanderbilt gave local onlookers a ray of hope, leading by one with just over three minutes to go. But the Lady Vols took control at the foul line, sinking 15 of 17 down the stretch to ice the game 67–57.

Midway through the second half, with both teams repeatedly swapping baskets, UT forward Sidney Spencer posted 10 points in five minutes en route to a game-high 26. Tennessee's hounding defense forced 25 Vandy turnovers, nine by point guard Dee Davis. Again, for VU, it was close but no cigar.

"At the end of the game, I think we did a great job of coming together and running our offense well," said Parker, who netted 19 points and bagged 11 rebounds. More than that, her defense helped trip Vandy at the end.

"Obviously, Candace is a go-to player for us," Summitt said. "I thought she stepped up and got some key rebounds for us and started the action for us on the defensive end. . . . The difference between this year's team and last year's is that the ball doesn't get stuck in certain players' hands. I think that's indicative of the commitment to play together as a team."

Wilting the SEC

The Lady Vols next took their show on the road to Tuscaloosa, Alabama, a 29-point breather, followed by South Carolina, whom UT manhandled by 36 points, back home.

No. 9 Georgia then came visiting on February 5. The great rivalry between the two SEC schools had produced 51 games to date, and though Tennessee owned an extensive 37–14 series lead, the contests always seemed to carry some manner of pay-back or revenge, their most memorable encounter coming in the 1996 NCAA finals, which the Lady Vols won for their fourth national championship.

On this night, surely Alexis Hornbuckle and Candace Parker flipped a coin to see who would take which half. While her teammates shot icicles from the floor, Hornbuckle conducted one of the most phenomenal halves of basketball ever recorded, figuring in on all but one scoring play for the entire first stanza. She posted 12 of her 14 total points in the first 20 minutes but also pulled down five rebounds, made four steals, and dished assists on four of the other five UT field goals that she didn't score to stake UT to a 27–21 halftime lead.

"She's the straw that stirs the drink," said Lady Bulldogs longtime coach Andy Landers, of Hornbuckle.

Parker then came on and lit up the second half, netting 18 of her game-high 22 points in the final 20 minutes. Earlier in the half, the Lady Vols went on a 14–2 run that cemented the game, with Sidney Spencer scoring the spurt's last nine points.

"We knew that they were going to come in here with a vengeance after we beat them on their home court [on January 14]," Hornbuckle said after the 73–57 win, Tennessee's sixth in a row over Georgia. "And the SEC was pretty much up for grabs."

In winning, UT secured a game-and-a-half lead over second place LSU, a team they were on track to meet head on in four games. But first, double-digit victories over Auburn, Kentucky, and Mississippi State took place before the Lady Vols landed in Bayou Country with a little more than gumbo at stake.

Running the tables

The SEC regular-season championship was on the line when Tennessee faced LSU before 9,146 at the Maravich Center, on February 19. The Lady Vols were looking to secure the crown with a win, their conference slate unblemished at 11-0. With a victory, UT would claim its first title in three years, retaking it from the SEC's two-time defending regular-season champions, the Lady Tigers of LSU.

It turned out to be an epic struggle.

While Candace Parker registered a double-double in the first half alone, her 20 points and 10 rebounds propelling UT to a 30–22 halftime lead, LSU came back fighting, twice tying the game in the second half, before a Parker foul shot pushed Tennessee to a one-point lead it never surrendered. Still, it remained for diminutive point guard Shannon Bobbitt to can two pressurized free throws with less than 12 seconds remaining to cement the 56–51 victory.

"This team has proven itself in so many big games," said Pat Summitt. "What they've done this season is testimony to their character and toughness and their ability to close out games."

Before LSU made its impressive runs at Tennessee in the second half, UT experienced a heightened performance from reserve Dominique Redding, who entered early in the half and netted eight points in eight minutes of play, including a pair of three-pointers. Redding's display held off the oncoming first surge by the Lady Tigers, who tied the game at 42 with 8:50 left and again at 49 with just 2:20 remaining.

Of Redding's production, Summitt said: "Those baskets were huge. We challenged Dom. We challenged the whole team to really step up."

Parker finished with a game-high 27 points and a team-high 13 rebounds, and Tennessee claimed its 14th regular-season

SEC championship. "We hadn't won a regular-season title in a while, that was a goal of ours," said Parker. "We've accomplished that. Now we want to run the tables."

At 12–0, the Lady Vols had some work ahead to remain undefeated as conference champions. That journey began three nights later in the Ozark Mountains of Arkansas, as Tennessee thumped the host Razorbacks 75–68. One more to go. The perfect conference season was within reach. The regular-season finale would be back home in Knoxville, pitting UT against instate rival Vanderbilt, traditionally an easy mark for the Lady Vols.

With one major difference: This year, Vandy was the second-hottest shooting team in the country.

Cooling Vandy

Before 19,201 at Thompson-Boling Arena, No. 12 Vanderbilt, scoring field goals at a 50.7 percent clip on the season, second best in the nation, got cooled off quick. The Lady Commodores shot a dismal 32.7 percent, 25.9 in the second half, and received a paralyzing dose of Tennessee defense, as the Lady Vols (27–2) romped to a 93–73 win.

"It was the best defensive effort that they've had against us," said Vanderbilt coach Melanie Balcomb, 0–11 versus Tennessee in five seasons. "They pressured the ball far better than they have. They took us out farther and took us out of our timing much better than they have in the past."

UT took a 40–29 halftime lead, then increased the bulge to 21 in the second half. Candace Parker demonstrated awesome ability, leading the way for the Lady Vols with 21 points and 14 rebounds. Her six blocked shots led to an intimidation of Vandy defensively. Shannon Bobbitt poured in 14 points and also added four steals, as Tennessee extended its consecutive winning streak over the Lady Commodores to 13. VU has never beaten the Lady Vols in Knoxville, where they are now 0–22 lifetime. If you're thinking, like a lot of folks, that this isn't really much of a rivalry, don't voice that sentiment around Alexis Hornbuckle.

"It's always going to be a rivalry," said the junior guard, from Charleston, West Virginia. "They're only a two-and-a-half-hour drive away. They don't like us, and we know that."

Summitt offered reflection on the overall series relative to the 2006 games between the two instate universities. "When we've played Vanderbilt, we've had some tough, hard-fought games," she said. "But in the games we've had this year, our defense has been able to separate us out."

Truth be told, the UT defense separated the team out from more than just Vandy. The regular-season finale victory also closed out a perfect SEC mark for the Lady Vols, who skated through the conference slate without a flaw at 14–0.

Vandy would have to wait another day for payback, but not Summitt. She would be repaying the shirtless Bruce Pearl, UT's men's hoops coach, who painted his chest orange with a large V on it in a display of support for Summitt and her troupe back on January 22, when the Lady Vols bowed to No. 1 Duke. Rumor had it that Summitt and her staff were going to dress as cheerleaders and deliver a special pregame performance to jack up the men's Tennessee-Florida crowd the following night. And that's exactly what happened. During the first timeout in the men's clash, Summitt hit the court with her staff members dressed in UT cheerleading outfits and led the boisterous crowd through a rousing rendition of "Rocky Top."

"I didn't get a chance to see it, but America got a chance to see a side of Pat Summitt that they probably haven't seen since eighth grade," Pearl said after his men defeated No. 5 Florida, the reigning (and future 2007) NCAA champs. "That's the way Pat is. Pat is a lot of fun to play for. She can be demanding and tough. But she's as kind and as sweet a person as I know, and she didn't disappoint."

The fun and games were the perfect elixir for the Lady Vols' mindset as they headed for the annual SEC Tournament being conducted in Duluth, Georgia

Tiger bait

Listed as the conference tourney's top seed, No. 2 Tennessee drew a first-round bye before pummeling South Carolina 81–63. The Lady Vols strode into the semifinals to face LSU, a series that had grown into the SEC's most anticipated matchup over the past few seasons. UT's five-point win over the Lady Tigers in Baton Rouge, on February 19, had clinched the regular-season

SEC title, the Lady Vols' 14th overall, and for the eighth time, Tennessee went through the SEC slate undefeated. In the two previous seasons, 2005 and 2006, LSU defeated UT during the regular season, but Tennessee came back to defeat the Lady Tigers both times and take the SEC Tournament titles.

A near-capacity crowd of 10,142 at the Gwinnett Center in Duluth, Georgia, was on hand to see UT's Alexis Hornbuckle turn in a phenomenal game, single-handedly carrying Tennessee with her 29 points and nine rebounds, but the lone Lady Vol's effort was not enough. Her more celebrated teammate, Candace Parker, and regular double-digit scorer Sidney Spencer stunk up the Center with a pathetic four of 22 from the floor, as UT fell to No. 11 LSU 63–54. Parker finished with just four points, a season low; Spencer totaled seven.

"I'm obviously very disappointed that we didn't match their intensity," said Summitt, "and when I say that, I'm talking about with five people on the floor at all times. LSU was much more inspired one through five and just really made a lot of great plays. Obviously Alexis had a super effort. But they were a better team tonight than we were."

Hornbuckle's valiant effort was UT's only bright light. "I came out tonight with the mindset that I wanted to give 110 percent no matter what," Hornbuckle said. "I wanted it to feel like I didn't let my teammates down. I got great looks, and I was able to knock them down."

LSU went on an 18–5 run, sparked by All-American Sylvia Fowles's six consecutive points, just before the end of the first half to take a 34–29 lead into the locker room. The Lady Tigers' game plan called for denying Parker the ball. The Lady Vol standout had been instrumental in beating LSU earlier in Baton Rouge, when she scored 27 points.

"We tried to limit some of the touches by Candace," noted LSU coach Pokey Chatman, a former Lady Tiger standout, who once scored 30 points as a player in the SEC Tournament finals to beat Tennessee back in 1991.

In hindsight, the loss would rate as the turning point of the 2006–07 season. The team conducted a three-hour heart-to-heart after the defeat, in hopes of identifying loose ends in need of adjustment. They found a major one: Parker.

"Candace said she was tired, that she couldn't get into it, and the other players called her out on it," associate head coach Holly Warlick said. "They were pretty tough on her. The message was, *We need you on both ends of the floor.*"

Holding at 28–3 on the season, the Lady Vols took comfort in a two-week hiatus before opening in the NCAA subregionals, where they would face Drake University.

Dayton Regional

It seems odd that a team that at one point in its season went through a 6–18 stretch would have any claim to a spot in the NCAAs. But that's the beauty, or curse, of the post-season conference tournaments. No. 16 Drake found itself opposite Summitt's troupe in the Dayton Regional opening rounds, held in Pittsburgh. The time-honored tradition of playing opening-round games in the comfort of their home arena was giving way to new NCAA policies. Every year from 1982 through 2003, Tennessee's first-round NCAA game had been played in Knoxville. But beginning in 2004, the trend began to alter. Three of the last four years—2004, 2006, and 2007—UT has played its opening tourney game elsewhere.

"The situation now with women's basketball is that teams [like ours] are sometimes going to have to travel and sometimes face opponents on *their* home floor," noted Summitt.

In Pittsburgh, the Lady Vols showed they could run their scintillating tournament hoops show elsewhere besides Thompson-Boling Arena. While Drake stayed close through the first 20 minutes, UT opened the second half with a blistering 25–0 run that totally silenced the Bulldogs, the Missouri Valley Conference tournament champion. The 76–37 whitewash kept intact the remarkable Lady Vols' skein of never having lost an opening-round NCAA tournament game in 26 straight appearances.

"We came into the first half a little anxious, having been off two weeks," said Candace Parker. "I feel we settled down in the second half and picked up our defensive intensity."

The facts bore that out. Drake shot an inexcusable 19.4 percent in the second half, in which the Bulldogs failed to register their first two points (on free throws) until almost 13 minutes were consumed on the clock.

The Lady Vols' second-rounder, against Pitt, was on the Panthers' home floor, and while the Pennsylvanians had the benefit of home support at the Peterson Events Center, their play showed obvious tightness plus an inability to cool a hot Parker, who poured in 30 points, shagged 12 boards, and had three blocks, in the 68–54 UT victory.

"We maybe felt like we couldn't compete or didn't belong," said a disappointed Agnus Berenato, Pitt coach.

Incredibly, UT was headed for the Sweet Sixteen for the 26th straight time. "We know Tennessee is built on a great tradition," noted Alexis Hornbuckle, "and we're just trying to continue that."

It was more of the same in Dayton, Ohio. A Cinderella Marist College team that only averaged 5-9 in height went with a three-guard backcourt to take advantage of its accomplished three-point shooting (the Red Foxes were averaging 45.5 percent from beyond the arc in the NCAAs) and its standing as the best ball-handling team in the country. But they converted only two of 10 three-pointers against the Lady Vols and turned the ball over 10 times in the first half. Parker, Hornbuckle, and center Nicky Anosike pummeled the boards for nine, eight, and seven rebounds respectively. Hornbuckle added five assists, to go along with Parker's game-high-tying 16 points, as Tennessee posted a 65–46 win.

In the regional final, Ole Miss announced that they would have no special plan in facing the Lady Vols, they would simply play their game. "We don't game plan a lot, and we're not going to deviate from what we do best," stated Ole Miss coach Carol Ross beforehand. "We're not going to let another team dictate how we play."

That lasted about three possessions for Ole Miss, which opened in a 2–3 zone but couldn't quell point guard Shannon Bobbitt's three-pointers from both corners for a 6-2 UT start. "They took us out of our comfort zone," remarked Rebels guard Ashley Awkward.

At the half, UT held a whopping 29-point lead and with under 13 minutes left raised that to a 39-point differential. For the game, Bobbitt hit all three of her three-point attempts, as UT posted 72.7 percent from three-point range, canning eight of 11 shots. Defensively, the Lady Vols revolved around Parker's presence in the middle. Five times the Naperville, Illinois, standout swatted away shots like so many bothersome flies, while pulling down a commanding 13 defensive boards. She also tossed in 24 points, on 10-of-14 shooting from the field. Tennessee got strong offensive rebound help from Anosike and reserve Alberta Auguste, who each collected five, and forward Sidney Spencer nearly matched Parker's points output, posting 22.

The 98–62 victory, with its 36-point margin, established an NCAA record for the most lopsided win in a regional final. "It was without a doubt our greatest offensive game of the tournament," admitted Summitt.

So it was now onto the Lady Vols' 17th Final Four appearance. The glow of the trio of consecutive national titles in the mid- to late '90s had long since receded. Summitt and her women had had to get back to the basics, grinding it out and persevering in the belief that at some point down the line more UT magic would reenter the picture and the national crowns would again come their way. Five times in the interim nine seasons Tennessee had been to the Final Four and lost, four times succumbing to hated Connecticut, three times in succession. The previous year, in 2006, they had been booted out of the Cleveland Regional by North Carolina, as happenstance would have it, their opponent this time in the Final Four semifinals, in of all places, Cleveland again.

"We've been to Cleveland before and came back pretty disappointed," Parker noted about the unlikely rematch of teams and location. "I just want to make sure on that short flight we return happy."

Final Four

But if the scenario seemed eerily similar to 2006, UT was aware of a substantial difference in the makeup of its 2007 team from the previous year.

"We always tried to take the short way out last year," said Alexis Hornbuckle, comparing the two Lady Vol squads. "We had a lot of offensive power, and a lot of times we came into games with the wrong intent: *Let's outscore this team.* How about,

Let's stop this team as well as outscore this team? That's the kind of mindset *this* team has. You can just feel it when you step onto the court. I know my teammates have my back. If I get beat, I know Candace or Nicky is going to be here. We weren't on that same page last year."

But the Tar Heels now had a two-game win streak going against Tennessee: the previous March in the NCAA regional finals and the 13-point victory in early December at Chapel Hill. But in another way, prophetically, the Lady Vols had posted one of their program's biggest wins ever against North Carolina in the 1998 Mideast Regional finals, a come-from-behind character-builder that propelled UT to its third successive NCAA crown and sixth overall. The possibilities and peculiarities were endless, but one thing was certain after the game began: any similarities to previous epic UNC-UT encounters were purely accidental. In other words, this contest was not holding up well under critical scrutiny. The game deteriorated into a slipshod affair, with both teams turning the ball over a total of 50 times, 29 for the Tar Heels.

"It's frustrating as a player to get so many open looks, and I had a lot of long layups that just rolled out," admitted Hornbuckle. "But at the same time I'm not the type of player that dwells on my offense. I just decided to pick it up on the defensive end and crash the boards." To that end, the UT guard gathered eight rebounds, fourth best on the evening among both schools. Parker, not enjoying a particularly productive game offensively with poor 3-of-12 shooting, also focused on defense and pulled down a game-high 13 rebounds, while logging three steals.

Yet even with Tennessee stepping it up defensively, North Carolina had pulled away to a 12-point lead with just a little over eight minutes to go in the game. Hornbuckle scored two straight buckets to cut it to an eight-point margin, when a media timeout with 7:13 remaining enabled Pat Summitt to stare and share. She stared that stare that only Summitt can emit, that freezes people like animals frozen by approaching car lights. And then she shared her vision with the squad.

"We're not leaving here without a national championship," Summitt said firmly. "Then we talked about what we

Candace Parker

had to do on the floor, and they responded. I said, 'We're going to have to win this with our defense.' I thought it was doable, and then I started to feel, with our defensive pressure, that it was beginning to be effective and we were starting to see the momentum change."

The Lady Vols walked Summitt's talk, shutting down North Carolina to just two free throws, while UT went on a 20–2 run to close out the game. Parker rose to the occasion, hitting six of her 14 points and grabbing three rebounds and a big steal in the last four and half minutes to help boost Tennessee to a come-from-behind 56–50 win. A major presence for the Lady Vols throughout was the often-overlooked Nicky Anosike. The 6-4 junior center from Staten Island, New York, tied Parker for game high in points scored, with 14, but also posted five steals, four blocked shots, and seven boards in a complete-game effort. Now, for the fourth time in the last nine years, Tennessee would attempt to win its seventh national championship in the NCAA finals.

"I think everybody wearing orange will say it's been way too long," said Parker. "It's been way too long since Tennessee has won a national championship. And I'm tired of going into Thompson-Boling Arena and playing on The Summit and not looking up and seeing a banner that has all our names written all over it. I want my legacy to be that we hung banners during my career. All of us came here to win championships. And we haven't done that since 1998."

Summitt, later, after her obligatory postgame press conference, had more to say about her 2006–07 Lady Vols. "I feel a real commitment to this team," she said, "and it's not about one person. It's all about this team. They want to win championships as much as any team I've coached in a long time, and they've demonstrated it through their commitment to defense and rebounding. They have great chemistry, and they are fun to coach. And we have Candace Parker. We haven't had a big go-to player since Holdsclaw and Catchings, when we won our last championship."

One more game to go. Against the Scarlet Knights of Rutgers, a team vaguely reminiscent of the 1995–96 Lady Vols that featured Holdsclaw and the Fab Four freshmen. But Rutgers had no Holdsclaw and they were starting five frosh, not four. They were a surprising finalist but had earned the right to be there, upsetting No. 1 Duke and pasting LSU in a 24-point shocker, in which Lady Tiger All-American Sylvia Fowles was held to five points. But Tennessee, as it had year in and year out for what seemed forever, had fought through the toughest schedule in the land. Few surprises existed on any horizon that UT would not be prepared for.

Seven

Rutgers head coach Vivian Stringer was no stranger to Pat Summitt. The two old friends and coaching rivals dated all the way back to 1984, when Stringer, then coaching at Pennsylvania's Cheyney State College, lost to Summitt's Vols in the 1984 Final Four semifinals in Los Angeles. Stringer eventually moved on to Iowa, where she claimed one of her two lifetime victories over Summitt—in the 1993 Mideast Regional finals to advance to the Final Four.

The Lady Vols coach owned a 7–1 career advantage over Stringer at Rutgers, including a 64–54 win over the Scarlet Knights in the 2000 Final Four to advance to the NCAA championship game. The 2007 NCAA finals would be their first-ever championship game encounter. The Lady Vols' all-time 5–0 mark over Stringer's Scarlet Knights in postseason play indicated a significant advantage, the skein including two victories in the last two NCAA tournaments.

While the number "7" had not appeared to be especially lucky in Tennessee's three previous NCAA finals appearances since their last national crown in 1998, given that they had lost each time, indications were sprouting everywhere with the 2007 troupe that this year, the seventh after the turn of the third millennium, would be different. For instance, the number of letters in both the first and last names of UT's two junior college transfers—Shannon Bobbitt and Alberta Auguste—each possessed seven letters. Add to that the last names of several others on the roster—Anosike, Spencer, McMahan, and Redding—plus coaches Warlick and Summitt, and you'd be forgiven if you raised an eyebrow. Then again, the name of Tennessee's finals foe, Rutgers, contained seven letters, too.

Omens and auguries aside, it likely would take another dose of UT's strength—pressure defense, superb rebounding, consistent scoring, and an all-out team effort—to defeat Stringer's 2007 edition of the Scarlet Knights.

Popping in on the Lady Vols in Cleveland to show their support were members of Summitt's first national championship team 20 years earlier. From that 1987 group, Shelley Sexton Collier, Melissa McCray Dukes, and Karla Horton Douglas enlightened the 2007 squad about the importance of team chemistry and the enduring friendships that develop from undergoing the rigors of a championship run. Collier noted the similarities between the two teams:

"There's a toughness there, and you can tell they are close," she said of the 2007 Lady Vols. "They really are a team."

The significance of the '87 trio's presence wasn't lost on Parker. "In 20 years we want to come back and have our banner in the rafters and be able to celebrate and tell famous Pat stories," Parker noted. "We'll roll her in, in a wheelchair."

Rolling is what Tennessee did to Rutgers midway through the opening period. Heading out on a 17-6 run, reserve forward Auguste tallied eight of her 10 points and swiped four rebounds during that points spurt to lead UT to a 29-18 halftime advantage. The 5-foot-2 munchkin Bobbitt highlighted a mid-second-period Tennessee run, in which she nailed three of her four treys to up the Lady Vols' margin to 16. Anosike, as she had against North Carolina, again asserted considerable presence under the boards, pulling down 10 of her 16 rebounds on the offensive end. Parker popped in 17 points and expertly carved up the Scarlet Knights, whose occasional sagging double and triple teams triggered some pinpoint Parker passing to open players for scores. Her performance drew the highest praise from Stringer.

"You are witnessing the best player in the world," the Rutgers coach stated respectfully. "There is nobody who comes close to her."

Summitt couldn't resist adding her own superlatives. "I think Candace Parker is the best player in the country. I'd be surprised if I don't see her as the best ever," Summitt pointed out, before discussing her superstar's extended effect on the team. "And having Candace Parker, yes, you've got a chance to win a national championship. But it's not because she's the only player on our team. It's because she makes everyone else better."

Behind a true team effort from eight leading Ladies, Tennessee finally brought home its elusive seventh national crown with the convincing 59–46 victory.

A triumphant Summitt climbed to cut the cords, with her now 16-year-old son Tyler. Nine long years had intervened between trips to the hoop with a pair of scissors for the two. Later, Summitt recounted the importance of one of her basketball maxims on the outcome.

"I've always believed that obviously rebounding wins championships," she said, in deference to the Lady Vols' 42–34 edge on the boards. "Tonight that effort was significant in this win."

Parker was elated, crediting teammates and a singular belief that permeated the team's season-long quest. "This is something that we have wanted from day one," said the Final Four MVP, "and we set our minds to it. Our focus was just one game and then the next and the next, and then we looked up and we were in the national championship game. It's amazing."

Pestered incessantly all season long by the press about her future pro plans, Parker took one last opportunity to underscore her commitment to return to The Hill for her junior season. "Yes, I'll be back," she said. "I'm coming back to Tennessee. I'll just say it one more time. I'll be back wearing orange next year to hang the banner in 2007."

Nicky Anosike, asked about her extraordinary board play in the title game win, mentioned a Summitt credo in her response. "Coach said before the game, offense sells tickets, defense wins games, and rebounding wins championships," said the Lady Vols' center, "and that really just stuck with me throughout the whole game." Alexis Hornbuckle, who posted seven boards, added, "Rebounding is not all about the height or who can jump the highest, it's about the heart and hustle and who wants the ball the most. And that's how we approached it."

Summitt explained that she felt it essential to be at her mentoring best in her squad's darkest hour, two days earlier.

"For me tonight it was all about helping this team. And that's why in our game against North Carolina I said, 'We're not leaving here without a national championship,' because I really believe this team deserved to be national champions."

If nine years between titles was any indication, the road to the top in women's college basketball was only going to get tougher in the future. "It's going to be difficult to win another championship," Summitt conjectured, "because there is more parity in the game. You just can't count on it every year by any means. We had some great runs at Tennessee, obviously in '96, '97, and '98. I don't know that we'll see that in the women's game again."

The woman who is *the* program at Tennessee, who came from humble rural beginnings to rise to the top of a sport that wasn't even on the radar when she took the helm at UT in 1974—a sport she almost single-handedly developed by herself—strode with pride and head held high from Cleveland's Quicken Loans Arena, a national champion yet again.

"This was not about winning number seven," Summitt said. "This is about this team winning their first. They were a team that did not want to be denied and they did what they had to do to make it happen."

And those Benzes? They multiplied. Summitt continued to receive one after each championship season, and after the 2007 coronation, the Mercedes treatment was extended to associate head coach Holly Warlick and assistants Nikki Caldwell and Dean Lockwood.

2006–07
(34–3, 14–0 SEC, 1st)
Final AP Ranking: 3rd
NCAA Dayton Regional Champions
NCAA NATIONAL CHAMPIONS

ROSTER

No.	Player	Yr	Pos.	Ht.	Hometown
00	**Shannon Bobbitt**	Jr	G	5–2	New York, NY
1	**Sidney Spencer**	Sr	F	6–3	Hoover, AL
2	Cait McMahan	Fr	G	5–4	Maryville, TN
3	**Candace Parker**	So	F/C/G	6–4	Naperville, IL
10	Elizabeth Curry	Sr	G	5–6	New Virginia, IA
13	Dominique Redding	Sr	F	6–1	Clearwater, FL
14	**Alexis Hornbuckle**	Jr	G	5–11	Charleston, WV
33	Alberta Auguste	Jr	F	5–11	Marrero, LA
44	Alex Fuller	So	F/C	6–3	Shelbyville, TN
55	**Nicky Anosike**	Jr	F/C	6–4	Staten Island, NY

(starters in bold)

SEASON STATS

Player	PPG	RPG	FG-Pct.	FT-Pct.
Candace Parker	19.6	9.8	.529	.712
Sidney Spencer	11.6	4.2	.421	.900
Alexis Hornbuckle	10.2	5.1	.440	.731
Shannon Bobbitt	8.7	1.6	.370	.790
Nicky Anosike	7.5	6.2	.427	.605
Alex Fuller	6.0	4.1	.497	.776
Alberta Auguste	5.0	2.3	.434	.671
Dominique Redding	3.5	1.4	.364	.813
Cait McMahan	2.4	1.2	.327	.444
Nicci Moats	0.8	0.9	.286	.300
Elizabeth Curry	0.4	0.0	.200	.667

2006–07 SCHEDULE

Date	Site	W/L	Score	Opponent
11/1/2006	H	W	104–49	Carson-Newman
11/5/2006	H	W-ex	101–51	Houston Jaguars
11/12/2006	H	W	102–72	Chattanooga
11/16/2006	H	W	83–60	UCLA
11/19/2006	A	W	83–74	Arizona State
11/24/2006	H	W	77–60	Stanford
11/26/2006	H	W	88–64	Middle Tenn. State
11/28/2006	A	W	71–50	Louisiana Tech
12/3/2006	A	L	70–57	North Carolina
12/5/2006	H	W	85–29	Tennessee-Martin
12/7/2006	H	W	85–62	George Washington
12/17/2006	A	W	67–46	Texas
12/20/2006	H	W	66–51	West Virginia
12/22/2006	A	W	75–59	Old Dominion
12/30/2006	H	W	78–54	Notre Dame
1/3/2007	H	W	72–36	Alabama
1/6/2007	A	W	70–64	Connecticut
1/11/2007	A	W	80–58	Florida
1/14/2007	A	W	52–41	Georgia
1/18/2007	A	W	73–44	Mississippi State
1/22/2007	H	L	74–70	Duke
1/25/2007	A	W	67–57	Vanderbilt
1/28/2007	A	W	80–51	Alabama
2/1/2007	H	W	72–36	South Carolina
2/5/2007	H	W	73–57	Georgia
2/8/2007	A	W	72–62	Auburn
2/11/2007	H	W	84–62	Kentucky
2/15/2007	H	W	81–69	Mississippi State
2/19/2007	A	W	56–51	LSU
2/22/2007	A	W	75–68	Arkansas
2/25/2007	H	W	73–53	Vanderbilt

SEC TOURNAMENT, Duluth, Ga.

Date	Site	W/L	Score	Opponent
3/2/2007	N	W	81–63	South Carolina
3/3/2007	N	L	63–54	LSU

NCAA SUBREGIONAL, Pittsburgh, Pa.

Date	Site	W/L	Score	Opponent
3/18/2007	N	W	76–37	Drake University
3/20/2007	A	W	68–54	Pittsburgh

NCAA DAYTON REGIONAL, Dayton, Ohio

Date	Site	W/L	Score	Opponent
3/25/2007	N	W	65–46	Marist
3/27/2007	N	W	98–62	Mississippi

NCAA FINAL FOUR, Cleveland, Ohio

Date	Site	W/L	Score	Opponent
4/1/2007	N	W	56–50	North Carolina
4/3/2007	N	W	59–46	Rutgers

8

The Lady Vols All-Time Championship Team

N O, THIS IS NOT A UT women's basketball all-time team. Behind this curtain stands a unit of Lady Vols selected strictly for meritorious service during the title years, an aggregate who stepped it up big during one or more of Tennessee's seven championship seasons.

While current Lady Vol watchers have their screens full of little else but Candace Parker these days, let it be said that the glowing junior-to-be may well deserve a place on this team with another impressive campaign similar to the one she posted in 2006–07. But if you can believe it, to this point, her efforts pale against the staggering stats and totals recorded by other forwards who have made their mark on Pat Summitt's legendary orange and white. And while higher-profile guards might be found among the array of fine back-court women who have brought the ball downcourt for Tennessee, the two on this team knew what to do come tournament time.

BRIDGETTE GORDON
forward (1985–89)

Let's face it, Bridgette Gordon's play, for all significant and historic purposes, is what put the Lady Vols on the national map. While not commanding the pre-buildup of a Holdsclaw or Parker, she simply went to work and became the highest scorer in NCAA Tournament history. Incredibly, nearly 20 years since her playing days at UT, she still ranks third on the NCAA's all-time list of tournament scorers.

Several years ago she was one of five women named to the prestigious NCAA 25th Silver Anniversary team, along with later Lady Vol Chamique Holdsclaw. Gordon was selected to the All-Final Four Tournament Team her sophomore season, when she helped elevate Tennessee to its first national crown, in 1987. Two years later she was named 1989 NCAA Tournament MVP, when the Lady Vols claimed their second national title. She also was selected as a two-time Kodak All-American, won a gold medal in Seoul, South Korea, in the 1988 Olympics, and set an NCAA record as the first four-year Final Four participant.

CHAMIQUE HOLDSCLAW
forward (1995–99)

If one player has come to embody the greatness of the Tennessee Lady Vols program it surely is the otherworldly athletic Holdsclaw. The high-profile recruit from Astoria, Queens, in New York City, was named the Naismith Player of the Century in 2000, and her awards list, if presented in its entirety, could run the length of a telephone directory.

Among her near-incomparable achievements are leading Tennessee to an unprecedented three straight NCAA championships, elite placement (along with Gordon) on the NCAA Silver Anniversary Team, one of only six four-time Kodak All-Americans, a two-time NCAA Tournament MOP (1997,

'98), the leading scorer (3,025) and rebounder (1,295) in Lady Vols history, and the all-time leading scorer (479) and rebounder (198) in NCAA Tournament history. Opposing coaches who faced her during her four dominant years at UT exclaimed that Holdsclaw was the greatest women's player they had ever seen.

DAEDRA CHARLES
center (1988–91)

She may have had a rough beginning at UT academically, running into Summitt's doghouse briefly early on, but Charles made quick corrections to become the greatest center in Lady Vols history and a Summitt player with true leadership skills.

With no real strong support from post players during her final two seasons, she was often ganged up on, the inside target of foes. But Charles only stepped up her powerful game even more, making the Kodak All-America team twice and earning the Wade Trophy as the women's college player of the year in 1991. That same year she also was picked SEC Woman Athlete of the Year. She helped Tennessee to two national championships, like Gordon, in both her sophomore and senior seasons. Charles closed out her august career as the No. 7 all-time scorer in Lady Vols history (1,495) and the school's sixth leading rebounder (858), while finishing second overall in blocked shots (97).

DENA HEAD
guard (1988–92)

Head's place in Lady Vol lore was secured as a freshman in 1989, when she was called upon to replace injured starting guard Tonya Edwards midway through the season. She wound up reenergizing the team with confidence at the point, clutch shooting, and stopper defense, as Tennessee drove to its second national title, with the young first-year player scoring 19 points in the championship game win over Auburn, 15 in the second half.

Head's crowning moment, however, was the last game of her junior season, in which she took over the NCAA championship game against Virginia, downing two pressure-packed free throws, before deflecting Lady Cav All-American Dawn Staley's potential game-winning shot to send the thriller into overtime. Head then netted half of her team's 10 points in the extra period en route to an NCAA championship game-record-tying 28 points, as UT beat Virginia 70–67 in 1991 for its third national title.

KELLIE JOLLY
guard (1995–99)

The 5–10 Sparta, Tennessee, sparkplug was the hustling point guard of the 1997 and '98 Tennessee championship teams. The tough, inspirational floor leader consistently stepped up in big games. She showed plenty of moxie in the 1997 Midwest Regional final, coming back from knee surgery earlier in the year and additionally playing on a defective ankle with torn ligaments to personally nail archrival Connecticut's coffin shut, ripping the nets for 19 points, her timely pair of second-half treys defusing UConn's rally. In the NCAA championship game win against Old Dominion, she set an NCAA finals record for assists, with 11.

The following year, her two tension-ridden free throws with 12 seconds left cemented the Lady Vols' improbable come-from-behind victory over North Carolina in the 1998 NCAA Mideast Regional final. Crowning her fabulous career, Jolly was the shooting star of the national championship game victory over Louisiana Tech that capped the perfect 39–0 season in '98, hitting her first five shots en route to a career-high 20 points that included four of five three-pointers.

References

Chapter One

Balloch, Jim. "Corn-fed Chicks: Pat Summitt's first championship team." Web.KnoxNews.com.http://web.knoxnews.com/special/0311cornfedchicks, March 9. 2007.

Balloch, Jim and Lauren Spuhler, prod. "Pat Summitt remembers her 1987 team." Web.KnoxNews.com. http://web.knoxnews.com/special/0311cornfedchicks/patsummitt.html, March 9, 2007.

Balloch, Jim and Lauren Spuhler, prod. "Shelley Sexton remembers the 1987 team." Web.KnoxNews.com. http://web.knoxnews.com/special/0311cornfedchicks/shelley.html, March 9, 2007.

Boatman, Kim. "Confident Lady Vols snap Texas streak." *Knoxville News-Sentinel*, Dec. 15, 1986: C1, C3.

Boatman, Kim. "UT's Gordon gets defensive." *Knoxville News-Sentinel*, Dec. 15, 1986: C3.

Boatman, Kim. "Coach agrees; Lady Vols No. 1." *Knoxville News-Sentinel*, Dec. 16, 1986: C1.

Boatman, Kim. "Lady Vols too much for Southern Cal." *Knoxville News-Sentinel*, Dec. 29, 1986: C1, C6.

Boatman, Kim. "Texas turns tables on No. 1 Lady Vols 88–74." *Knoxville News-Sentinel*, Dec. 30, 1986: C1, C2.

Boatman, Kim. "Poor facilities, Texas rain on Lady Vols' trip." *Knoxville News-Sentinel*, Dec. 31, 1986: C3.

Boatman, Kim. "UT women beaten at Auburn." *Knoxville News-Sentinel*, Jan. 15, 1987: C1, C3.

Boatman, Kim. "Vandy upsets Lady Vols." *Knoxville News-Sentinel*, Feb. 5, 1987: C1, C4.

Boatman, Kim. "Lady Techsters defeat Lady Vols again, 72–60." *Knoxville News-Sentinel*, Feb. 10, 1987: C1, C2.

Boatman, Kim. "Run-happy Auburn knocks out Lady Vols 102–96." *Knoxville News-Sentinel*, March 7, 1987: B1, B5.

Boatman, Kim. "Summitt plans shakeup." *Knoxville News-Sentinel*, March 8, 1987: C3.

Boatman, Kim. "Stokely Showdown: Pressure is on Lady Vols to solve Auburn press." *Knoxville News-Sentinel*, March 21, 1987: B1, B5.

Boatman, Kim. "Lady Vols reach Final Four." *Knoxville News-Sentinel*, March 22, 1987: C1, C3.

Boatman, Kim. "Long Beach is talking a good game." *Knoxville News-Sentinel*, March 27, 1987: C1, C3.

Boatman, Kim. "Tennessee gains NCAA title game with 74–64 win." *Knoxville News-Sentinel*, March 28, 1987: B1, B5.

Boatman, Kim. "McCray deals State long-range surprise." *Knoxville News-Sentinel*, March 28, 1987: B5.

Boatman, Kim. "Lady Vols say NCAA title is within their reach." *Knoxville News-Sentinel*, March 29, 1987: C1, C6.

Boatman, Kim. "Adoption of three-point shot puts smile on Summitt's face." *Knoxville News-Sentinel*, March 29, 1987: C6.

Boatman, Kim. "Lady Vols fulfill Summitt's dream of NCAA crown." *Knoxville News-Sentinel*, March 30, 1987: Page one, back page.

Boatman, Kim. "Summitt gets title with ease." *Knoxville News-Sentinel*, March 30, 1987: C1, C3.

Boatman, Kim. "Edwards delivers on her promise." *Knoxville News-Sentinel*, March 30, 1987: C2.

Boatman, Kim. "Champions are 'mentally drained' by victory." *Knoxville News-Sentinel*, March 30, 1987: C3.

Boatman, Kim. "Lady Vols' dream win scores points with recruits." *Knoxville News-Sentinel*, March 31, 1987: C1.

Browning, Al. "A special day for Summitt, Sexton." *Knoxville News-Sentinel*, March 30, 1987: C1, C2.

Diskey, Jay. "Fans welcome Summitt, Lady Vols." *Knoxville News-Sentinel*, March 31, 1987: Page one, back page.

Hyams, Jimmy. "Free-throw shooting, fouls doom Auburn." *Knoxville News-Sentinel*, March 22, 1987: C3.

Minium, Harry. "Lady Vols sink late foul shots to slip by ODU." *Knoxville News-Sentinel*, Jan. 8, 1987: C1.

Summitt, Pat Head and Debby Jennings. *Basketball*. Dubuque, Iowa: Wm. C. Brown Publishers, 1991.

Summitt, Pat with Sally Jenkins. *Reach for the Summitt*. New York City: Broadway Books, 1998.

utladyvols.com. "Lady Vol History." http://www.utladyvols.com/old_site/photos/sports/w-baskbl/auto_pdf/06bk-mediaguide-10.pdf.

utladyvols.com. "Lady Vol Records." http://www.utladyvols.com/old_site/photos/sports/w-baskbl/auto_pdf/06bk-mediaguide-11.pdf.

Chapter Two

Associated Press. "Top powers move to women's Final Four." *Knoxville Journal*, March 27, 1989: 3C.

Balloch, Jim. "Stalk of the Town: 'Corn-fed chicks' still wear nickname proudly 20 years later." KnoxNews.com. http://www.knoxnews.com/kns/local_news/article/0,1406,KNS_347_5409787,00.html, March 11, 2007.

Bigold, Pat. "Lady Vols avenge Final Four loss." *Knoxville Journal*, Nov. 28, 1988: C1, C7.

Byrd, Ben. "Signs of success for Lady Vols: wins and traffic jams." *Knoxville Journal*, Jan. 16, 1989: C4.

Byrd, Ben. "Lady Vols in tough company at Tacoma." *Knoxville Journal*, March 27, 1989: 4C.

Fleser, Dan. "Lady Vols move inside, bounce 49ers." *Knoxville News-Sentinel*, Dec. 4, 1988: C1, C3.

Fleser, Dan. "Lady Vols' win adds zest to growing rivalry." *Knoxville News-Sentinel*, Dec. 5, 1988: C1, C3.

Fleser, Dan. "Auburn layups paved way for Lady Vols' downfall." *Knoxville News-Sentinel*, Jan. 8, 1989: C3.

Fleser, Dan. "Lady Vols rally to clip Ole Miss." *Knoxville News-Sentinel*, Jan. 15, 1989: C1, C3.

Fleser, Dan. "Lady Vols on road to Tacoma again." *Knoxville News-Sentinel*, March 26, 1989: C1, C3.

Fleser, Dan. "Gordon hit all angles in leading Lady Vols." *Knoxville News-Sentinel*, March 26, 1989: C3.

Seremetis, Angelique. "They're one big, happy family." *Knoxville Journal*, Nov. 29, 1988: C1.

Seremetis, Angelique. "Life's no beach for Lady Vols." *Knoxville Journal*, Dec. 5, 1988: C5.

Seremetis, Angelique. "USC could give Lady Vols a run." *Knoxville Journal*, Dec. 6, 1988: C1.

Seremetis, Angelique. "Lady Vol freshmen come off the bench to finish off USC." *Knoxville Journal*, Dec. 7, 1988: C1, C4.

Seremetis, Angelique. "Gordon leads UT rout." *Knoxville Journal*, Dec. 19, 1988: C1, C7.

Seremetis, Angelique. "Lady Vols romp." *Knoxville Journal*, Dec. 31, 1988: B1, B3.

Seremetis, Angelique. "State: no rest for the weary." *Knoxville Journal*, Jan. 16, 1989: C1, C3.

Seremetis, Angelique. "Gordon saves best for Georgia." *Knoxville Journal*, Jan. 30, 1989: C1, C4.

Seremetis, Angelique. "Davis leads Texas victory." *Knoxville Journal*, Feb. 1, 1989: C1, C6.

Seremetis, Angelique. "Gordon, Lady Vols rise to occasion at La. Tech." *Knoxville Journal*, Feb. 15, 1989: C1, C6.

Seremetis, Angelique. "La. Tech coach gives no apology for his outburst." *Knoxville Journal*, Feb. 15, 1989: C6.

Seremetis, Angelique. "Lady Vols hope to stuff tourney jinx." *Knoxville Journal*, March 6, 1989: 1C, 5C.

Seremetis, Angelique. "Lady Vols claw Auburn, may be top seed in East." *Knoxville Journal*, March 7, 1989: 1C.

Seremetis, Angelique. "Dena playing heads-up ball." *Knoxville Journal*, March 7, 1989: 6C.

Seremetis, Angelique. "Long Beach State a changed team." *Knoxville Journal*, March 25, 1989: 1B, 3B.

Seremetis, Angelique. "Lady Terps give Summitt an eyeful." *Knoxville Journal*, March 27, 1989: 1C, 4C.

Seremetis, Angelique. "Lady Vol seniors continue upward." *Knoxville Journal*, March 30, 1989: 5C.

Seremetis, Angelique. "Maryland: new kid on block." *Knoxville Journal*, March 31, 1989: 1C, 7C.

Seremetis, Angelique. "Gordon repeats as All-American." *Knoxville Journal*, March 31, 1989: 6C.

Seremetis, Angelique. "Frost, Lady Vols chill Terps." *Knoxville Journal*, April 1, 1989: 1B.

Summitt, Pat with Sally Jenkins. *Reach for the Summit*. New York City: Broadway Books, 1998.

utladyvols.com. "Lady Vol History." http://www.utladyvols.com/old_site/photos/sports/w-baskbl/auto_pdf/06bk-mediaguide-10.pdf.

utladyvols.com. "Lady Vol Records." http://www.utladyvols.com/old_site/photos/sports/w-baskbl/auto_pdf/06bk-mediaguide-11.pdf.

Chapter Three

Associated Press. "N.C. State 90, Tennessee 77." *Nashville Tennessean*, Dec. 2, 1990: 8C.

Adams, John. "Home games won't ensure Lady Vol wins." *Knoxville News-Sentinel*, Jan. 30, 1991: D1, D3.

Adams, John. "Lady Vols set winning pace other UT teams only envy." *Knoxville News-Sentinel*, Feb. 24, 1991: C1, C6.

Adams, John. "Lady Vols rattle Lady Tigers—and their coach." *Knoxville News-Sentinel*, March 4, 1991: C1, C3.

Adams, John. "Summitt sets tone for charge to New Orleans." *Knoxville News-Sentinel*, March 24, 1991: C1, C11.

Adams, John. "Head must be UT's stopper at Final Four." *Knoxville News-Sentinel*, March 30, 1991: C1, C5.

Adams, John. "Beating Virginia will be sweetest revenge of all." *Knoxville News-Sentinel*, March 31, 1991: C1, C4.

Adams, John. "Head kept her head under pressure at end." *Knoxville News-Sentinel*, April 1, 1991: C1, C4.

Adams, John. "Many factors play role in conquering Cavaliers." *Knoxville News-Sentinel*, April 1, 1991: C1, C5.

Cavalaris, Chuck. "Lady Vols topple Stanford for Shootout title." *Knoxville News-Sentinel*, Dec. 31, 1990: C1, C3.

Cavalaris, Chuck. "Lady Vols falter, but win in OT." *Knoxville News-Sentinel*, Jan. 17, 1991: C1, C3.

Cavalaris, Chuck. "Auburn overtakes Lady Vols." *Knoxville News-Sentinel*, Jan. 20, 1991: C1, C6.

Cavalaris, Chuck. "No. 4 Lady Vols clip LSU 79–77." *Knoxville News-Sentinel*, Jan. 22, 1991: C1, C3.

Cavalaris, Chuck. "Georgia gets key SEC win over Lady Vols." *Knoxville News-Sentinel*, Jan. 29, 1991: C1, C3.

Cavalaris, Chuck. "Sexy uniforms a poor cure for apathy toward women's game." *Knoxville News-Sentinel*, Feb. 24, 1991: C2.

Cavalaris, Chuck. "Lady Vols leave Texas with big win." *Knoxville News-Sentinel,* Feb. 24, 1991: C1, C6.

Cavalaris, Chuck. "Lady Vols leave Texas with big win." *Knoxville News-Sentinel*, Feb. 24, 1991: C1, C6.

Cavalaris, Chuck. "SEC tourney a tough test for Lady Vols." *Knoxville News-Sentinel*, March 2, 1991: C1, C3.

Cavalaris, Chuck. "Victory over Auburn puts UT in finals." *Knoxville News-Sentinel*, March 4, 1991: C1, C3.

Cavalaris, Chuck. "Chatman shoots LSU by Lady Vols." *Knoxville News-Sentinel*, March 5, 1991: C1, C3.

Cavalaris, Chuck. "Defense to have final say: Intimidators UT, Auburn to fight for Final Four shot." *Knoxville News-Sentinel*, March 23, 1991: C1, C4.

Cavalaris, Chuck. "Lady Vols block Auburn's path: Adams steps in, draws foul that seals UT's 69–65 victory." *Knoxville News-Sentinel*, March 24, 1991: C1, C11.

Cavalaris, Chuck. "Lady Vols aim to go 3-for-3 against Cardinal." *Knoxville News-Sentinel*, March 25, 1991: C1, C4.

Cavalaris, Chuck. "UT must beat Stanford for another shot at title." *Knoxville News-Sentinel*, March 30, 1991: C1, C5.

Cavalaris, Chuck. "Lady Vols seek third NCAA crown." *Knoxville News-Sentinel*, March 31, 1991: C1, C4.

Cavalaris, Chuck. "Summitt sought, got help at half." *Knoxville News-Sentinel*, March 31, 1991: C4.

Cavalaris, Chuck. "Lady Vols Champs: 'We were a family,' says coach Summitt." *Knoxville News-Sentinel*, April 1, 1991: Front page.

Cavalaris, Chuck. "Champs again: Lady Vols first to win three titles." *Knoxville News-Sentinel*, April 1, 1991: C1, C5.

Cavalaris, Chuck. "Lady Vols back with game to remember." *Knoxville News-Sentinel*, April 1, 1991: C5.

Cavalaris, Chuck. "Lady Vols' 1991 script is amazing." *Knoxville News-Sentinel*, April 2, 1991: C1, C4.

Cavalaris, Chuck and Dan Fleser. "Summitt pushing for more fans at today's Mideast final." *Knoxville News-Sentinel*, March 23, 1991: C1, C4.

Fleser, Dan. "Lady Wolfpack overpowers, outhustles Lady Vols, 90–77." *Knoxville News-Sentinel*, Dec. 2, 1990: C1, C12.

Fleser, Dan. "Auburn stalls on road to 4th Final Four." *Knoxville News-Sentinel*, March 24, 1991: C10.

Gelin, Dana. "Vandy trips No. 6 Lady Vols." *Nashville Banner*, Dec. 7, 1990, E-1, E-8.

Segrest, Doug. "Evans answers questions." *Nashville Banner*, Nov. 26, 1990: E-3.

Sullivan, Nick. "Lady Vols edge VU behind Charles' 27." *Nashville Tennessean*, March 3, 1991: 1C, 2C.

Summitt, Pat with Sally Jenkins. *Reach for the Summitt*. New York City: Broadway Books, 1998.

utladyvols.com. "Lady Vol History." http://www.utladyvols.com/old_site/photos/sports/w-baskbl/auto_pdf/06bk-mediaguide-10.pdf.

utladyvols.com. "Lady Vol Records." http://www.utladyvols.com/old_site/photos/sports/w-baskbl/auto_pdf/06bk-mediaguide-11.pdf.

Wikipedia, the free encyclopedia. "Larry Johnson (basketball)." http://en.wikipedia.org/wiki/Larry_Johnson_(basketball)

wnba.com. "The History of Women's Basketball." http://www.wnba.com/liberty/news/WomBBhist.html

Chapter Four

Adams, John. "Lady Vols return to finals: UT gangs up on stubborn Connecticut." *Knoxville News-Sentinel*, March 30, 1996, C1, C3.

Adams, John. "Championship a crowning moment for UT." *Knoxville News-Sentinel*, April 1, 1996, C1, C4.

Adams, John. "Whatever strength Georgia had just fell apart." *Knoxville News-Sentinel*, April 1, 1996, C4.

Adams, John. "Marciniak named outstanding player." *Knoxville News-Sentinel*, April 1, 1996, C4.

Associated Press. "UT, Holdsclaw shred up Purdue." *Nashville Tennessean*, Dec. 4, 1995: 6C.

Associated Press. "Impressive No. 2 Vols impressed by Penn St." *Nashville Tennessean*, Dec. 5, 1995: 4C.

Associated Press. "Georgia bulldogs Lady Vols." *Nashville Tennessean*, Jan. 9, 1996: 4C.

Associated Press. "Lady Vols rally past Gamecocks." *Nashville Tennessean*, Feb. 16, 1996: 4C.

Coleman, Anthony. "The duel before the real deal." *Nashville Tennessean*, Jan. 19, 1996: 6C.

Coleman, Anthony. "VU's foul trouble helps UT grab boards, victory." *Nashville Tennessean*, Jan. 20, 1996: 4C.

Coleman, Anthony. "Lady Vols' encore: Beating No. 1." *Nashville Tennessean*, Jan. 23, 1996: 1C.

Fleser, Dan. "Virginia versus UT: The rivalry resumes." *Knoxville News-Sentinel*, March 25, 1996: C1, C8.

Fleser, Dan. "Next stop: Final Four." *Knoxville News-Sentinel*, March 26, 1996: D1, D4.

Fleser, Dan. "Who wants to be the favorite?" *Knoxville News-Sentinel*, March 29, 1996: C1, C4.

Fleser, Dan. "UConn finally falls, 88–83 in overtime." *Knoxville News-Sentinel*, March 30, 1996: C1, C3.

Fleser, Dan. "Court decision is clear: SEC's best." *Knoxville News-Sentinel*, March 31, 1996: C4.

Fleser, Dan. "It's a Tennessee waltz." *Knoxville News Sentinel*, April 1, 1996: C1, C4.

Fleser, Dan. "No place like home for Tiffani." *Knoxville News-Sentinel*, April 1, 1996: C4.

Fleser, Dan. "Lady Vols relish title, but what about next year?." *Knoxville News-Sentinel*, April 2, 1996: D1, D3.

Patton, Maurice. "UT pounds boards, knocks out Virginia." *Nashville Tennessean*, Nov. 20, 1995: 1C.

Patton, Maurice. "UT Conk-lins Purdue." *Nashville Tennessean*, Dec. 9, 1995: 1C.

Patton, Maurice. "UT steps up, takes VU down." *Nashville Tennessean*, Jan. 20, 1996: 1C.

Patton, Maurice. "Lady Vols escape Auburn's claws." *Nashville Tennessean*, Feb. 19, 1996: 4C.

Patton, Maurice. "Lady Vols pass their boards." *Nashville Tennessean*, March 4, 1996: 1C.

Patton, Maurice. "Two for the tournament: Lady Vols tip Alabama to win SEC." *Nashville Tennessean*, March 5, 1996: 1C.

Patton, Maurice. "Holdsclaw has teammates holding hearts." *Nashville Tennessean*, March 5, 1996: 4C.

Summitt, Pat with Sally Jenkins. *Reach for the Summitt*. New York City: Broadway Books, 1998.

utladyvols.com. "Lady Vol History." http://www.utladyvols.com/old_site/photos/sports/w-baskbl/auto_pdf/06bk-mediaguide-10.pdf.

utladyvols.com. "Lady Vol Records." http://www.utladyvols.com/old_site/photos/sports/w-baskbl/auto_pdf/06bk-mediaguide-11.pdf.

Wood, Tom. "Connecticut snaps UT's home run." *Nashville Tennessean*, Jan. 7, 1996: 1C.

Wood, Tom. "Boards, foul shots hurt UT." *Nashville Tennessean*, Jan. 7, 1996: 7C.

Woody, Larry. "Patterned for Success." *Nashville Tennessean*, Jan. 19, 1996: 1C, 6C.

Chapter Five

Adams, John. "Fifth in SEC, but No. 1 in the country." *Knoxville News-Sentinel*, March 31, 1997, C1, C4.

Associated Press. "Lady Vols fall to ODU." *Nashville Tennessean*, Jan. 8, 1997: 3C.

Associated Press. "Lady Vols break Tide's record win streak at 14." *Nashville Tennessean*, Jan. 27, 1997: 4C.

Climer, David. "Lady Vols back where they belong." *Nashville Tennessean*, Jan. 20, 1997: 1C.

Davy, Jimmy. "Best foot forward: Conklin plays with injured toe." *Nashville Tennessean*, Jan. 20, 1997: 4C.

Fleser, Dan. "Lady Vols need OT for win at Texas." *Knoxville News-Sentinel*, Dec. 22, 1996: C1, C7.

Fleser, Dan. "Lady Vols brace for UConn." *Knoxville News-Sentinel*, March 24, 1997: C1, C4.

Fleser, Dan. "UT's Going Back: Lady Vols return to Final Four after rocking No. 1 UConn 91–81." *Knoxville News-Sentinel*, March 25, 1997: D1, D3.

Fleser, Dan. "Jolly's toughness sparks UT win." *Knoxville News-Sentinel*, March 26, 1997: D1, D4.

Fleser, Dan. "Pressure was too heavy for UConn." *Knoxville News-Sentinel*, March 26, 1997: D1, D4.

Fleser, Dan. "Surprise, it's Notre Dame vs. UT." *Knoxville News-Sentinel*, March 28, 1997: C1, C4.

Fleser, Dan. "UT returns to final." *Knoxville News-Sentinel*, March 29, 1997: C1, C5.

References

Fleser, Dan. "It's 5 the hard way." *Knoxville News-Sentinel*, March 31, 1997: C1, C4.

Fleser, Dan. "Tough regular-season road a key to title." *Knoxville News-Sentinel*, April 1, 1997: D1, D3.

Fleser, Dan. "More vocal leadership for Holdsclaw?" *Knoxville News-Sentinel*, April 1, 1997: D3.

Lundy, Gary. "Holdsclaw finds proper motivation." *Knoxville News-Sentinel*, March 29, 1997: C5.

Morrow, Mike. "Tennessean of the Year: Pat Summitt." *Nashville Tennessean*, Dec. 22, 1996: 1 D, 2D.

Organ, Mike. "Working OT: UT too much for Vandy." *Nashville Tennessean*, Jan. 20, 1997: 1C, 4C.

Patton, Maurice. "Holdsclaw holds up under load, but Lady Vols fall." *Nashville Tennessean*, Dec. 9, 1996: 1C.

Patton, Maurice. "Lady Vols not yet up to task." *Nashville Tennessean*, Jan. 6, 1997: 1C.

Patton, Maurice. "Lady Vols win in OT." *Nashville Tennessean*, March 2, 1997: 1C, 7C.

Summitt, Pat with Sally Jenkins. *Reach for the Summitt*. New York City: Broadway Books, 1998.

utladyvols.com. "Lady Vol History." http://www.utladyvols.com/old_site/photos/sports/w-baskbl/auto_pdf/06bk-mediaguide-10.pdf.

utladyvols.com. "Lady Vol Records." http://www.utladyvols.com/old_site/photos/sports/w-baskbl/auto_pdf/06bk-mediaguide-11.pdf.

Chapter Six

Adams, John. "When Lady Vols smell trouble, ball goes to Holdsclaw." *Knoxville News-Sentinel*, Feb. 8, 1998, C1, C6.

Adams, John. "Geter a leading Lady in her role of great escape." *Knoxville News-Sentinel*, March 24, 1998, D1, D4.

Adams, John. "Arkansas leaves island for life in (K) city." *Knoxville News-Sentinel*, March 27, 1998, C1, C4.

Adams, John. "Razorbacks can't keep UT's pace; Tech different story." *Knoxville News-Sentinel*, March 28, 1998, C6.

Adams, John. "Clockwork Orange: UT is best team ever." *Knoxville News-Sentinel*, March 30, 1998, C1, C10.

Adams, John. "Tech's mistakes in early moments were devastating." *Knoxville News-Sentinel*, March 30, 1998, C10.

Associated Press. "No. 1 Vols rally back, beat No. 2." *Nashville Tennessean*, Nov. 22, 1997: 1C.

Associated Press. "Lady Vols end Stanford streak." *Nashville Tennessean*, Nov. 30, 1997: 6C.

Associated Press. "Holdsclaw's 29 puts UT in Northern Lights finals." *Nashville Tennessean*, Dec. 21, 1997: 10C.

Cavalaris, Chuck. "Big crowd, big win: 24,597 watch Lady Vols rip Huskies." *Knoxville News-Sentinel*, Jan. 4, 1998: C1, C6.

Climer, David. "Lady Vols just want to have fun." *Nashville Tennessean*, Feb. 17, 1998: 1C.

Cornelius, Maria M. "The Champs: Lady Vols down Louisiana Tech 93–75 to go 39–0." *Knoxville News-Sentinel*, March 30, 1998: A1, A6.

Davy, Jimmy. "Just ask Vandy: Lady Vol defense wears down foes." *Nashville Tennessean*, Feb. 17, 1998: 6C.

Fleser, Dan. "Tennessee winner at home." *Knoxville News-Sentinel*, Feb. 8, 1998: C1, C6.

Fleser, Dan. "A Titanic win for Vols: UT (37–0) going to Kansas City after 76–70 victory." *Knoxville News-Sentinel*, March 24, 1998: D1, D4.

Fleser, Dan. "A comeback that ranks as a No. 1 effort." *Knoxville News-Sentinel*, March 25, 1998: D1, D4.

Fleser, Dan. "Holdsclaw has a Kodak smile." *Knoxville News-Sentinel*, March 27, 1998: C1, C4.

Fleser, Dan. "Summitt receives Coach-of-Year award from AP." *Knoxville News-Sentinel*, March 27, 1998: C4.

Fleser, Dan. "38 down, one to go: UT's 86–58 victory sets up showdown against La. Tech for championship." *Knoxville News-Sentinel*, March 28, 1998: C1, C6.

Fleser, Dan. "Holdsclaw, Summitt sweep Naismiths." *Knoxville News-Sentinel*, March 28, 1998: C6.

Fleser, Dan. "Lady Vols, Lady Techsters may get physical: Historic rivals meet for title." *Knoxville News-Sentinel*, March 29, 1998: C1, C4.

Fleser, Dan. "A perfect ending: It's a three-peat for Lady Vols (39–0); Techsters no match, 93–75." *Knoxville News-Sentinel*, March 30, 1998: C1, C10.

Low, Chris. "Super Sunday for Lady Vols." *Nashville Tennessean*, Jan. 26, 1998: 1C, 8C.

Low, Chris. "Lady Vols beat LSU to cap perfect season." *Nashville Tennessean*, Feb. 23, 1998: 4C.

Low, Chris. "Lady Vols discover yet another level." *Nashville Tennessean*, March 1, 1998: 1C, 4C.

Low, Chris. "Lady Vols get second scare from Alabama." *Nashville Tennessean*, March 2, 1998: 1C, 4C.

McAfee, Paul. "Attendance record boost for women's basketball." *Knoxville News-Sentinel*, Jan. 4, 1998: C6.

Organ, Mike. "UT just perfect: Lady Vols roll by Commodores." *Nashville Tennessean*, Feb. 17, 1998: 1C, 6C.

Organ, Mike. "Vandy devastated by 61-point loss." *Nashville Tennessean*, March 1, 1998: 4C.

Organ, Mike. "SEC leaving Columbus, back at UTC next year." *Nashville Tennessean*, March 1, 1998: 4C.

Organ, Mike. "Ezell says Lady Vols merely great." *Nashville Tennessean*, March 2, 1998: 4C.

Strange, Mike. "Starting five seldom sits for Lady Techsters." *Knoxville News-Sentinel*, March 29, 1998: C4.

Strange, Mike. "Was Jolly disguised as a 'Meek'?" *Knoxville News-Sentinel*, March 30, 1998: C10.

Summitt, Pat with Sally Jenkins. *Raise the Roof: The Inspiring Story of the Tennessee Lady Vols' Groundbreaking Season in Women's College Basketball.* New York City: Broadway Books, 1998.

utladyvols.com. "Lady Vol History." http://www.utladyvols.com/old_site/photos/sports/w-baskbl/auto_pdf/06bk-mediaguide-10.pdf.

utladyvols.com. "Lady Vol Records." http://www.utladyvols.com/old_site/photos/sports/w-baskbl/auto_pdf/06bk-mediaguide-11.pdf.

Chapter Seven

Adamec, Carl. "Lady Vols' guards get best of Montgomery." *Knoxville News-Sentinel*, Jan. 7, 2007, D6.

Anderson, Kelli. "2007 Final Four: About a Team." *Sports Illustrated Presents: Lady Vols 2007 National Champions*: 45, 46, 48–50, 52.

Burke, Garance. "Female coaches are leaving collegiate ranks." Associated Press/Yahoo! Sports. http://sports.yahoo.com/top/news?slug=ap womencoaches&prov=ap&type=lgns, July 4, 2007.

Callahan, Ryan. "Tennessee dunks Stanford." *Nashville Tennessean*, Nov. 25, 2006: http://0-infoweb.newsbank.com.waldo.library.nashville.org/iw-search/we/InfoWeb?p_action=doc&p_docid=116362445764B178&p_docnum=1&p_queryname=6&p_product=NTNB&p_theme=aggregated4&p_nbid=T4AX50RHMTE4NjA3NDQ4Ni4yMzk5MTg6 MToxMzoxNzAuMTkwLjQwLjIw.

Callahan, Ryan. "Lady Vols have edge: Fuller knowledge of Insell's system helps rout MTSU." *Nashville Tennessean*, Nov. 25, 2006: http://0-infoweb.newsbank.com.waldo.library.nashville.org/iw-search/we/InfoWeb?p_action=doc&p_docid=11636246843AF260&p_docnum=1&p_queryname=8&p_product=NTNB&p_theme=aggregated4&p_nbid=T4AX50RHMTE4NjA3NDQ4Ni4yMzk5MTg6MTox MzoxNzAuMTkwLjQwLjIw.

Callahan, Ryan. "Lady Vols' slow start ends hopes vs. Duke." *Nashville Tennessean*, Jan. 23, 2007: http://0-infoweb.newsbank.com.waldo.library. nashville.org/iw-search/we/InfoWeb?p_action=doc&p_docid= 11804DDCECDCC590&p_docnum=2&p_queryname=25&p_product=NTNB&p_theme=aggregated4&p_nbid=T4AX50RHMTE4NjA3N DQ4Ni4yMzk5MTg6MToxMzoxNzAuMTkwLjQwLjIw.

Callahan, Ryan. "Hornbuckle upset over mental game." *Nashville Tennessean*, Jan. 23, 2007: http://0-infoweb.newsbank.com.waldo. library.nashville.org/iw-search/we/InfoWeb?p_action=doc&p_docid= 11804DDBD21A1C08&p_docnum=1&p_queryname=25&p_ product=NTNB&p_theme=aggregated4&p_nbid=T4AX50RHMTE4Nj A3NDQ4Ni4yMzk5MTg6MToxMzoxNzAuMTkwLjQwLjIw.

Callahan, Ryan. "Lady Vols maintain hold over Georgia: Parker scores 22 in sixth straight win over Bulldogs." *Nashville Tennessean*, Feb. 6, 2007: http://0-infoweb.newsbank.com.waldo.library.nashville.org/iw-search/ we/InfoWeb?p_action=doc&p_docid=11848EA395123DC8&p_ docnum=1&p_queryname=2&p_product=NTNB&p_theme=aggregated 4&p_nbid=R4DD53CKMTE4NjExMjYzNi45NDA2MjA6MToxMzox NzAuMTkwLjQwLjIw.

Callahan, Ryan. "Vandy overpowered by Lady Vols' defense." *Nashville Tennessean*, Feb. 26, 2007: http://0-infoweb.newsbank.com.waldo. library.nashville.org/iw-search/we/InfoWeb?p_action=doc&p_docid= 118C776F05018268&p_docnum=1&p_queryname=2&p_product= NTNB&p_theme=aggregated4&p_nbid=F4DT52QJMTE4NjE4Njk0M S42NTY0MzA6MToxMzoxNzAuMTkwLjQwLjIw.

Callahan, Ryan. "Summitt has plans for Pearl." *Nashville Tennessean*, Feb. 26, 2007: http://0-infoweb.newsbank.com.waldo.library.nashville.org/ iw-search/we/InfoWeb?p_action=doc&p_docid=118C776EA3AEA8A8 &p_docnum=2&p_queryname=3&p_product=NTNB&p_theme= aggregated4&p_nbid=Y45S49PAMTE4NjIwMTAzOS4xMDk5NToxO- jEzOjE3MC4xOTAuNDAuMjA.

Climer, David. "Lady Vols completed by Parker." *Nashville Tennessean*, Jan. 26, 2007: http://0-infoweb.newsbank.com.waldo.library.nashville.org/ iw-search/we/InfoWeb?p_action=doc&p_docid=1180F4D7B185B048 &p_docnum=3&p_queryname=2&p_product=NTNB&p_theme=aggre gated4&p_nbid=F4FV55AMMTE4NjA5NTUyNy4xNjMzODk6MTox MzoxNzAuMTkwLjQwLjIw.

Cornelius, Maria M. "More than a Dunk." *Rocky Top News*, Spring 2007: 6, 31.

Davis, Elizabeth A. "Lady Vols' coaches rewarded for title." USATODAY.com, April 4, 2007: http://www.usatoday.com/sports/ college/womensbasketball/2007-04-04-1035026492_x.htm.

Deitsch, Richard. "100 Greatest Female Athletes: No. 51, Nera White." *Sports Illustrated for Women*. http://sportsillustrated.cnn.com/ siforwomen/top_100/51/.

Fleser, Dan. "Defensive intensity: Lady Vols use strong half to beat Louisiana Tech." *Knoxville News-Sentinel*, Nov. 29, 2006: C1, C4.

Fleser, Dan. "Singing Carolina blues: No. 2 Tar Heels hand Lady Vols first defeat." *Knoxville News-Sentinel*, Dec. 4, 2006: C1, C4.

Fleser, Dan. "No answer for Parker: Another dunk keys huge start; finish is even bigger." *Knoxville News-Sentinel*, Jan. 7, 2007: D1, D6.

Fleser, Dan. "Retaking SEC title: Lady Vols now want to 'run the table.'" *Knoxville News-Sentinel*, Feb. 20, 2007: D1, D5.

Hale, Monte Jr. "MTSU looks like new team: Blue Raiders have come long way with Coach Insell." *Nashville Tennessean*, Nov. 27, 2006: http://0-infoweb.newsbank.com.waldo.library.nashville.org/iw-search/we/InfoWeb?p_action=doc&p_docid=116362468C7C1738&p_docnum=2&p_queryname=8&p_product=NTNB&p_theme=aggregated4&p_nbid=T4AX50RHMTE4NjA3NDQ4Ni4yMzk5MTg6MToxMzoxNzAuMTkwLjQwLjIw

Lawrence, Andrew. "Hitting the Road." *Sports Illustrated Presents: Lady Vols 2007 National Champions*: 32, 35.

Lawrence, Andrew. "Two Over Easy." *Sports Illustrated Presents: Lady Vols 2007 National Champions*: 38, 41.

Lawrence, Andrew. "The Belle of the Ball." *Sports Illustrated Presents: Lady Vols 2007 National Champions*: 55, 56, 58.

Low, Chris. "Summitt cheers men on to victory." *Nashville Tennessean*, Feb. 28, 2007: http://0-infoweb.newsbank.com.waldo.library.nashville.org/iw-search/we/InfoWeb?p_action=doc&p_docid=118DCA0750378CE0&p_docnum=2&p_queryname=4&p_product=NTNB&p_theme=aggregated4&p_nbid=Y45S49PAMTE4NjIwMTAzOS4xMDk5NToxOjEzOjE3MC4xOTAuNDAuMjA.

Mullen, Bryan. "Fulmer sees Lady Vol as role model for his QB." *Nashville Tennessean*, Aug. 5, 2007: http://www.tennessean.com/apps/pbcs.dll/article?AID=2007708050394.

Organ, Mike. "UT still owns Vandy." *Nashville Tennessean*, Jan. 26, 2007: http://0-infoweb.newsbank.com.waldo.library.nashville.org/iw-search/we/InfoWeb?p_action=doc&p_docid=1180F4D369168E00&p_docnum=1&p_queryname=38&p_product=NTNB&p_theme=aggregated4&p_nbid=T4AX50RHMTE4NjA3NDQ4Ni4yMzk5MTg6MToxMzoxNzAuMTkwLjQwLjIw

Organ, Mike. "Hornbuckle's 29 not enough to carry Lady Vols into final." *Nashville Tennessean*, March 4, 2007: http://0infoweb.newsbank.com.waldo.library.nashville.org/iwsearch/we/InfoWeb?p_action=doc&p_docid=118F6F43A558BEC8&p_docnum=2&p_queryname=6&p_product=NTNB&p_theme=aggregated4&p_nbid=V56W5ALRMTE4NjI1NDExOS400OTkwMzE6MToxMzoxNzAuMTkwLjQwLjIw.

utladyvols.com. "Lady Vol History." http://www.utladyvols.com/old_site/photos/sports/w-baskbl/auto_pdf/06bk-mediaguide-10.pdf.

utladyvols.com. "Lady Vol Records." http://www.utladyvols.com/old_site/photos/sports/w-baskbl/auto_pdf/06bk-mediaguide-11.pdf.

Index

A

Adams, Jody, 85, 93, 95, 98, 101, 105, 109, 112

Ainge, Erik, 206

Akron Zips, 172, 196

Alabama Crimson Tide, 30, 46, 68, 82, 89, 113, 125, 127-128, 139, 151-152, 165, 177-179, 184, 186, 190, 196, 209, 225

Alabama-Birmingham Lady Blazers, 118

Albany Civic Center, 69, 103

Anosike, Nicky, 198, 204, 215-216, 219-222, 224

Argentinian Natl. Team, 47

Arizona State Sun Devils, 198, 225

Arkansas Lady Razor-

backs, 121, 139, 144, 165, 172, 189-190, 196, 211, 225

Associated Press, 18, 189, 233-234, 237-241

Atlanta Tipoff Club, 189

Auburn Lady Tigers, 25-27, 30-35, 37-38, 40, 44, 46-47, 58-60, 62, 68-70, 74, 76-80, 82, 91, 93-96, 100-106, 113, 125-126, 134, 139, 152, 155, 165, 179, 196, 210, 225

Auguste, Alberta, 201, 216, 220-221, 224

Auriemma, Geno, 119-120, 131, 157-159, 172, 175, 204-205

Austin Peay Lady Governors, 165

Awkward, Ashley, 215

B

Baby Vols, 56

Balcomb, Melanie, 211

Baltimore Colts, 40

Barmore, Leon, 29, 39-41, 50-51, 65-66, 124, 169, 191-194

Baroody, Helene, 27, 33

Barry, Ceal, 156

Bell Atlantic Holiday Tournament, 57

Berenato, Agnus, 215

Blair, Gary, 190

Boatman, Kim, 51

Bobbitt, Shannon, 198, 210-211, 215, 220-221, 224

Bolton, Mae Ola, 26, 34

Bolton, Ruthie, 77

Bonvicini, Joan, 37-38, 53, 72-73

Boucek, Jenny, 129
Brazilian tour, 47
Brown Athletic Center, 57
Brown, Al, 174
Brown, Cindy, 36, 38, 54
Bullett, Vicky, 74
Butts, Niya, 42, 161, 163-164, 195
Byrd, Ben, 60

C
Caldwell, Nikki, 85, 89-90, 93, 99-100, 112, 223
Cal-Santa Barbara Gauchos, 36
Carmichael Auditorium, 202
Carson-Newman Lady Eagles, 225
Carver, Tamara, 112
Carver-Hawkeye Arena, 156-157
Casteel, Kelli, 52, 55, 81, 85, 98, 105-106, 112
Catchings, Tamika, 12, 168-171, 174-175, 177, 179, 181, 183, 186, 188-193, 195, 219
Catchings, Tauja, 171
CBS Sports, 97, 203
Chancellor, Van, 68
Charles, Daedra, 12, 53, 56, 58, 60-61, 79, 81, 84, 86-91, 94, 98-100, 102, 104, 106, 108, 110, 112, 229
Charlotte Coliseum, 132
Charlotte Hornets, 107
Chatman, Dana "Pokey", 94, 103, 213
Cheyney State College, 220
Chicago Bulls, 177
Ciampi, Joe, 26, 35, 70,

77-78, 80, 93, 100, 103-105
Clark, Regina, 52, 55, 81, 85, 112
Clement, Kristen "Ace", 168-169, 172, 181, 187, 195
Clemson Lady Tigers, 129
Cloud, Doug, 26
Colorado Buffaloes, 156, 165
Columbus Civic Center, 182
Conklin, Abby, 116-119, 123-124, 126, 128, 131, 136, 138, 141-143, 146-147, 149-152, 155, 157, 159-162, 164, 167
Connecticut Lady Huskies, 119-121, 131-135, 139, 147, 149, 156-159, 162, 165, 172, 174-176, 193, 196, 203-205, 216, 225
Conradt, Jody, 22, 145
Corteau, June, 26
Cronan, Joan, 97-98
Cunningham, Mara, 123
Curry, Elizabeth, 224

D
Dangerfield, Rodney, 131
Darsch, Nancy, 17
Davis, Clarissa, 22, 62-63
Davis, Dee, 208
Davis, Latina, 116, 118-119, 123-124, 126-127, 129, 131, 138, 141, 167
Davy, Jimmy, 180
Dayton Flyers, 46
DeMoss, Mickie, 20, 42, 108, 133, 136, 158, 161-162, 189, 191, 193
DePaul Blue Demons,

113, 119, 139, 165, 176, 196
Diddle Arena, 71
Drake Lady Bulldogs, 214, 225
Duke Blue Devils, 180, 189, 194, 206, 208, 212, 220, 225
Dunn, Lin, 21, 119
Duran, Amy, 158
Durham, Kris, 54, 79, 81

E
Edwards, Tonya, 19, 24-25, 31, 34, 37-38, 40, 42, 45, 50-51, 53-54, 56-58, 62-63, 65, 69, 71, 79, 81, 229
Elzy, Kyra, 154, 160-161, 164, 169-170, 174, 177, 179, 190, 193, 195
Erwin Center, 18, 37, 40, 62, 97, 143
ESPN, 104, 176
ESPY award, 156
Evans, Peggy, 85-86, 91, 94, 108, 110, 112
Everly Brothers, 71
"Eyes of Texas, The" 22
Ezell, Brittney, 152, 186

F
Fab Four, 168, 181, 194, 219
Fenway Park, 4
Florida Lady Gators, 19-20, 24, 27, 34, 46, 57, 68, 82, 89-91, 94-95, 113, 119, 127, 139, 151, 165, 176, 196, 201, 206, 212, 225
Foster, Jim, 122-123, 145, 151, 177, 180, 183
Fowles, Sylvia, 213, 220
French Natl. Team, 82
Frett, Keshia, 135

Frost, Sheila, 19, 21-22, 28-31, 34, 40, 43, 45, 50, 52-53, 55-61, 63-64, 68-69, 72-73, 75-78, 81

Fuller, Alex, 199, 224

Fulmer, Phil, 205-206

G

Gaither, Katryna, 159-160

George Mason Pariots, 196

George Washington Colonials, 225

Georgia Lady Bulldogs, 33, 46, 61-62, 82, 91, 95-97, 99, 101, 106, 113, 120-121, 134-135, 139, 142-143, 165, 176-177, 196, 206, 209, 225

Georgia Tech Yellow Jackets, 27, 46, 68, 82

Geter, Teresa "Tree", 168-169, 187-188, 190, 192, 195

Gillingham, Heidi, 88, 100

Gordon, Bridgette, 12, 18-19, 21-22, 25, 27-31, 34-38, 40-42, 45, 50-53, 55-65, 67, 69-70, 73-78, 80-81, 228-229

Gorsica, Angela, 123

Grambling State Lady Tigers, 156, 158, 165

Greene, Misty, 138, 164, 195

Griffith, Mimi, 44

Gunter, Sue, 12, 68, 103, 181

Gwinnett Center, 213

H

Harrison, Lisa, 85, 90-91, 99, 108, 110, 112

Hartford Civic Center, 147, 203

Hatchell, Sylvia, 149

Hawhee, Debbie, 52, 81, 112

HBO, 142, 149, 184

Head, Dena, 12, 52, 55-56, 63, 65-66, 69-71, 73, 75, 79, 81, 84-85, 87, 89, 90, 93-94, 96-98, 101-102, 107-112, 229

Head, Hazel, 122

Head, Richard, 122

Holdsclaw, Chamique, 12-13, 115-119, 121, 123-129, 131-133, 135, 137-139, 141-144, 147-148, 151-152, 154-164, 167-172, 173, 174-175, 177-180, 183-184, 186-190, 192-195, 197, 206, 219-220, 228-229

Hornbuckle, Alexis, 198-199, 201-202, 209, 211, 213, 215-216, 222, 224

Horton, Karla, 22, 28-30, 34, 44-45, 221

Houston, Charde, 204

Houston Jaguars, 225

I

Illinois Fighting Illini, 52, 82, 88, 113, 171, 196

Indiana Hoosiers, 111, 145

Insell, Rick, 199

Iowa Hawkeyes, 46, 220

J

Jackson, Tamicha, 191

Jenkins, Sally, 172

Jeter, Marlene, 112

Johnson, Larry, 107

Johnson, Shannon, 125

Johnson, Tiffani, 116, 118-119, 128, 133, 135, 138, 141, 150, 152, 156, 159-160, 162, 164, 167

Jolly, Kellie, 138, 144, 153, 157-159, 162, 164, 171, 187-188, 190, 192, 195

Jones, Carolyn, 93, 102, 104-105

K

Kansas Lady Jayhawks, 128, 139, 142, 165

Kemper Arena, 189-190, 192

Kentucky Lady Wildcats, 25, 46, 61, 82, 89, 113, 139, 145, 149, 165, 176, 180, 196, 210, 225

Klum Gym, 50

Knight, Bob, 111, 145

Knight Complex, 20-21

Kodak All-America Team, 132, 189, 229

Kona Basketball Classic, 118-119

L

La Salle Explorers, 70, 82

Lady Bulldogs, 60-61, 89, 96-97, 121, 134-135, 142-143, 152, 177, 209, 237

Lady Tigers, 25-27, 29, 31-35, 44, 58-59, 69-70, 76-78, 91, 93-94, 96, 100, 103-106, 126, 154-155, 181, 210, 212-213, 235

Lakefront Arena, 108, 111

Landers, Andy, 61, 96-97, 121, 134, 143, 209

Lang, Erika, 90

Larry, Wendy, 161

Lawson, Kara, 12, 197

Laxton, Brynae, 138, 164, 195

Lee, Phil, 28, 88

Lewis, Nora, 41, 66

Liberty Basketball Association, 95

Lithuania, 117-118, 139

Littlejohn, Cheryl, 45

Lloyd, Andrea, 18-19, 22

Lockwood, Dean, 223

Long Beach State 49ers, 35-40, 44, 47, 52-54, 57, 71-73, 82, 234

Louisiana State (LSU) Lady Tigers, 12, 28-30, 46, 64, 68, 82, 94-95, 101-103, 113, 127, 139, 152, 154, 165, 181, 183, 194, 196, 198, 210, 212-213, 220, 225

Louisiana Tech Lady Techsters, 20, 28-31, 38-41, 44, 46-47, 49-50, 64-66, 76, 82, 91, 96-97, 113, 121, 124-125, 139, 142, 148, 154, 165, 168-169, 190-194, 196, 198, 201-202, 225, 230

M

Maine Black Bears, 88, 113

Manhattan Lady Jaspers, 171

Manning, Gus, 145

Maravich Center, 210

March Madness, 131

Marciniak, Michelle "Spinderella," 12, 116-119, 123-126, 128-129, *130*, 131-138, 141, 146, 167, 203

Marist Red Foxes, 215, 225

Marquette Golden Eagles, 165

Marsh, Dawn, 19, 21, 25, 33, 45

Maryland Lady Terrapins, 74-76, 82, 88, 113

McCray, Melissa, 37-38, 45, 52, 61, 66, 73, 75, 77-78, 81, 86, 221

McCray, Nikki, 86

McGhee, Carla, 24, 29, 43, 45, 79, 81

McMahan, Cait, 220, 224

McNeil, Diann, 34

Meeks (Three Meeksketeers), 170, 172, 177, 180, 183, 186

Memorial Coliseum, 25, 31

Memorial Gym, 27-28, 121, 179, 187, 208

Memphis (State) Lady Tigers, 27, 46, 82, 113, 119, 139, 165, 179, 196

Michigan Wolverines, 55

Middle Tennessee State Blue Raiders, 122, 198-199

Miller, Cheryl, 21, 73, 124

Milligan, Laurie, 138, 147, 164, 171, 181, 193, 195

Mink, Patsy T., 12

Mississippi (Ole Miss) Lady Rebels, 27, 46, 59-60, 68, 82, 95, 113, 125, 127, 133, 139, 152, 165, 168, 177, 196, 215, 225

Mississippi State Lady Bulldogs, 30, 46, 60-61, 82, 89, 113, 125, 139, 152, 165, 179, 182, 196, 206, 210, 225

Missouri Valley Conference, 214

Moats, Nicci, 224

Montgomery, Renee, 205

Moore, Pearl, 81

Morgan, Beth, 159-160

Morris, Laticia, 126

Mott, Sabrina, 45

N

Naismith awards, 189, 194, 228

Namath, Joe, 40

Nashville Banner, 236

Nashville Tennessean, 144, 180, 234, 236-243

Natl. Basketball Assn. (NBA), 94, 107, 143, 180, 192

Natl. Collegiate Athletic Assn. (NCAA), 12, 33, 36-37, 42, 73, 97, 120, 157, 174, 216, 228

NCAA Division I, 91, 170, 181, 192

NCAA Silver Anniversary Team, 228

NCAA Women's Basketball Tournament, 32, 46, 73, 81, 99, 103-104, 109, 112, 128-129, 138, 155-156, 159, 162, 164, 188, 191, 195, 199, 214-15, 228-229

NCAA Cleveland Regional, 198, 202, 216

NCAA Dayton Regional, 214-215, 224-225

NCAA East Regional, 70-72, 81-83, 91, 99, 109, 128-129, 139, 194

NCAA Final Four, 18, 21, 27, 32-33, 35-37, 39-40, 43-44, 47, 49-50, 52, 54, 68, 71-76, 82-83, 85, 88, 103, 105-107, 109, 113, 131-132, 134-136, 139, 147, 155-156, 158-160, 162, 165, 184, 188-190, 192, 196, 216, 220, 222,

225, 228, 232-233, 235-238, 241

NCAA Mideast Regional, 32-35, 45, 47, 103, 105, 112-113, 119, 131, 186, 196, 217, 220, 230

NCAA Midwest Regional, 156, 158, 165, 172, 230

NCAA West Regional, 35, 74, 106, 189

Natl. Invitation Tournament (NIT), 158

Nelson, Cherie, 55

New Jersey Nets, 197

New Orleans, University of, 108

New York Times, 141

New York Yankees, 12

North Carolina Lady Tar Heels, 24, 46, 149, 186-188, 190, 196, 198, 202, 216-217, 219, 221, 223, 225, 230

North Carolina State Lady Wolfpack, 46, 86-88, 113, 190, 208

Northern Lights Invitational, 172

Northwestern Lady Wildcats, 27, 46

Notre Dame Fighting Irish, 46, 68, 82, 113, 137, 158-160, 165, 225, 238

Nygaard, Vanessa, 171

O

ODU Fieldhouse, 24

Ohio State Lady Buckeyes, 35, 89, 113, 128, 139

Ohio Valley Conference, 95

Old Dominion Lady Monarchs, 24-25, 46, 58, 82, 89, 113, 121,

134, 139, 148-149, 161-162, 165, 178-179, 196, 203, 225, 230

Olympics, 56, 228

Orange Bowl Invitational Tournament, 20-22

Oregon Ducks, 156, 165

Orr, Vickie, 34

Ostrom, Lisa, 183

P

Parker, Candace, 12-13, 197-199, *200*, 201-206, 208-211, 213-217, *218*, 219, 221-222, 224, 227-228

Parton, Dolly, 98

Paul, Brenda, 60

Pearl, Bruce, 206, 212

Penicheiro, Ticha, 148, 161, 178-179

Penn State Lady Nittany Lions, 119, 139

Peterson Events Center, 215

Pittsburgh Panthers, 215

Portland, Rene, 119

Portland Pilots, 171, 196

Prague Univ., 47

Pringle, LaToya, 202

Providence Friars, 46

Purdue Lady Boilermakers, 118-119, 139, 150, 165, 170, 194

Q

Quicken Loans Arena, 223

R

Radford Highlanders, 128, 139

Rainbow Wahine Classic, 50-51

Ralph, Shea, 157

Randall, Semeka, 168-171, 174-175, 177, 179, 183-184, 186, 188, 190, 195

Reach for the Summit, 17, 77, 84, 116, 122, 133

Redding, Dominique, 201, 210, 220, 224

Redman, Paige, 151

Reynolds Coliseum, 86

Richmond Spiders, 89, 113

Riverfront Coliseum, 159, 161

Rizzotti, Jennifer, 133

Roane State Raiderettes, 134

Roberts, Patricia, 12

"Rocky Top," 22, 134, 212, 242

Ross, Carol, 91, 127, 215

Roundtree, Saudia, 135

Rupp Arena, 54

Rupp, Adolph, 145

Rutgers Scarlet Knights, 57-58, 82, 186, 196, 219-221, 225

Ryan, Debbie, 129

S

Sales, Nykesha, 132, 174

Sam, Sheri, 123

San Jose Arena, 170

San Jose State Spartans, 36

Sao Paulo, 47

Sauer, Paige, 157

Scholtens, Wendy, 88, 99-100

Scott, Debbie, 52, 81

Seabiscuit, 187

Sexton, Shelley, 20, *23*, 25-29, 31, 42-43, 45, 75, 106, 221

Smallwood, Kim, 138

Smith, Ashley, 180

Snow, Michelle, 12, 197

South Carolina Game-
cocks, 46, 64, 82, 113,
125, 139, 152, 154,
165, 176, 196, 209,
212, 225

South Korean Natl.
Team, 47

Southeastern Confer-
ence (SEC), 25, 27-28,
30-31, 42, 59-60, 68,
70, 76, 88-89, 93, 95-
97, 99-101, 103-104,
117, 121, 127, 134,
149, 151, 160, 163,
186, 193, 196, 198,
206, 208-213, 225, 229

SEC Tournament, 30-31,
35, 46, 68-70, 81-82,
99-105, 113, 127, 139,
155-156, 159, 165, 182,
184, 186, 194-196, 212-
213, 225

Southeastern Louisiana
Lady Lions, 41

Southern California
Trojans, 21, 24, 43, 46,
53-55, 57, 73, 124, 231

Southern Illinois
Salukis, 61, 82

Southwest Conference,
37

Southwest Missouri
State Lady Bears, 103

Spencer, Sidney, 198-
199, 203-205, *207*, 208-
209, 213, 216, 220, 224

Spinks, Kathy, 31, 36, 45

St. Joseph's Hawks, 21,
46, 118, 139, 146, 165

Staley, Dawn, 110-111

Stallworth, LaQuan, 191

Stanford Lady Cardinal,
53, 56-57, 82, 85-86,
89, 106-109, 113, 119,
139, 142-143, 165, 170-
171, 196, 198, 225

Stephens, LaShonda,
164, 195

Stetson Hatters, 82

Stevens, Trisha, 107

Stokely Athletic Center,
25, 32, 34, 52, 60, 96

Stringer, Vivian, 220-221

Sullivan Award, 194

Summitt, Pat Head, 12-
13, 17-22, 24-29, 31-33,
36-44, 49, 51-54, 57-58,
60, 62-66, 68-72, 74-79,
83-91, *92*, 93-111, 116-
129, 131-133, 135-137,
141-152, 154-155, 157-
163, 167-172, 174-184,
185, 186-194, 199, 201-
206, 209-210, 212-214,
216-217, 219-223, 227,
229

Super Bowl III, 40

Super Shootout, 89

T

Tacoma Dome, 49, 76-
77

Taurasi, Diana, 205

Tennessee Sports Hall of
Fame, 99

Tennessee-Martin Sky-
hawks, 196, 225

Tennessee Tech Golden
Eagles, 29, 31-32, 39-
40, 47, 91, 95, 113, 148,
192, 198

Texas A&M Aggies, 172,
196

Texas Lady Longhorns,
18-22, 24, 29, 34-36,
38-39, 44, 46-47, 62-66,
74, 79, 82, 96-98, 102,
113, 119, 139, 143-145,
165, 168, 171, 196,
203, 225

Texas Tech Lady Raiders,
96, 118, 139, 143, 165

Thomas Assembly Cen-
ter, 65, 201

Thompson, Pashen, 116,
118-119, 123, 133-136,

138, 146, 150, 159-160,
162, 164, 167

Thompson-Boling
Arena, 24, 52-53, 55,
59, 61-62, 72, 83, 85,
95-96, 104, 119, 124,
142, 150, 156, 168,
174, 178, 198, 201, 211,
214, 219

Title IX, 11-12, 145

Toler, Penny, 71

Townson, Gay, 45

Tuggle, Jennifer, 45

U

UCLA Bruins, 20, 46, 53,
57, 82, 88, 113, 180,
225

UNC-Charlotte, 30, 46

UNIMEP, 47

U.S. Armed Forces, 196

U.S. Congress, 11

U.S. Natl. Team, 139

UNLV Runnin' Rebels,
107

V

Vanderbilt Lady Com-
modores, 27-28, 29, 46,
61, 82, 88, 99-101, 113,
121-123, 127, 131, 139,
145, 148-152, 165, 176-
177, 179-180, 182-184,
196, 208-209, 211-212,
225

VanDerveer, Heidi, 51

VanDerveer, Tara, 56,
107

Vermont Catamounts,
165, 170, 196

Virginia Lady Cavaliers,
32, 47, 71, 82-83, 87,
91, 109-110, 113, 117-
118, 128-129, 131, 139,
230

Virginia Tech Hokies,
87-88, 113

Index

W

Wade Trophy, 84, 198, 229

Waites, Traci, 54, 71, 73

Wake Forest Lady Deacons, 57, 82

Warlick, Holly, 12, 18, 20, 42, 108, 145, 214, 220, 223

Washington Lady Huskies, 52, 82

Weatherspoon, Teresa, 39

Webb, Lisa, 22, 26, 31, 45

Weller, Chris, 75

West Virginia Mountaineers, 225

Western Kentucky Hilltoppers, 68, 71, 82, 103, 106, 113, 186, 196

Western Michigan Lady Broncos, 58, 82

White, Nera, 12, 242

Wilson, Amanda, 192

Wilson, Nancy, 125

Wisconsin Badgers, 125, 139, 165, 172, 196

Women's Natl. Basketball Assn. (WNBA), 12, 95, 143, 194

Wolters, Kara, 132-133, 157, 159

Women's Basketball Coaches Assn., 189

Y

Yow, Kay, 87

Z

Zaharias, Babe Didrikson, 12

Zeilstra, Julie, 107

Zolman, Shanna, 12, 197